TREE DETAILING

Michael Littlewood

Butterworth Architecture
London Singapore Sydney Wellington

First published in 1988 by
Butterworth Architecture,
an imprint of Butterworth Scientific

British Library Cataloguing in Publication Data

Littlewood, Michael
    Tree Detailing
    1. Trees 2. Landscape architecture
    I. Title
    715'.2   SB435

ISBN 0 408 50002 6

Printed and bound in England by
Anchor-Brendon Ltd., Tiptree, Essex

CONTENTS

FOREWORD

The reasons for this book are many and varied, but little did I realise when I began it seven years ago that it would prove such a challenge. A considerable amount of material was available about trees, and I thought the task of compiling, collecting and sifting data to produce detail sheets would be reasonably easy. The problem is that on some topics there is too much material, and on others there is not enough or none at all.

The purpose of this book has been to produce a handbook containing detail sheets and guidance notes that could be used for contract documentation. I and many of my professional colleagues felt that while the hard landscape works have been covered quite adequately the soft landscape was not given the same degree of attention. Certainly when one sees contract documents for soft landscape works the amount of information given for the detailing of stock, planting, protection etc. has usually been covered very briefly by drawings and specifications.

Consequently, it comes as no surprise that landscape architects do not always achieve their final design expectations owing perhaps to landscape contractors and nurseries supplying the wrong stock or the stock being planted or protected incorrectly.

If it is necessary to give a contractor details for a paved area, it is just as important to give details about trees. It is essential to be more specific in future when compiling documents for tender to avoid disappointments and misunder-standings.

Another purpose of the detail sheets is to enable soft landscape works to be properly priced by quantity surveyors at the design/budget stage. It has far too often been the experience of landscape architects that too little money is given to soft works - it is usually treated as being of minor importance to a project. It is far better for the quantity surveyor to price adequately for all aspects of soft landscape works based on all the details assembled than to put in a provisional sum as so often happens. If a budget has to be cut, do not let it be at the expense of good stock and establishment. Fewer trees, all growing successfully, should then be the objective.

I have been told that publication of this book could open a can of worms, after it is published but then, if it gets everyone in the business - both horticulture and landscape - to come to an agreement on many of the aspects in the book it will have been well worth while. After all, revised editions can always take any changes into account.

I know too from my teaching experience that the book will be useful to many students, and I hope that the details will also save them time during periods of pressure. The guidance notes should also be a help when writing specifications.

Acknowledgements

Just as no man is an island, neither is an author, particularly one who is involved with technical aspects. This book could never have been produced without the help of many people, including some who have worked in my practice. Some have moved on; others are still with me; and one or two joined in at a later stage but have still made a valuable contribution. I trust that they too will have gained from the experience and hope that the final printed version will come up to their expectations. Tim Linnington, who more than anyone in the practice has provided the main support, along with Graham Slocombe, Frances Ward, Jane Irwin, Bernard Clark, Janette Tillotson and Christine Cordrey - I thank you all.

I must also thank Rodney Helliwell for supplying valuable information, checking text and drawings on numerous occasions, and putting up with so many questions from my office. Without his encouragement I would not have continued.

To James St J Wilson for being so helpful in checking drawings and text and giving considerable helpful advice at short notice.

Also to John Chetham, formerly with Bristol City Council, and now in Australia, who spent a considerable amount of time in the early days helping me with visits to nurseries to photograph tree stock, especially tree roots.

To Derek Patch of the Forestry Commission for inspiring me to publish and be damned when I was at the crossroads five years ago and was wondering if it was really worth while.

To the many landscape architects and horticulturalists, too numerous to name, with whom I have discussed the contents of these chapters.

I must add that my publishers, in particular Maritz Vandenberg, have been very patient and understanding, especially in waiting for such a long time for the final manuscript and drawings.

I cannot end without acknowledging the many hours of typing and word processing as well as often correcting the text, put in by our secretaries, Jane Yeates and Emma Parker. They have provided tremendous support.

While so many people have kindly assisted me on this interesting and worthwhile assignment, any errors, omissions, or inadequacies must be my responsibility. I can only hope that readers will be tolerant and help me to make sure that the next edition is even better.

INTRODUCTION

These detail sheets and guidance notes have been produced to assist landscape architects, designers, contractors and any others associated with landscape contract documents. It is to be hoped that they will save them considerable time in drawing standard details, and will avoid needless repetition.

It is envisaged that the detail sheets could be used at both the design and contract stages of a project. It is possible to use them without alteration, but in some cases minor modifications and additions to dimensions or specification may be necessary. Lettering has been standardised by the use of a stencil (italic 3.5 mm).

The notes which precede each section are intended to be of assistance especially when specifications are necessary. For more detailed guidance, the publications listed should be consulted. Details should not be used without a knowledge of the content of the British Standards. Some British Standards contain alternative specifications which may prove to be more suitable in a particular case.

Use of the detail sheets

The collection of detail sheets, as published, may be photocopied, punched, and stored in a ring binder. The sheets have been laid out in such a way as to facilitate this. In the form of individual leaves the details can easily be traced or copy negatives be made.

Some of the sheets should be used in conjunction with a planting plan or schedule, especially those concerning size, planting, staking etc. (see Figures 1-2).

Production of new detail sheets

Where the use of a detail not included in the original collection of detail sheets is required, the new detail is produced on A4 tracing paper using a standard format. This allows it to be added to the original collection and easily re-used. New details are assigned a reference number by the Design Office, using their own reference system. The title of the new detail, as shown in the centre label at the foot of the drawing, is then added to the contents list prefacing each section.

Issue of detail sheets

Detail sheets can be used in two ways. A set of photocopies can be issued to the contractor and/or quantity surveyor of the selected details, after completion of the title panel reference, and each detail can be number-stamped with the office stamp and collated in a binder with the specifications.

The second method is to trace or copy a batch of details, grouped according to type and identified with key numbers, on to an A1 sheet of tracing paper and include the drawing with the contract set in the normal way.

Standards

British Standards and Codes of Practice are referred to where necessary. Users of this book in countries where British Standards are not used should delete the reference to the British Standard and, if they feel it necessary, either insert a reference to an equivalent national standard or describe in empirical terms what is required.

TYPICAL PLANTING PLAN

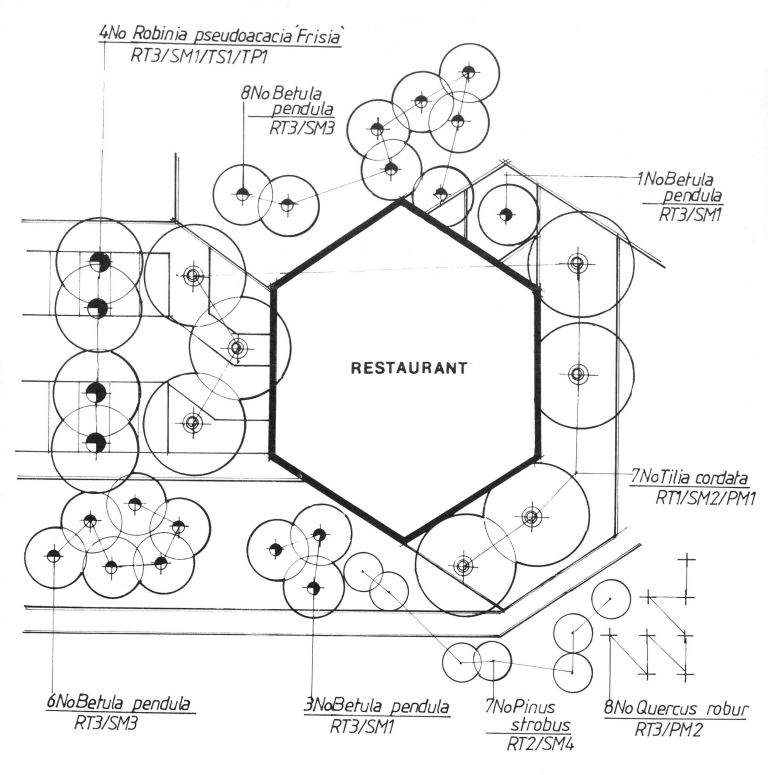

4No Robinia pseudoacacia 'Frisia'
RT3/SM1/TS1/TP1

8No Betula
pendula
RT3/SM3

1No Betula
pendula
RT3/SM1

RESTAURANT

7No Tilia cordata
RT1/SM2/PM1

6No Betula pendula
RT3/SM3

3No Betula pendula
RT3/SM1

7No Pinus
strobus
RT2/SM4

8No Quercus robur
RT3/PM2

Figure 1

TYPICAL PLANT SCHEDULE

PLANT NAME	PLANT SIZE	PLANT SPACING	TOTAL	ROOT TYPE	SECURING METHOD	PROTECTION METHOD	NOTES
TREES							
Betula pendula	Tall standard	As shown	4	RT3	SM1		
Betula pendula	Standard	As shown	14	RT3	SM3		
Pinus strobus		As shown	7	RT2	SM4		
Quercus robur	Transp	As shown	8	RT3		PM2	
Robinia pseudoacacia 'Frisia'	Tall standard	As shown	4	RT3	SM1		TS1 / TP1
Tilia cordata	Semi -	As shown	7	RT1	SM2	PM1	

KEY

ROOT TYPE
RT1	Root balled
RT2	Container grown
RT3	Bare root

SECURING METHOD
SM1	Double staking
SM2	Timber deadman
SM3	Single stake
SM4	Short stake

PROTECTION METHOD
PM1	Hessian wraping
PM2	Tuley tubes

TREE SURROUNDS
TS1	Grid detail
TP1	Pit detail

PLANT SYMBOLS
	Standard
	Semi-mature
	Tall standard
	Transplant

DETAIL SHEETS

STAKING advanced stock double stake, crossbar
ANCHORAGE semi-mature tree
STAKING advanced stock low single stake
STAKING advanced stock low single stake

TRANSPLANTING tree wrapping
TREE PROTECTION tree shelter

TREE SURROUNDS cast iron
TREE PIT in filled ground

STOCK standard

STOCK semi-mature

STOCK tall standard

STOCK transplant

Figure 2

1 STOCK AND SIZES

This chapter sets out general points which need to be considered when selecting and specifying stock. The main considerations are specific requirements on origin, condition, form, dimensions and plant handling. The British Standard recommendations for nursery stock are in BS 3936. Part 1 (1980) covers trees and shrubs, and Part 4 (1966) deals with forest trees. These recommendations may not be sufficiently detailed for all circumstances.

Origin

When selecting stock, it is useful to obtain information on its origin and growing conditions. A supplier will usually be required to declare whether or not plants offered for sale are UK-grown. If plants which are normally propagated vegetatively have been grown from seed or vice versa, this fact should also be stated by the supplier. Other information on the method of propagation will usually be provided by the supplier on request.

Whenever possible, it is useful to inspect trees while they are growing in the nursery. An inspection of growing conditions in the nursery may also give an indication of the quality of stock.

Growing conditions

Trees which have been grown at too close a spacing will be spindly and lacking in vigour. They will also have root systems which are small and likely to be extensively damaged during lifting. As a general rule, trees in the nursery should be at a spacing which is not less than one third of their height. For example, trees 450 mm tall should be not less than 150 mm apart, and trees 3 m tall should be not less than 1 m apart.

Trees which have been grown at closer spacings will probably be cheaper and may be adequate for a particular job, but they must be regarded as second-rate trees. Most trees currently produced by the nursery trade fall into this second-rate category, owing to strong competition within the trade. It is hoped that this situation will change in future, for the cost of the trees is often a very small proportion of the total cost of a job. It would be well worth paying more for first-rate trees that will grow immediately, more rapidly and more successfully.

Polythene tunnels and glasshouses

Trees which have been grown under cover should be adequately hardened off outside, for a minimum of eight growing-season weeks, before being planted on any exposed or open site. Polythene tunnels can cause excessive height increment out of proportion with stem girth increment. Betula species are very susceptible to this and are often so weak they bend above the point of attachment at the top of the stake.

Grafted trees

Some cultivars need to be grafted onto a closely related rootstock; sometimes this is done merely for convenience, because the rootstock plants are easier and quicker to grow.

Points on which to be cautious include:

1.
Trees which have been grafted on to a rootstock which may cause problems,

1

e.g. *Sorbus* cultivars grafted on to hawthorn rootstock, shoots from which will require frequent cutting. It is better, whenever possible, to select cultivar stock grafted on to a rootstock of the *same* genus.

2.
Trees which have been grafted at more than a few centimetres above ground level. Some trees which have been grafted at about 1 m will tend to look unsightly in later years, particularly if the stock increases in girth at a greater or lesser rate than the scion, giving an obvious bulge in the stem.
Weeping trees, such as weeping ash (*Fraxinus excelsior 'Pendula'*), are often grafted at about 2 m, in order to obtain a straight stem below the pendulous branches, and certain cherries are often grafted at this height. This is usually acceptable, as the graft tends to be obscured by the main branches, but it can still occasionally be unsightly.

When selecting grafted stock, it is recommended that information on the name or designation of rootstock be obtained from the supplier.

Provenance

There can be marked differences in growth rates, frost-hardiness and other characteristics within the geographical range of tree species. Trees grown from seed of unknown or untried provenance represent a greater risk than those from seed from a tried and tested origin or from parent trees in the locality.

Condition of stock

When inspected in the nursery, trees should be visually free from pest and disease disorder and materially

undamaged. The trees should have been cultivated so as to ensure that they have an adequate root system conducive to successful transplantation. To this end, the root system should be well balanced in relation to the size of the plant.

It is preferable to inspect trees while in leaf. Trees should be of the desired size and form, with the size and colour of leaves typical for the species, or if not in leaf, they should have firm healthy buds. A strong tapered trunk is most desirable for adequate support, and a good leader is important for continued growth.

Choice of stock

For each project the size of stock should be selected with regard to the conditions for establishment on site, the initial impact required from the planting, and the capital cost of stock. It is better to buy high-quality smaller stock than second-rate larger stock, as growth will catch up within the first few years.

Type of stock available

The traditional emphasis on standard-formed larger stock reflects economics of production. The "lollipop" shape is in fact unnatural for most species, but good for street trees. Feathered forms are more natural; these are generally available in smaller sizes. Feathered trees develop a strong trunk more rapidly because of the stimulating effect of branches growing all the way up the stem.

There is potentially a demand amongst landscape architects for larger feathers and multi-stemmed trees, but availability of these is limited as yet.

2

As a general rule, properly grown and carefully handled field-grown trees are likely to be cheaper and better than container-grown trees. Exceptions include *black* pines (*Pinus nigra*) and mulberries (*Morus* species). The roots of trees in containers very quickly develop a spiral growth pattern, unless the container is large, and this can give problems of poor growth and instability in later years.

Container-grown trees transplanted in midsummer will need watering in dry weather. The soil volume from which the plant can take up moisture is limited because of the restricted root growth at first. Watering is therefore vital.

Semi-mature trees (transplanted)

The main reasons for transplanting large stock are associated with design effect. Large trees provide an immediate landscape feature, with predictable form and good visual impact. The techniques may also be used to transfer an existing tree threatened by development. The use of standard stock may be more cost-effective and ultimately successful, especially in cases where an intensive maintenance programme is difficult.

In Britain and Europe, stock which is transplanted is generally under 12.5 m in height. Species vary considerably in their suitability for transplanting at large sizes (see BS 4043, the Civic Trust references in the Bibliography to this chapter, and the tables on pp.7-11). In general it is best to relate the species chosen to the conditions prevailing at the new site, as with planting standard nursery stock. The form of the tree will change little after planting, so stock of an appropriate growth form should be selected initially.

Form and dimensions

The dimensions of stock should be in accordance with Tables 1-4 on pp. 7-11. Specific requirements for form and size of different types of nursery stock are outlined in the details and summarised below.

Transplant
Trees transplanted or roots undercut or transplanted at least once to develop fibrous root system

Age and height stated

Whip
Transplanted (or undercut) at least once to develop root system

Without significant feather growth and without head

Overall height stated

Feathered
Transplanted (or undercut) at least once to develop root system

Reasonably straight stem

Head well developed for its type and evenly balanced, with no main branches crossing the crown and with a central leader

Overall height stated, as well as stem circumference measured 1 m from ground level

Standards
All standards supplied as: bare root; rootballed; or container grown

Plants should have been previously

3

transplanted at least once during their life

Plants should have reasonably straight stems, bottom worked trees should have no more than a slight bend at the union, temporary feathering should have been removed flush with the stem

The head should be well developed for its type and evenly balanced, with no main branch crossing the crown, with a central leader, or alternatively with a branched head

Standards, excluding half standards, are designated by size of stem circumference, measured 1 m from ground level, and overall height should be stated for standards other than weeping standards. Weeping standards should have minimum clear stem height stated

Advanced nursery stock

Advanced nursery stock are those transplanted from their original site and grown on for transplanting to their final site at an advanced stage of growth

Girth measurements 10-12 cm up to 20+ cm

Height is normally between 3.6 m and 6.0 m in the case of deciduous trees, and between 2 m and 3.5 m in the case of conifers

Requirements for form as for standards; size of advanced standards designated by size of stem circumference measured 1 m from the ground and overall height stated as for standards
Broadleaf evergreen
Supplied as container - or field-grown, balled and wrapped in hessian. Ball

sizes should be of a diameter and depth to encompass enough fibrous and feeding roots necessary for recovery of plant

Container grown plants should be well established in the container in which they are sold with their roots to the bottom of the pot

Plants should be vigorous and healthy, with good-sized, well-formed leaves on all branches

Ratio of height to spread should be no less than 3:2

Height and spread to be stated as well as ball diameter or container size

Conifers
Supplied either container-grown or grown in open ground with roots balled and wrapped in hessian. Conifers grown in open ground should have been transplanted or undercut sufficiently often in relation to their age to ensure well-developed fibrous root system

Container grown conifers should have been established in the container long enough for substantial new growth to have been produced within the container; the size of the container should be in reasonable proportion to the size and mass of the plant, with the volume capacity of the container stated

Upright growing conifers are measured by overall height from ground level, excluding roots, rootball or container: spreading conifers measured by mean diameter of spread

Semi-mature
A tree at an advanced stage of growth

4

which is to be transplanted with an earth rootball and is of such combined size and weight that special equipment is needed for transplanting operations. Trees are generally between 5 and 12 m tall, but certain shorter trees may be included

Plant handling

Quality of stock must be maintained by proper handling. All trees should be adequately and carefully packed and protected against drying out, mechanical damage and extremes of temperature, from the moment they are lifted until they are planted.

Bare rooted trees up to 14 cm in girth are generally bundled, with all shoots facing in the same direction and with foliage surface as dry as possible. Trees up to 45 cm tall are then packed in loose bundles within plastic film bags. Trees in excess of 14 cm girth are supplied without soil adhering to the roots but with roots packed with moist straw or other suitable material and enclosed in hessian or plastic film. It is important to note that hessian is not an adequate protection against drying out.

Container-grown or rootballed plants must not be bundled. The rootballs of rootballed plants must be supported to prevent collapse and protected against drying out. Additional packaging is not normally necessary for container plants. Conifers and evergreens may be treated with anti-desiccant before delivery to the site, but this is not usual. The period between lifting and despatch and between receipt and planting should be limited as far as possible. Bare-rooted plants may be stored for a few weeks with a covering of suitable material such as moist sand to keep the roots moist. The permeable wrappings of rootballed plants should be kept moist and polythene wrappings protected from direct sunlight. Container-grown plants should be kept upright and watered.

All plant material to be transported should be carefully handled to avoid mechanical damage. If transport is to be by open lorry, the consignment should be completely sheeted; closed lorries are preferred. The shoots or foliage of plants to be transported in closed lorries or containers should be as surface dry as possible.

Plant handling in general should be in accordance with the *General Conditions, Specification and Schedules of Quantity for the Supply and Delivery of Plants* (Joint Liaison Committee for Plant Suppliers, 1982. revised 1986) and *Plant Handling*, a booklet published by the CPSE (1985).

Labelling (specification as included in the *Plant Handling* booklet)

Each plant, or bundle of single species or cultivar, should be legibly labelled with its full botanical name.

Each consignment should give particulars so as to provide easy and adequate identification at the point of delivery, i.e. name of plants and supplier.

Checklist

Origin
All trees should be true to name.
Plants grown outside the UK should be stated.
Name or designation of rootstock for grafted trees should be stated by the

supplier if requested.

Condition
Trees should be visibly free of pest or disease and materially undamaged. The root system should be well balanced in relation to the plant and conducive to successful transplantation.

Dimensions
The size of tree should conform with the dimensions set out in the tables. Dimensions should be correctly stated for the type of stock.

Packaging
and handling
Packaging should be adequate to protect the plants and prevent extremes of temperature or drying out.

Labelling
Each plant should be adequately labelled with plant name, each consignment with name of supplier.

Bibliography

AMERICAN ASSOCIATION OF NURSERYMEN (ANS1 Z60. 1-1973) American Standard for Nursery Stock

BRITISH HARDIPLANTS LTD, The Good Planting Guide

BRITISH STANDARDS INSTITUTION BS 3936: Nursery stock. Part 1 - Trees and shrubs (1980); Part 4 - Forest trees (1966)
BRITISH STANDARDS INSTITUTION (1978) BS 4043: Recommendations for transplanting semi-mature trees

BRITISH STANDARDS INSTITUTION (1969) BS 4428: Recommendations for general landscape operations

BRITISH STANDARDS INSTITUTION (1975) BS 5236: Cultivation and planting of trees in the advanced nursery stock category

CIVIC TRUST The Civic Trust Trees Campaign - Practice Notes on the Transplanting of Semi-mature Trees

CIVIC TRUST The Civic Trust Trees Campaign

CIVIC TRUST Moving Big Trees

COMMITTEE FOR PLANT SUPPLY AND ESTABLISHMENT (1986) Plant Handling

DAVIES, A. (1983) Making the grade, *CG and HTJ*, December

JOINT LIAISON COMMITTEE FOR PLANT SUPPLIERS (1982) General Conditions, Specification and Schedules of Quantity for the Supply and Delivery of Plants (revised 1986)

SPRAY, M. (1983) Tasteful trees, *CG and HTJ*, July

Tables 1-4: Dimensions for nursery stock

Table 1 Deciduous stock: metric

Stock type	Circumference of stem (in)	Min diameter of stem (in) at 3'2" height (BS 3936)	Height overall (ft) in	Height from ground to branch: Min clear (ft) in	Min root depth (in)	Min root width (ft) in	Balled and burlapped min Ball width (ft) in
Younger stock							
Transplant			2' - 4'0"		6	4	6
Whip A/B			4' - 6'0"		7¾	7¾"	7¾"
Feathered	2¼		6' - 10'0"		11¾	11¾"	11¾"
Standard stock							
Half standard	1½ - 2¼	½	6' - 7'0"	4' - 4'6"	11¾	11¾"	11¾"
Three-quarter standard	2¼ - 3	¾	7' - 8'0"	4'6" - 5'0"	11¾	1' 5¾"	1' 3¾"
Light standard	2¼ - 3	¾	8' - 9'0"	5'0" - 5'6"	11¾	1' 7¾"	1' 5¾"
Standard	3 - 4	1	9' - 10'0"	5'6" - 6'0"	11¾	1' 9½"	1' 5¾"
Tall standard	3 - 4	1	10' - 11'9"	6'0"	11¾	1' 11¾"	1' 7¾"
Selected standard	4 - 4¾	1¼	10' - 11'9"	6'0"	13¾	1' 11¾"	1' 7¾"
Advanced stock							
Heavy standard	4¾ - 5½	1½	11'9" - 13'6"	6'0"	15¾	2' 3½"	1' 11½"
Extra H std A	5½ - 6½	1¾	13'6" - 15'6"	6'0"	17¾	2' 7"	2' 3½"
Extra H std B	6½ - 7¾	2	15'6" - 17'6"	6'0"	17¾	2' 11"	2' 7"
Extra H std c	7¾ - 9¼	2½	17'6" - 19'6"	6'0"	17¾	3' 3"	2' 11"

Table 1 Deciduous stock: imperial

Stock type	Circumference of stem (cm)	Min diameter of stem (mm) at 1m height (BS 3936)	Height overall	Height from ground to branch: min clear	Min root depth	Min root width	Balled and burlapped min ball width
Younger stock							
Transplant			600-1200		150	100	150
Whip A/B			1200-1800		200	200	200
Feathered	6		1800-3000		300	300	300
Standard stock							
Half standard	4-6	13	1800-2100	1200-1400	300	300	350
Three-quarter standard	6-8	19	2100-2400	1400-1600	300	450	400
Light standard	6-8	19	2400-2700	1600-1700	300	500	450
Standard	8-10	25	2700-3000	1700-1800	350	550	450
Tall standard	8-10	25	3000-3600	1800 min	350	600	500
Selected standard	10-12	32	3000-3600	1800 min	400	600	500
Advanced stock							
Heavy standard	12-14	38	3600-4200	1800 min	450	700	600
Extra H std A	14-16	45	4200-4800	1800 min	500	800	700
Extra H std B	16-18	51	4800-5400	1800 min	500	900	800
Extra H std c	18-20	57	5400-6000	1800 min	500	1000	900

Table 2 Broadleaf evergreen stock, domed & conical: metric				
Average height (mm)	*Average spread (mm)*	*Ball depth (mm)*	*Ball width (mm)*	*Minimum pot size for C G stock (litres)*
750	500	225	300	3
1000	660	260	350	8
1250	825	300	400	10
1500	1000	325	500	15
2000	1300	350	550	35

Ratio of height to spread should be no less than 3:2

Examples of species of this form:

Domed:
Cotoneaster cornubia
Davidia involucrata

Conical:
Eucalyptus gunnii (when young)

Broadleaf evergreen stock, domed & conical: imperial				
Average height (ft in)	*Average spread (ft in)*	*Ball depth (ft in)*	*Ball width (ft in)*	*Minimum pot size for C G stock (Imp gal) (=1 2 US gal)*
2' 6"	1' 6"	8¾"	11¾"	.5
3' 6"	2' 0"	10½"	1' 1¾"	1.75
4' 0"	2' 3"	11¾"	1' 3¾"	2.25
5' 0"	3' 3"	1' 0¾"	1' 7¾"	3.25
6' 5"	4' 3"	1' 1¾"	1' 9½"	7.75

Ratio of height to spread should be no less than 3:2

Table 3 Conifer stock pyramidal and broad upright: metric

Height (mm)	Spread (mm)	Minimum pot size for C G stock (l)	Minimum root diameter for balled and burlapped stock (mm)
300- 375	200- 300	1.5	
375- 450	225- 375	1.5	
450- 600	300- 450	3	200
600- 750	375- 525	3	250
750- 900	450- 600	3	300
900-1200	525- 750	8	350
1200-1500	750- 900	15	400
1500-1800	900-1050	25	500
1800-2100	1050-1200	35	550

Ball depth ratio for balled and burlapped stock:

Ball diameter   l - 500 mm: depth not less than 75% of width
Ball diameter 500-750 mm: depth not less than 66% of width
Ball diameter 750-120 mm: depth not less than 60% of width

Examples of species of this form:
Abies
Cedrus deodara
Chamaecyparis lawsoniana 'allumii'
Picea abies (conical types)
Pinus (except dwarf varieties)
Thuja occidentalis, T orientalis (conical types)

Conifer stock pyramidal and broad upright: imperial

Height (ft in)	Spread (ft in)	Minimum pot size for C G stock (gal) (Imp.) (US)	Minimum root diameter for balled and burlapped stock (ft in)
1' - 1'3"	8" - 1'0"	.3	
1'3" - 1'6"	9" - 1'3"	.3	
1'6" - 2'0"	1'0" - 1'5"	.6	7¾"
2'0" - 2'6"	1'3" - 1'9"	.6	9¾"
2'6" - 3'0"	1'0" - 2'0"	.6	11¾"
3'0" - 4'0"	1'9" - 2'6"	2.1	1' 1¾"
4'0" - 5'0"	2'6" - 3'0"	4.5	1' 3¾"
5'0" - 6'0"	3'0" - 3'6"	6.6	1' 7¾"
6'0" - 7'0"	3'6" - 4'0"	9.3	1' 9½"

Ball depth ratio for balled and burlapped stock:

Ball diameter   l   - 1' 7.75": depth not less than 75% of width
Ball diameter 1' 7.75" - 2' 5.5" : depth not less than 66% of width
Ball diameter 2' 5.5" -   4.75": depth not less than 60% of width

Table 4 Conifer stock columnar: metric

Height (mm)	Spread (mm)*	Minimum pot size for C G Stock (litres)	Minimum root diameter for balled & burlapped (mm)
300- 375	75-150	1.5	
375- 450	100-175	1.5	
450- 600	125-200	3	250
600- 750	150-225	4	300
750- 900	174-250	4	300
900-1200 .	225-300	8	325
1200-1500	300-375	8	350
1500-1800	375-450	15	400
1800-2100	450-525	35	450

*For regular-growing species
Ball depth ratio : see note to Table 3

Examples of species of this form:
Thuja occidentalis, orientalis (columnar types)
Juniperus virginiana 'Skyrocket'

Conifer stock, columnar: imperial

Height (ft in)	Spread (ft in)*	Minimum pot size for C G Stock (gal) (Imp.) (US)	Minimum root diameter for balled & burlapped (in)
1' - 1'3"	3 - 6	.30	
1'3" - 1'6"	4 - 7	.30	
1'6" - 2'0"	5 - 8	.6	9¾"
2'0" - 2'6"	6 - 9	.9	11¾"
2'6" - 3'0"	7 - 10	.9	11¾"
3'0" - 4'0"	9 - 11.75	2.1	1' 0¾"
4'0" - 5'0"	11.75 - 1'2.75"	2.1	1' 1¾"
5'0" - 6'0"	1'2.75"-1'5.75"	4.5	1' 3¾"
6'0" - 7'0"	1'5.75"-1'8.5"	9.3	1' 5¾"

*For regular-growing species
Ball depth ratio : see note to Table 3

Detail sheets

1.1
Stock - main parts of a tree
1.2
Stock - transplant
1.3
Stock - whip A/B
1.4
Stock - feathered
1.5
Stock - half standard
1.6
Stock - three-quarter standard
1.7
Stock - light standard
1.8
Stock - standard
1.9
Stock - tall standard
1.10
Stock - selected standard
1.11
Stock - heavy standard
1.12
Stock - extra heavy standard A
1.13
Stock - extra heavy standard B
1.14
Stock - extra heavy standard C
1.15
Stock - semi-mature tree A
1.16
Stock - semi-mature tree B
1.17
Stock - broadleaf evergreen - domed
1.18
Stock - broadleaf evergreen - conical
1.19
Stock - conifer - pyramidal
1.20
Stock - conifer - broad
1.21
Stock - conifer - columnar

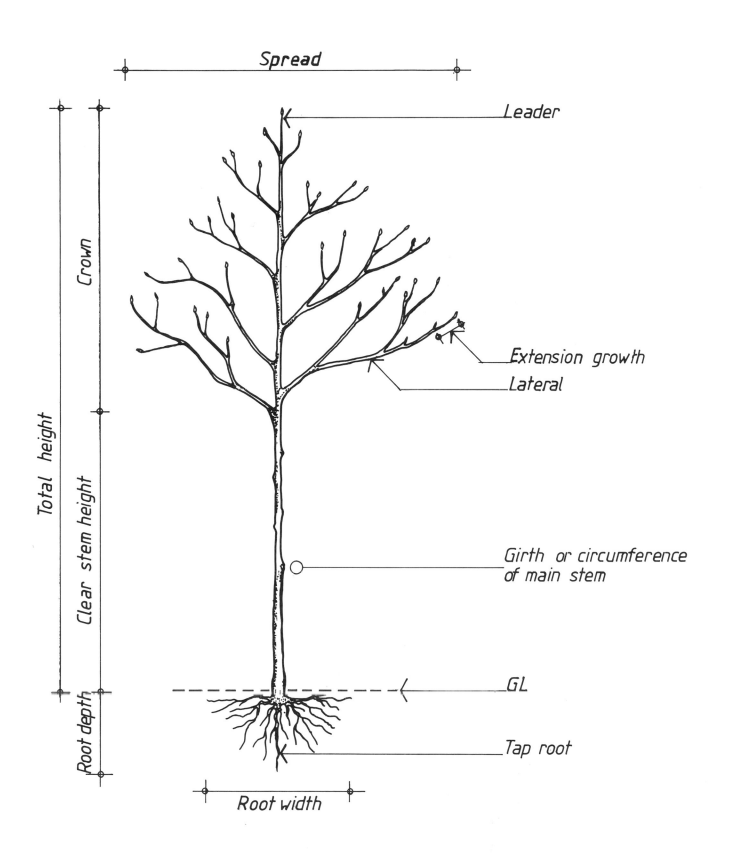

Spread

Leader

Crown

Total height

Clear stem height

Root depth

Extension growth

Lateral

Girth or circumference
of main stem

GL

Tap root

Root width

NTS

STOCK

main parts of a tree

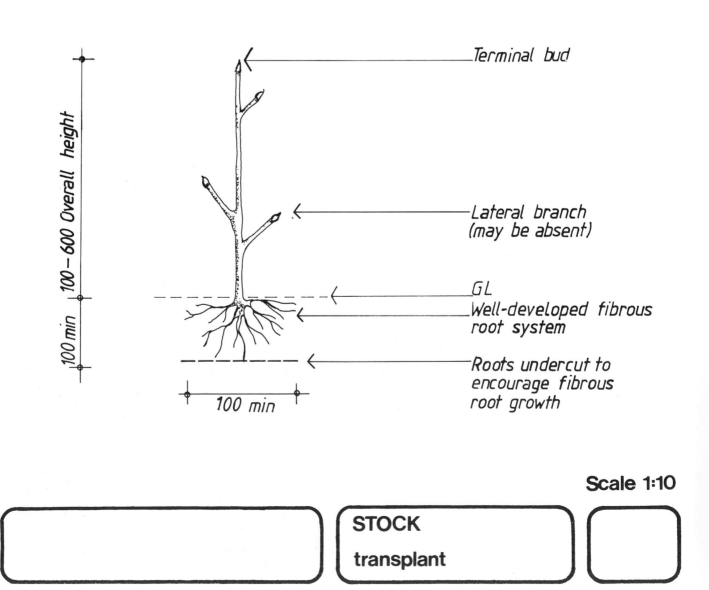

Terminal bud

Lateral branch
(may be absent)

GL
Well-developed fibrous
root system

Roots undercut to
encourage fibrous
root growth

100 – 600 Overall height

100 min

100 min

Scale 1:10

STOCK

transplant

14

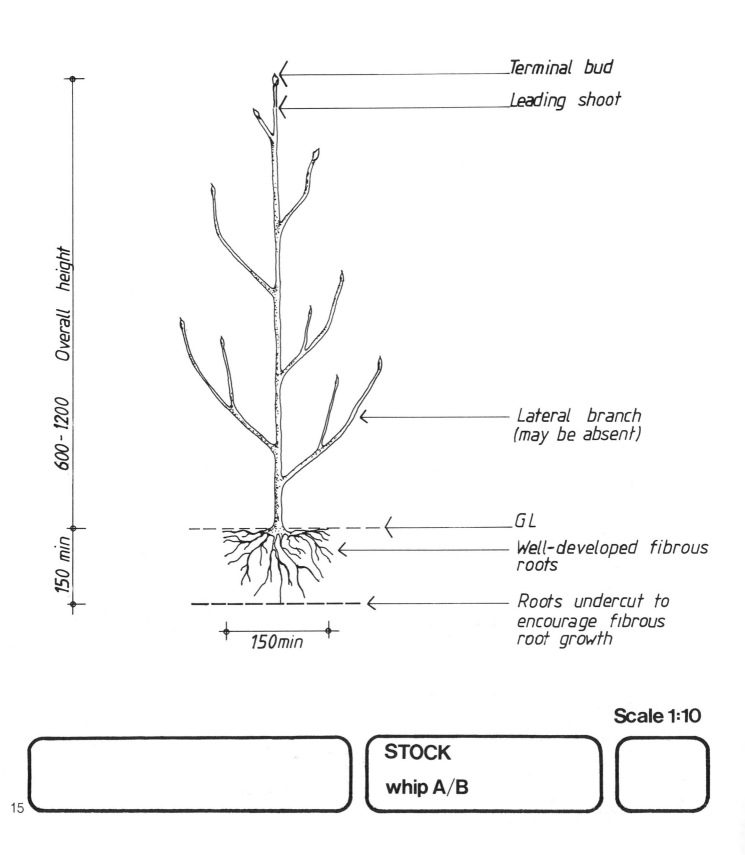

Terminal bud

Leading shoot

Overall height

600 - 1200

150 min

Lateral branch
(may be absent)

GL

Well-developed fibrous
roots

Roots undercut to
encourage fibrous
root growth

150min

Scale 1:10

STOCK

whip A/B

15

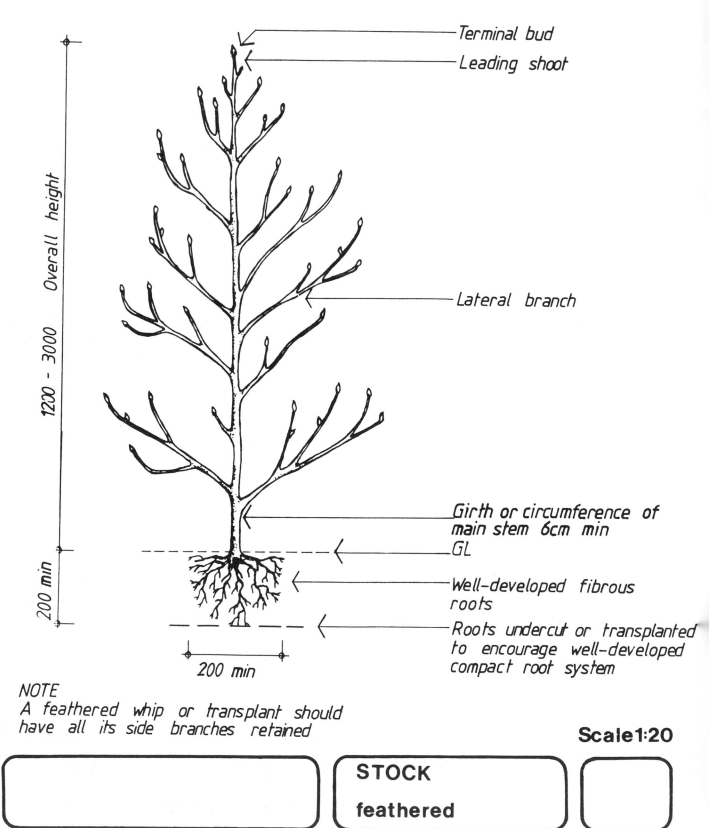

Terminal bud

Leading shoot

Overall height

1200 - 3000

Lateral branch

Girth or circumference of main stem 6cm min

GL

Well-developed fibrous roots

200 min

Roots undercut or transplanted to encourage well-developed compact root system

200 min

NOTE
A feathered whip or transplant should have all its side branches retained

Scale 1:20

STOCK

feathered

16

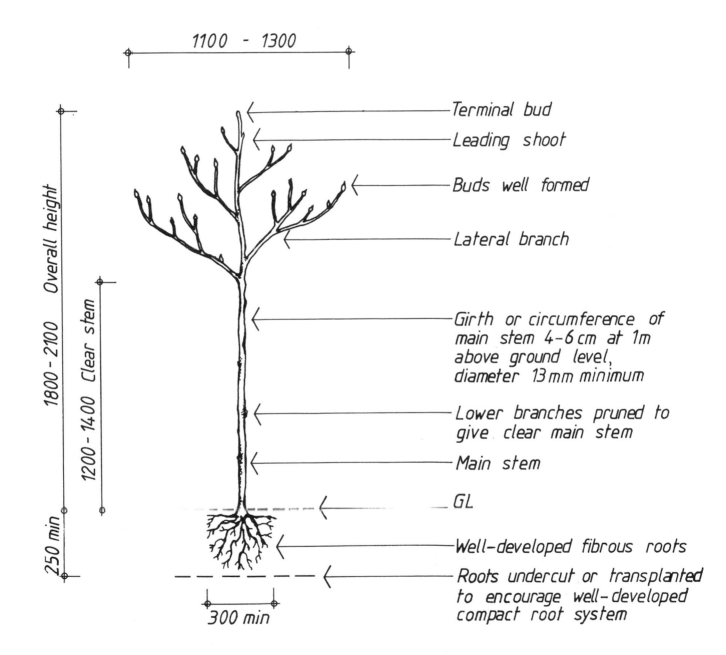

1100 - 1300

Terminal bud

Leading shoot

Buds well formed

Lateral branch

Girth or circumference of main stem 4-6cm at 1m above ground level, diameter 13mm minimum

Lower branches pruned to give clear main stem

Main stem

GL

Well-developed fibrous roots

Roots undercut or transplanted to encourage well-developed compact root system

Overall height

1800 - 2100

1200 - 1400 Clear stem

250 min

300 min

Scale 1:20

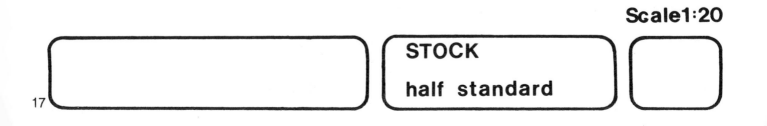

STOCK

half standard

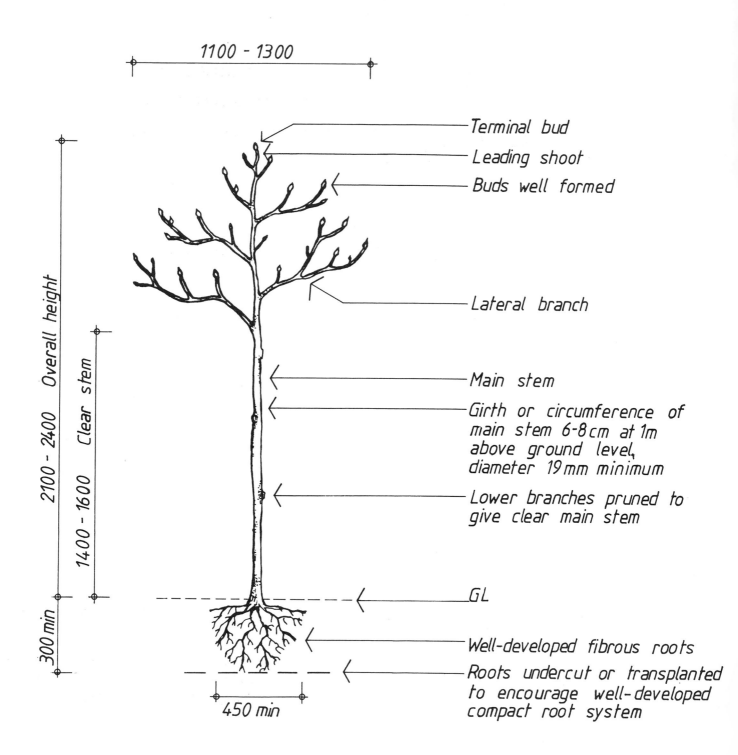

1100 - 1300

Terminal bud
Leading shoot
Buds well formed

Lateral branch

Main stem

Girth or circumference of
main stem 6-8 cm at 1m
above ground level,
diameter 19 mm minimum

Lower branches pruned to
give clear main stem

GL

Well-developed fibrous roots

Roots undercut or transplanted
to encourage well-developed
compact root system

2100 - 2400 Overall height

1400 - 1600 Clear stem

300 min

450 min

Scale1:20

**STOCK
three-quarter
standard**

18

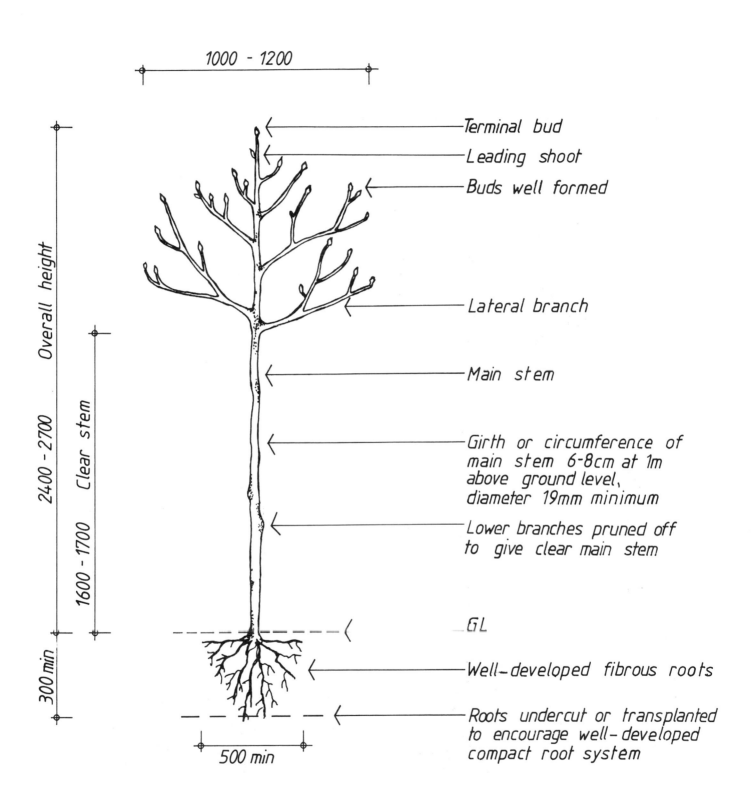

1000 - 1200

Terminal bud

Leading shoot

Buds well formed

Lateral branch

Main stem

Girth or circumference of
main stem 6-8cm at 1m
above ground level,
diameter 19mm minimum

Lower branches pruned off
to give clear main stem

GL

Well-developed fibrous roots

Roots undercut or transplanted
to encourage well-developed
compact root system

Overall height

Clear stem

2400 - 2700

1600 - 1700

300 min

500 min

Scale1:20

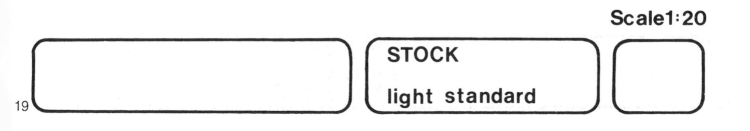

STOCK

light standard

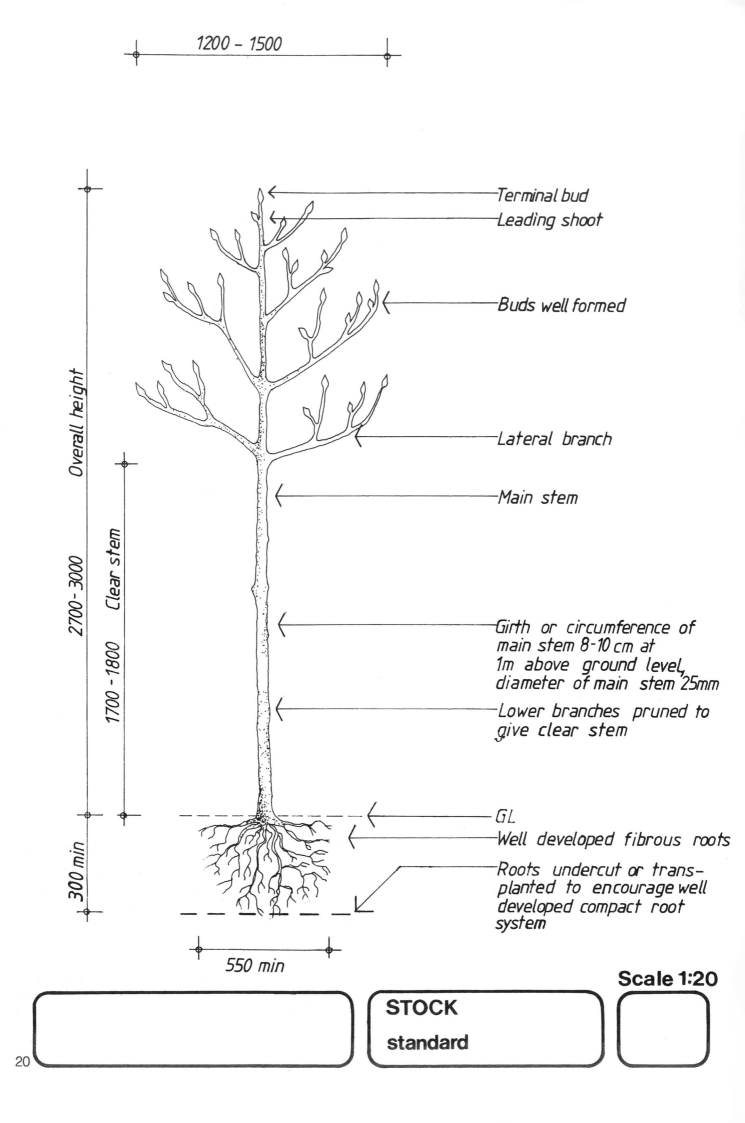

1200 - 1500

Terminal bud
Leading shoot

Buds well formed

Lateral branch

Main stem

Girth or circumference of
main stem 8-10 cm at
1m above ground level,
diameter of main stem 25mm

Lower branches pruned to
give clear stem

GL
Well developed fibrous roots

Roots undercut or trans-
planted to encourage well
developed compact root
system

Overall height

2700 - 3000

Clear stem

1700 - 1800

300 min

550 min

Scale 1:20

STOCK

standard

20

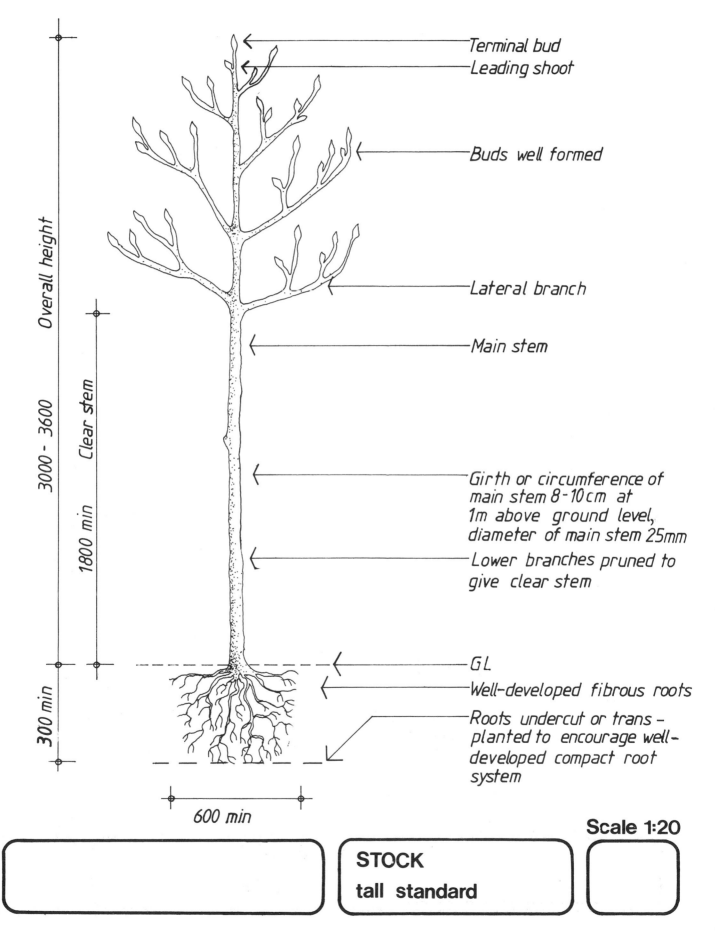

1200 - 1500

Terminal bud
Leading shoot

Buds well formed

Lateral branch

Main stem

Girth or circumference of
main stem 8-10 cm at
1m above ground level,
diameter of main stem 25mm

Lower branches pruned to
give clear stem

GL

Well-developed fibrous roots

Roots undercut or trans-
planted to encourage well-
developed compact root
system

Overall height

3000 - 3600

Clear stem

1800 min

300 min

600 min

Scale 1:20

STOCK
tall standard

21

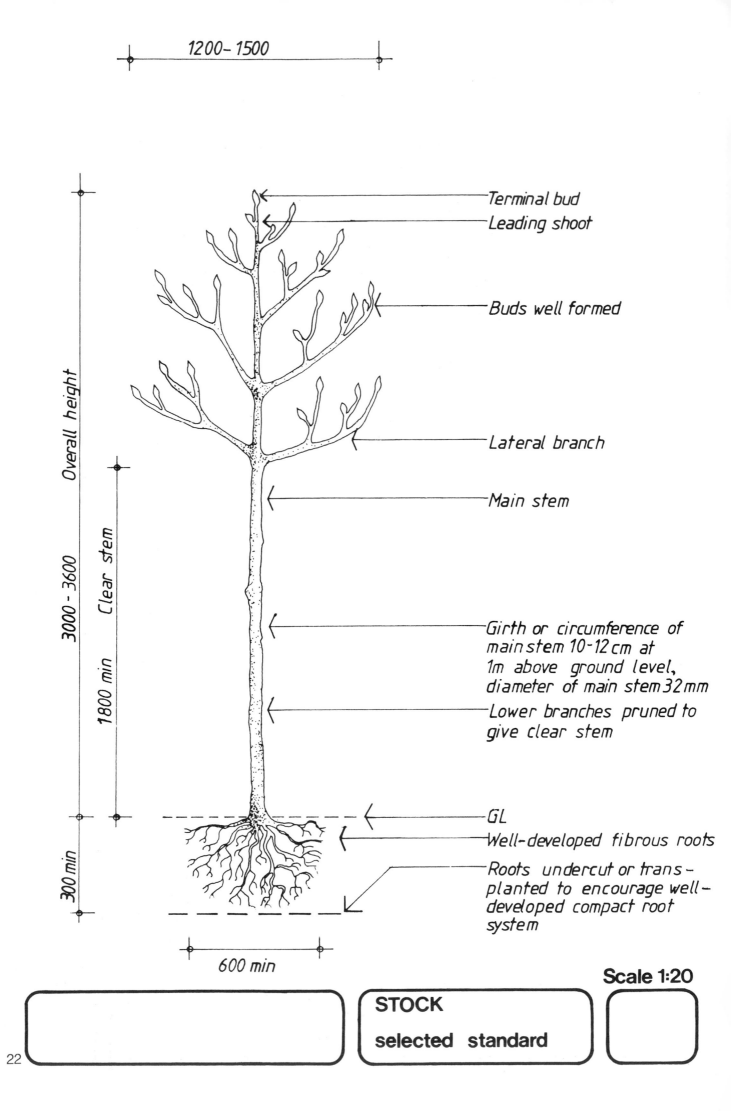

1200–1500

Terminal bud

Leading shoot

Buds well formed

Lateral branch

Main stem

Girth or circumference of main stem 10-12 cm at 1m above ground level, diameter of main stem 32mm

Lower branches pruned to give clear stem

GL

Well-developed fibrous roots

Roots undercut or trans- planted to encourage well- developed compact root system

Overall height

3000 - 3600

Clear stem

1800 min

300 min

600 min

Scale 1:20

STOCK

selected standard

22

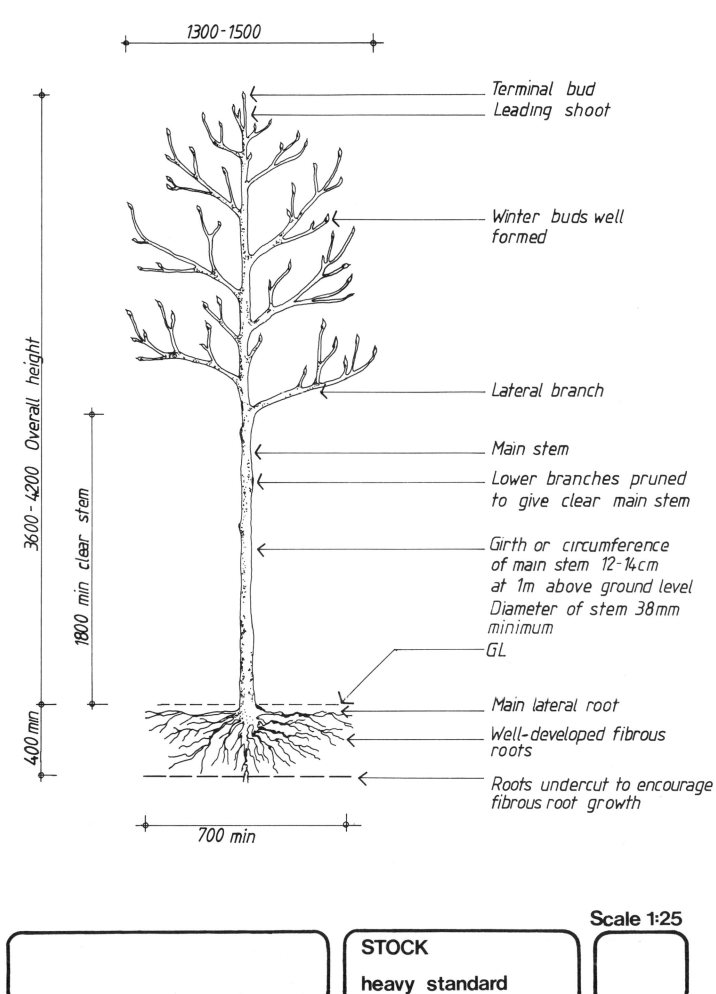

1300 - 1500

Terminal bud
Leading shoot

Winter buds well formed

Lateral branch

Main stem

Lower branches pruned to give clear main stem

Girth or circumference of main stem 12-14 cm at 1m above ground level
Diameter of stem 38mm minimum

GL

Main lateral root

Well-developed fibrous roots

Roots undercut to encourage fibrous root growth

3600 - 4200 Overall height

1800 min clear stem

400 min

700 min

Scale 1:25

STOCK

heavy standard

23

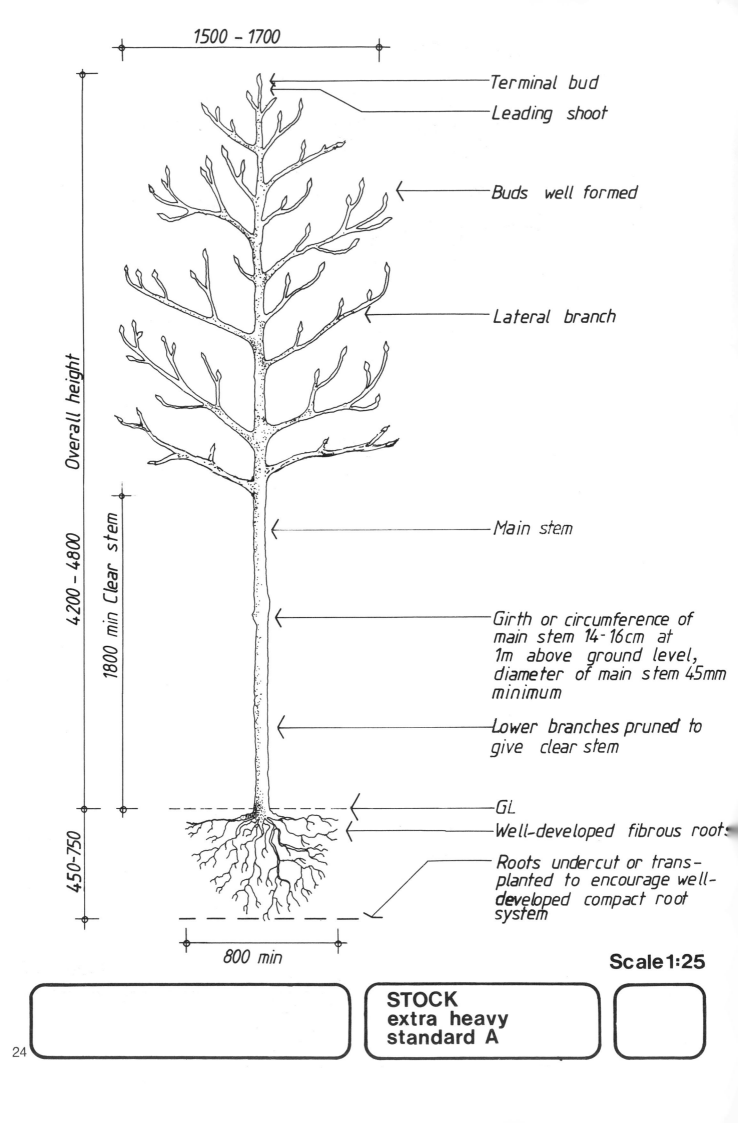

1500 – 1700

Terminal bud

Leading shoot

Buds well formed

Lateral branch

Overall height

4200 – 4800

1800 min Clear stem

Main stem

Girth or circumference of main stem 14-16cm at 1m above ground level, diameter of main stem 45mm minimum

Lower branches pruned to give clear stem

GL

Well-developed fibrous roots

450-750

Roots undercut or transplanted to encourage well-developed compact root system

800 min

Scale 1:25

**STOCK
extra heavy
standard A**

24

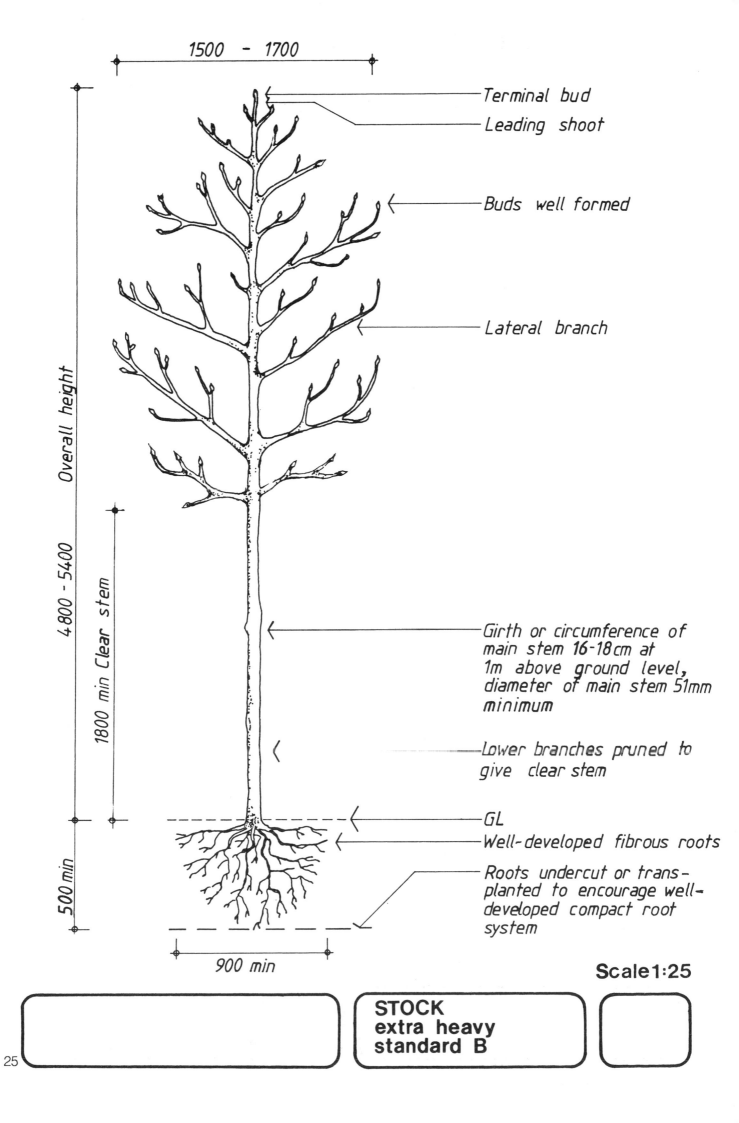

1500 – 1700

Terminal bud

Leading shoot

Buds well formed

Lateral branch

Overall height

4800 – 5400

1800 min Clear stem

Girth or circumference of main stem 16-18cm at 1m above ground level, diameter of main stem 51mm minimum

Lower branches pruned to give clear stem

GL

Well-developed fibrous roots

Roots undercut or trans- planted to encourage well- developed compact root system

500 min

900 min

Scale 1:25

STOCK
extra heavy
standard B

25

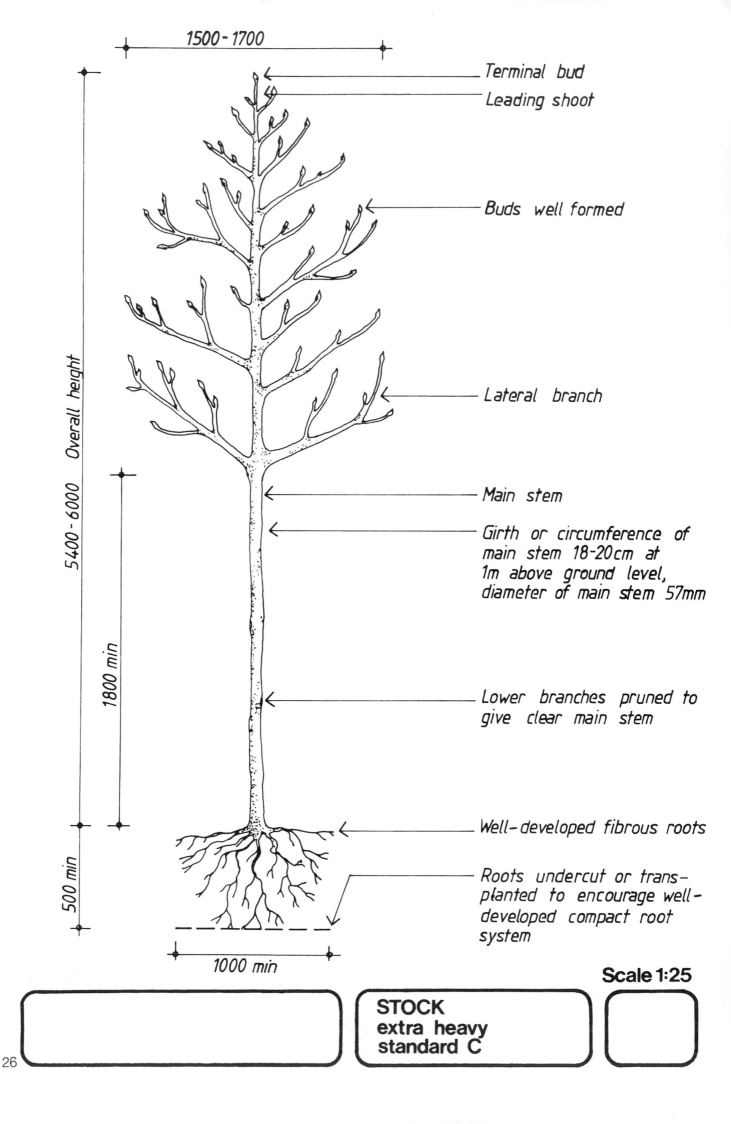

1500-1700

Terminal bud

Leading shoot

Buds well formed

Lateral branch

Main stem

Girth or circumference of main stem 18-20cm at 1m above ground level, diameter of main stem 57mm

Lower branches pruned to give clear main stem

Well-developed fibrous roots

Roots undercut or transplanted to encourage well-developed compact root system

5400-6000 Overall height

1800 min

500 min

1000 min

Scale 1:25

STOCK
extra heavy
standard C

26

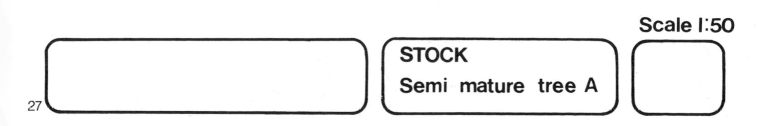

Sound central leader

Well-formed crown

Main stem

Girth of main stem 20 cm +
at 1m above ground

Length of main stem varies
according to species

Rootball wrapped in
hessian

5000 - 6500

1800 min

450 min

1000 min

Scale 1:50

STOCK
Semi mature tree A

27

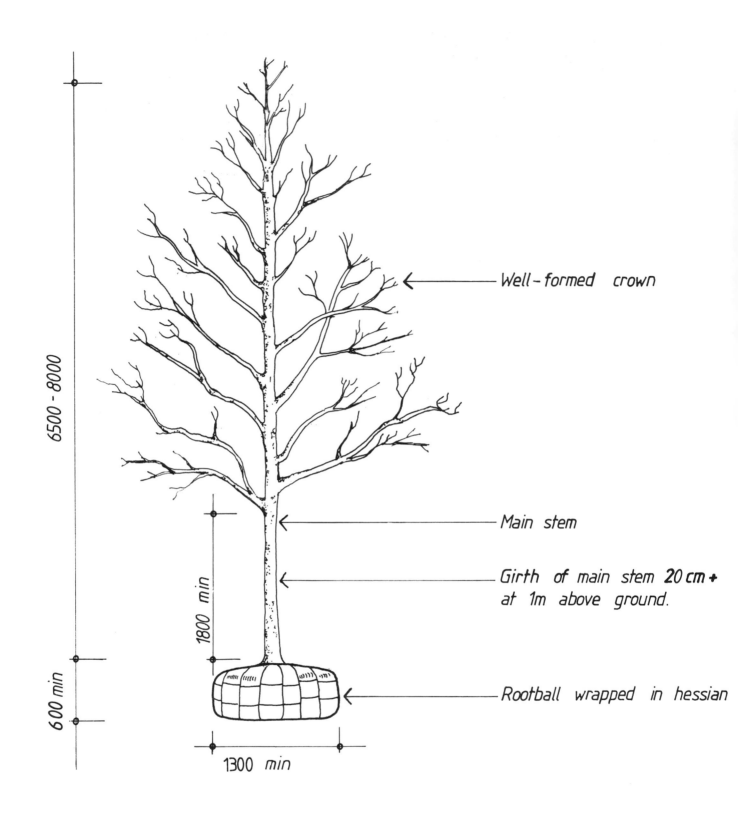

6500 - 8000

Well-formed crown

1800 min

600 min

Main stem

Girth of main stem **20 cm +** at 1m above ground.

Rootball wrapped in hessian

1300 min

Scale 1:50

STOCK
Semi mature tree B

Average height	Average spread	Ball depth	Ball width
750	500	225	300
1000	660	260	350
1250	825	300	400
1500	1000	325	500
2000	1300	350	550

NOTE
Ratio of height to spread should generally be no less than 3:2 but variations can occur depending on the species

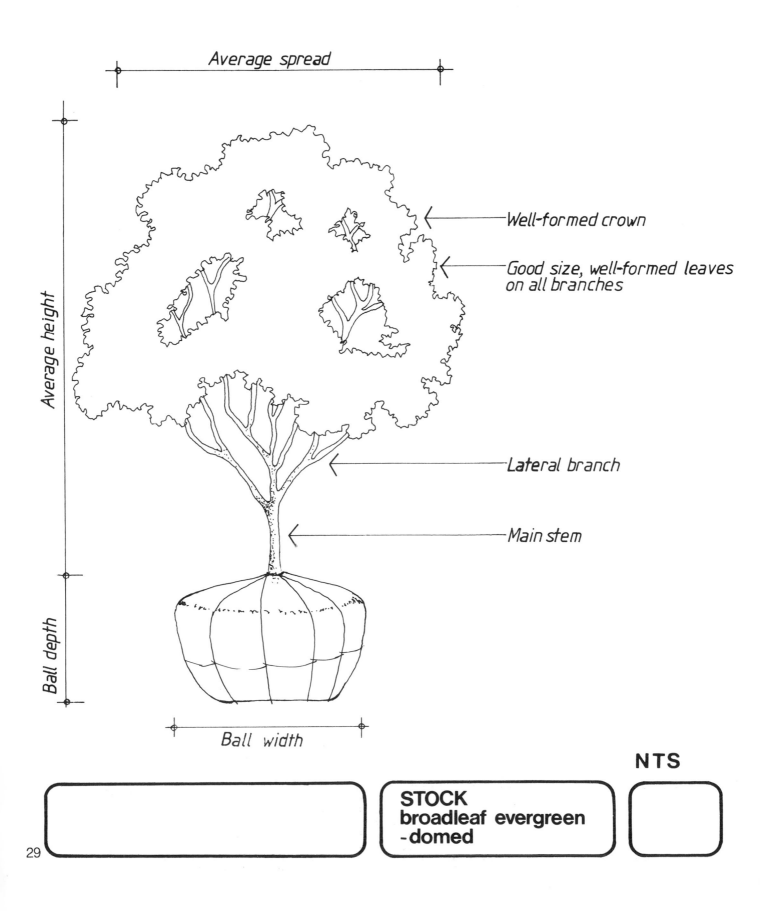

Average spread

Average height

Well-formed crown

Good size, well-formed leaves on all branches

Lateral branch

Main stem

Ball depth

Ball width

NTS

STOCK
broadleaf evergreen
-domed

29

Average height	Average spread	Ball depth	Ball width
750	500	225	300
1000	660	260	350
1250	825	300	400
1500	1000	325	500
2000	1300	350	550

<u>NOTE</u>
Ratio of height to spread should be no less than 3:2

Length of clear stem should **not** exceed 20% of overall height

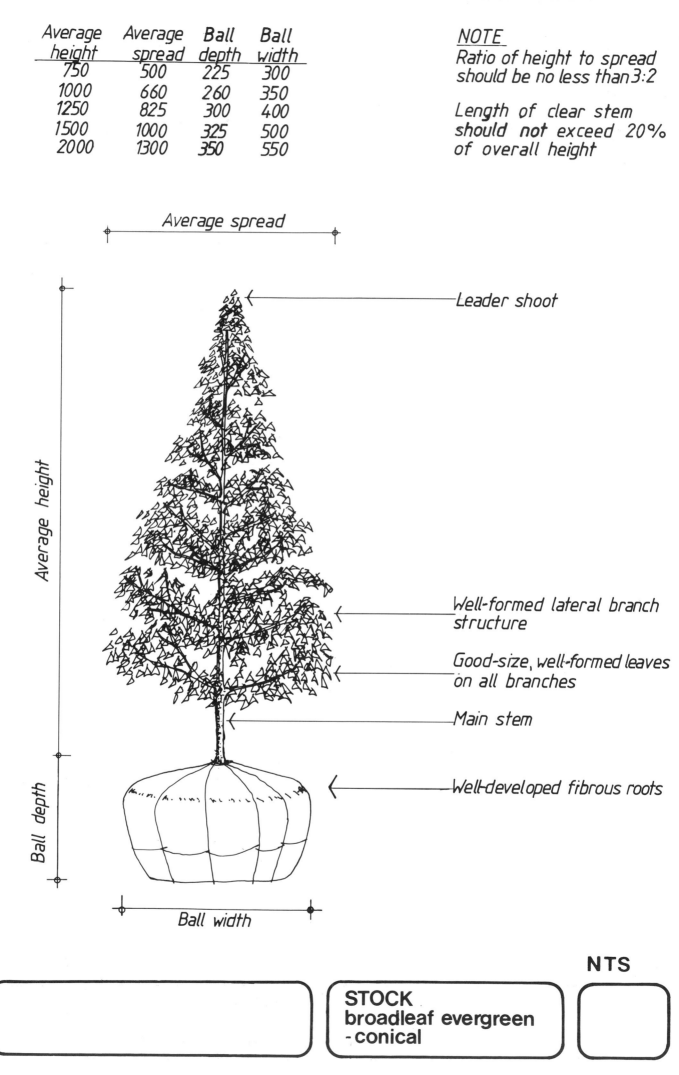

Average spread

Leader shoot

Average height

Well-formed lateral branch structure

Good-size, well-formed leaves on all branches

Main stem

Ball depth

Well-developed fibrous roots

Ball width

NTS

STOCK
broadleaf evergreen
- conical

30

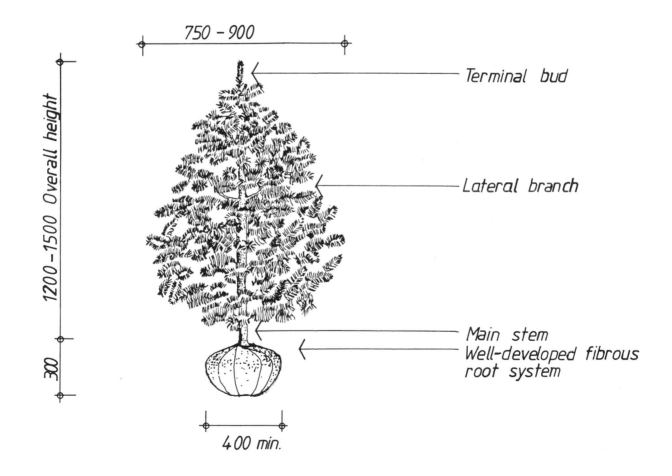

750 - 900

1200 - 1500 Overall height

300

400 min.

Terminal bud

Lateral branch

Main stem
Well-developed fibrous
root system

Scale 1:20

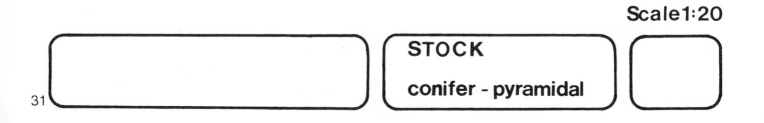

STOCK

conifer - pyramidal

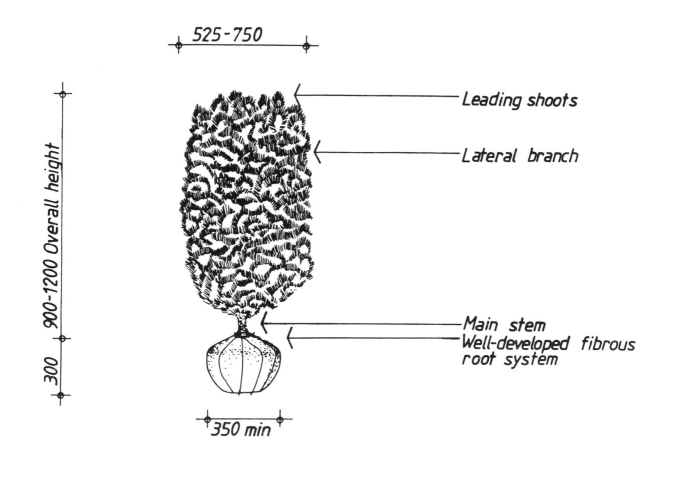

525-750

900-1200 Overall height

300

Leading shoots

Lateral branch

Main stem
Well-developed fibrous
root system

350 min

Scale 1:20

STOCK

conifer - broad

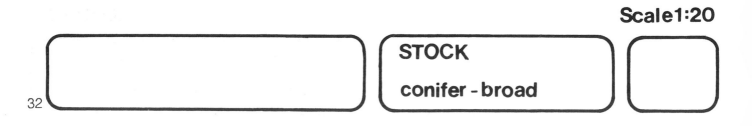

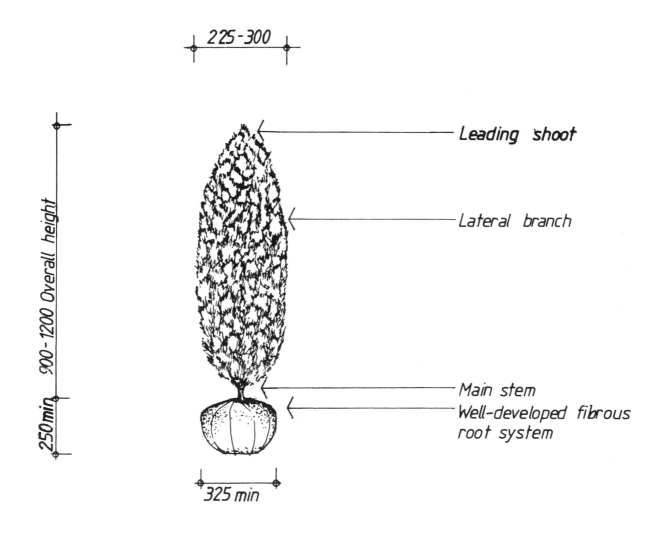

225-300

Leading shoot

Lateral branch

900 - 1200 Overall height

250min

Main stem
Well-developed fibrous
root system

325 min

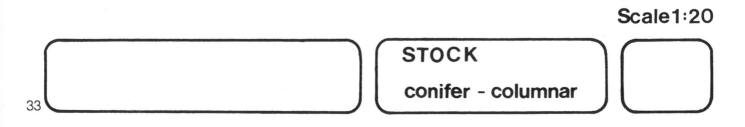

Scale 1:20

STOCK

conifer - columnar

33

2 PLANTING

This chapter gives guidance notes for planting of the nursery stock described in Chapter 1 and includes a section on transplanting semi-mature trees from nursery to site, or from one site to another. The major considerations when specifying planting procedure are adequate protection of stock on site; proper preparation of the ground and tree pits for planting; proper planting techniques; and adequate after-planting care of trees.

Protection of stock on site

Trees which are not to be planted immediately after delivery to a site should be stored in an area specially set aside for storage and properly protected.

Always keep roots moist and covered, as they are irreparably damaged by drying out and frost if left unprotected. For a few hours' delay on site, polythene is a very effective material to protect roots; if the delay is longer, heeling in stock in moist friable soil is necessary. The rootballs of "balled and burlapped" and container-grown stock may require moistening while stock is waiting, especially if roots are in sandy material. In general, a high standard of plant handling is vital, as detailed in the Joint Liaison Committee for Plant Suppliers' *General Conditions, Specification and Schedules of Quantity for the Supply and Delivery of Plants*, (1982; revised 1986) and the booklet *Plant Handling* (1985).

As a protection against moisture loss, anti-desiccant spray can be specified for evergreens, to be applied before leaving the nursery or after planting. There is more likely to be a need for the spray in dry planting seasons, if plants are very large or if they are to be planted in exposed positions.

Transplanting of semi-mature trees

Preparation of large stock is particularly important. It is not possible to transfer a complete natural root system with the tree, so more fibrous root development needs to be encouraged near the trunk before moving.

Some stock is specially grown up to the semi-mature size categories with modified root systems. Otherwise, particularly when moving trees within a site, a period of special root preparation is required. This may take two or three years, time varying with the age and species of the tree. See the detail sheets for root preparation methods.

It is essential to water a tree's rootball thoroughly 24 hours before lifting and to prepare the tree for transport by wrapping the rootball, wrapping the trunk to reduce water loss and spraying with anti-desiccant where appropriate.

Various types of equipment are available for moving semi-mature stock: the tree lever (e.g. Newman), tree spade (e.g. Michigan 85), tree digger (e.g. Vermeer TM 700) or crane lifting gear with cradle. The equipment varies in the size of stock and type of conditions that it can deal with. The tree spade and tree digger, for instance, are larger, heavier types of plant which can be used only where ground conditions permit. Access for equipment may be the deciding factor on whether semi-mature planting is feasible.

Preparation for planting

Ground preparation

The preferred time for ground preparation is late summer/early autumn, preceding the planting season. If ground preparation must take place during the planting season, great care should be taken to prevent excess disturbance or compaction to the topsoil. Heavy soil should be allowed to settle before planting. Operations involved in preparation depend on the nature and scale of the scheme and the state of the ground.

In general

Clear unwanted vegetation
Break up soil compacted during construction etc. to required depth,
Pick up and remove stones and rubbish. Replace or spread topsoil if required
Treat to eradicate perennial weeds

Drainage

No planting of intolerant species should be carried out in waterlogged soil

These are possible solutions:

Break up any hard pan
Use field drainage or other techniques to lower a high water table
Mound planting technique
Select tolerant species (e.g. Salix, Alnus)
Select small adaptable planting stock

Soil and ameliorants

The main requirement of a tree is for a growing medium which:

i
is well drained and well aerated

ii
retains sufficient moisture for adequate survival and growth of trees

iii
is free from toxic materials and of a pH somewhere between about 3.5 and 8.5

Amelioration of some soil types may be necessary before planting to improve growing conditions. Soil type will determine working seasons and the need for additional drainage. The characteristics of major soil types are listed below.

Loam: Straightforward for planting

Sandy soil: Well drained generally. Long working season, can become improverished with a low pH

Possible additions to soil: organic matter, clay size material, fertiliser, lime where applicable

Clay: Poor drainage, season of working limited to autumn and early winter

Conditions for planting may be improved by various means as listed under *Drainage*, or by adding organic matter and/or sand to existing soil

Chalk/limestone: Drainage usually good. Soil may be improved by additions of organic manure

Peat/fenland: Possible poor drainage, which can be difficult to improve. Some nutrients may be 'locked up'

Analysis of the soil can identify a lack of certain nutrients available for plant

36

growth, or an incorrect pH level. Nitrogen is the most commonly deficient soil nutrient. Nutrients can be added to the soil in the form of a suitable compost or well-rotted manure and/or as an inorganic fertiliser applied to the surface, or in a slow-release form before planting. If a soil is too acid or alkaline, its pH can be increased by adding lime or decreased by adding sulphur, although species selection should be appropriate to the soil type.

Tests for pH, chemical, physical and biological conditions should be carried out by an approved source. The facilities of authorities such as the National Agricultural Advisory Service or local Farm Institutes, and private consultants should be used to pinpoint deficiencies.

The desirable characteristics of various soils and ameliorants are listed below.

Imported topsoil

Imported topsoil should be suitable for specific location and purpose but free from weeds and other extraneous matter as far as possible, with pH value and soil type as required for the planting purpose and approved by the supervising officer.

Imported subsoil

Imported subsoil should be suitable for specific location and purpose but always free from extraneous matter.

Sewage sludge

Before the delivery of sludge, the contractor should submit for approval of the supervising officer a certificate stating the source of supply, content of the sludge and absence of toxic levels of heavy metals or other contaminants.

Sludge should be friable, with all large lumps broken down, and with a maximum of 10 per cent moisture with nutrient contents of not less than 6 per cent N, 3 per cent P_2O_5, 5 per cent K_2O.

Leaf mould

Leaf mould should generally be from broad-leaved trees and be well rotted.

Peat

Peat should be sphagnum peat in accordance with BS 4156. Peat for calcifuge plants should be of pH value not exceeding 6.0.

Alkaline peat shall not be used unless expressly specified.

Manure

Well rotted farmyard or vegetable manure, garden compost, spent hops or spent mushroom compost; or a mixture. Manure should be past the stage of most rapid decay.

Lime

Fine ground limestone containing not less than 50 per cent of CaO equivalent, spread evenly on the soil surface and worked deeply into the soil.

Bonemeal

Medium coarse texture, containing not less than 20 per cent soluble potash and 3-5 per cent nitrogen.

Fishmeal

Finely ground, free from large particles and containing not less than 8 per cent nitrogen, 8 per cent phosphate and up to 1.5 per cent potash.

Hoof and horn

Medium fine, with particle size 3 mm down to dust, containing not less than 12 per cent nitrogen and 5 per cent phosphate.

Inorganic nitrogen fertiliser

Inorganic nitrogen fertiliser can be applied in the form of ammonium nitrate or ammonium sulphate, to an area 1 square metre around each tree after planting.

Slow release fertiliser

Ficote 140 is blue-coated pellets, therefore visible to the supervising officer, but expensive.

Useful where plantings are inconvenient or expensive to fertilise regularly. Place deep in planting pit prior to planting and backfill with approximately 100 mm topsoil; or use according to manufacturers' instructions.

Preparation of tree pits

For each tree to be planted an area should be cleared free of weeds and rubbish prior to excavation of the tree pit. A separate hole should be excavated for each tree. The pit should be at least 75 mm deeper than the root system and wide enough to allow adequate clearance between the root ends or sides of rootball and the side of the pit. Dimensions for the tree pits for different types of stock are shown in the detail sheets.

On sites with no proper soil (e.g. shale tips), a pit which can hold at least 0.5 cubic metres of topsoil to supply moisture is preferred.

Pits for advanced stock and semi-mature trees should be at least 250 mm deeper and 500 mm (advanced stock) or 600 mm (semi-mature) wider than rootstock.

Topsoil excavated from the pit should be set aside for re-use. Excavated subsoil should be removed and not mixed with the topsoil.

The bottom of the pit should be broken up to a depth of 150 mm, to assist drainage and firm root development. If the sides of the pit are glazed, these should also be broken up or roughened.

Planting

Season and conditions for planting

Whenever possible it is advisable to plant most trees during the winter season, this being the dormant period. In other seasons container-grown stock should be used and particular attention paid to watering.

For deciduous stock autumn or early winter is the best period. For evergreen and conifer stock, April is preferred; otherwise September-October. Conifer transplants are, however, usually planted in the dormant season.

All transplanting of semi mature trees should be carried out during the dormant season for the species, usually between October and mid-March. For details, reference can be made to Civic Trust notes (see the Bibliograpy to Chapter 1).

Certain weather conditions are detrimental to new planting. Do not plant when:

Soil is waterlogged owing to wet weather

Drought conditions prevail

Weather is frosty

Persistent cold or drying winds are likely to occur

Planting procedure

Pit planting

This method can be used for all stock categories, including transplants.

Erect stakes where appropriate (see Chapter 4).

The bottom of the planting pit should be covered with 50-75 mm of soil.

All plastic wrapping and imperishable containers should be removed before planting.

Hessian around rootballed plants should be loosened and twine removed from the ball before placing in the pit. Particular care should be taken to remove rootball wraps at the latest possible time, to reduce the risk of roots drying out.

Plant trees upright in the centre of the pit and at original soil depth. The soil mark on the stem is an indication of original depth and it should be maintained on the finished level, allowing for settling of the soil after planting.

Damaged roots should be clean pruned.

Bare roots should be spread evenly in the planting pit; a small mound in the centre of the pit on which the roots are placed will aid an even spread.

Soil should be placed around the roots, gently shaking the tree to allow the soil particles to sift into the root system to ensure close contact with all roots and to prevent air-pockets.

Backfill soil should be firmed in layers as filling proceeds. Firm heavier soils lightly, and light soils firmly. Backfill soil should incorporate any necessary organic matter or other ameliorants.

Notch planting

This method can be used for bare-rooted transplants and whips up to about 90 mm, applicable to large schemes involving forestry planting. Notch planting can be economical and effective in suitable ground. Care needs to be taken not to cramp up the roots. (see the detail sheet). On clay soils the notch can open in dry weather; pit planting is preferred on such sites.

After planting

Watering after planting is very important because of the reduction in root surface area. On light soils, a watering basin formed around the stem(about 50 mm rim on the soil surface) aids moisture supply in the first growing season. Trees need watering immediately after planting and they will benefit from watering during prolonged dry periods in their first one or two growing seasons. A large amount of water, to be applied slowly, may usefully be specified, e.g.

20 litres per standard tree.

A pre-emergent herbicide may be applied before mulching to prevent weed growth.

A mulch gives a higher chance of successful planting and quicker early growth through retaining moisture in the soil, controlling temperature and preventing weed growth. Choice of mulch will usually be determined by: availability; ease of application and maintenance; appearance; stability under windy and wet conditions; freedom from contamination by weed seeds etc.; slow decomposition; and permeability.

Loose organic mulches are usually applied in a layer 50-100 mm thick around each plant. In most situations mulches should remain on the surface and not be incorporated with the soil. They should not be so thick or dense as to prevent air or moisture reaching the soil easily.

Trees in grassed areas to be kept free of grass for two growing seasons at 1-2 m diameter depending upon size.

Checklist

Protection of stock

Keep roots moist and covered by use of protective material, watering or heeling in.

Transplanting semi-mature trees

Prepare for transplanting over one or two years, according to the detail sheets. Wrap rootball properly and transport with approved equipment.

Ground preparation

Remove all unwanted vegetation, rubbish and stones. Break up soil to required depth and spread topsoil.

Drainage

Do not plant intolerant species in waterlogged soil. Carry out ameliorating measures where appropriate.

Soil and ameliorants

Ensure that all topsoil and ameliorants are specified in proper quantities and mixes according to specific site requirements.

Tree pits

Excavate tree pits to appropriate dimensions for size of stock. Break up sides and bottom of pit.

Planting

Plant in appropriate season and not in adverse conditions.

Carefully plant tree upright and at original soil depth. Spread roots evenly and backfill with topsoil mix in layers, firming as filling proceeds.

After planting

Water plants thoroughly, apply herbicide as applicable, and mulch to required depth and area.

40

Bibliography

ARBORICULTURAL ASSOCIATION (1987) Arboricultural Handout No 2, Guide to tree planting

BRITISH STANDARDS INSTITUTION (1965) BS3882: Recommendations and classification for top soil

BRITISH STANDARDS INSTITUTION (1978) BS 4043: Recommendations for Transplanting semi-mature trees

BRITISH STANDARDS INSTITUTION (1975) BS 5236: Cultivation and planting of trees in the advanced nursery stock category

COMMITTEE FOR PLANT SUPPLY AND ESTABLISHMENT (1985) Plant Handling

COUNTRYSIDE CONSERVATION HANDBOOK, Leaflet 3, The Planting and After Care of Trees and Shrubs

DRURY, SALLY (1982) Planting to last, *GC and HTJ*, October 1

HARRIS, R W (1983) Arboriculture, Prentice-Hall

JOINT LIAISON COMMITTEE FOR PLANT SUPPLIERS (1982) General Conditions, Specification and Schedules of Quantity for the Supply and Delivery of Plants (revised 1986)

WELLS, D. V., Trees - Site Preparation and Planting

Detail sheets

2.1
Transplanting - tree wrapping
2.2
Transplanting - semi-mature trees: preparation, 1 season
2.3
Transplanting - semi-mature trees: preparation, 2 seasons
2.4
Planting - younger stock
2.5
Planting - standard stock
2.6
Planting - advanced stock
2.7
Planting - semi-mature A
2.8
Planting - semi-mature B
2.9
Planting - broadleaf evergreen
2.10
Planting - conifer - columnar
2.11
Planting - conifer - pyramidal
2.12
Planting - notch planting
2.13
Planting - on slopes

Conversion Table			
mm	ft. in	mm	ft. in
50	2"	450	1' 5¾"
100	4"	550	1' 9½"
200	7¾"	650	2' 1½"
250	10"	700	2' 3½"
300	11¾"	800	2' 7"
325	1' 0¾"	900	2' 11"
350	1' 1¾"	1000	3' 3"
400	1' 3¾"	1100	3' 6"

Double thickness wrapping

Cord binding

Rootball wrapping

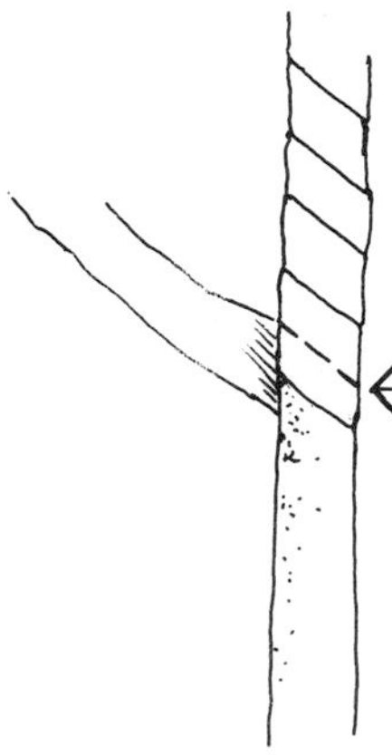

Wrapping overlap

DETAIL OF WRAPPING

NTS

TRANSPLANTING

tree wrapping

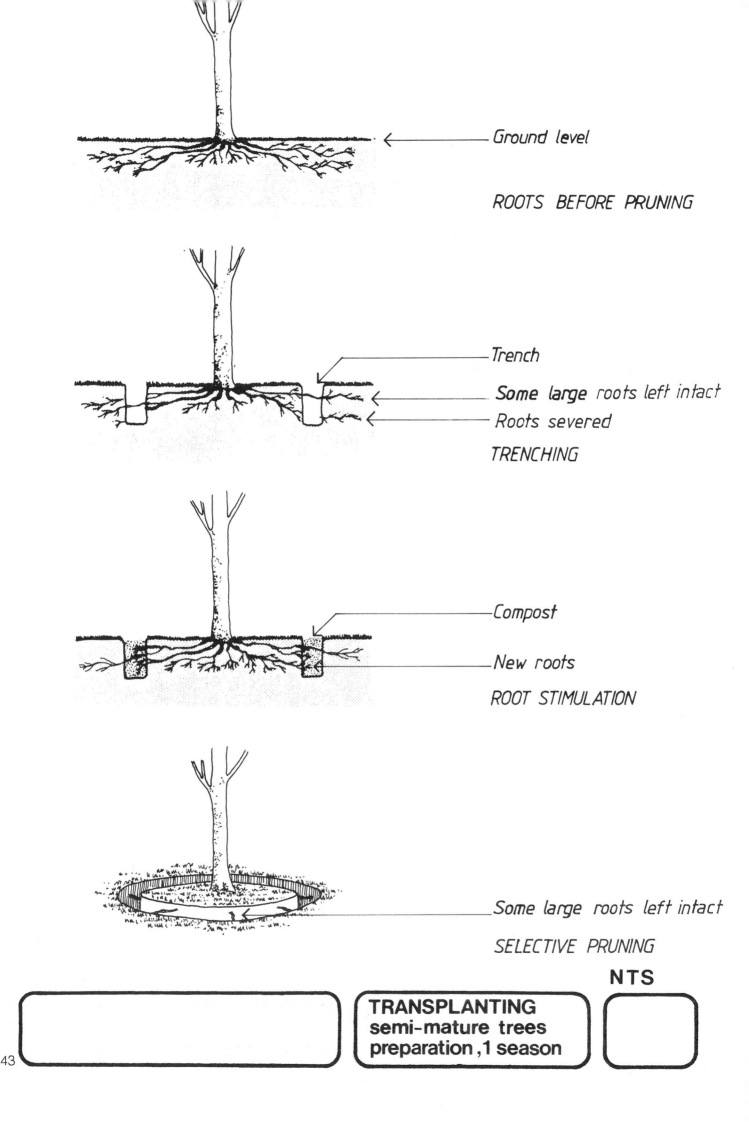

Ground level

ROOTS BEFORE PRUNING

Trench

Some large roots left intact

Roots severed

TRENCHING

Compost

New roots

ROOT STIMULATION

Some large roots left intact

SELECTIVE PRUNING

NTS

TRANSPLANTING
semi-mature trees
preparation ,1 season

43

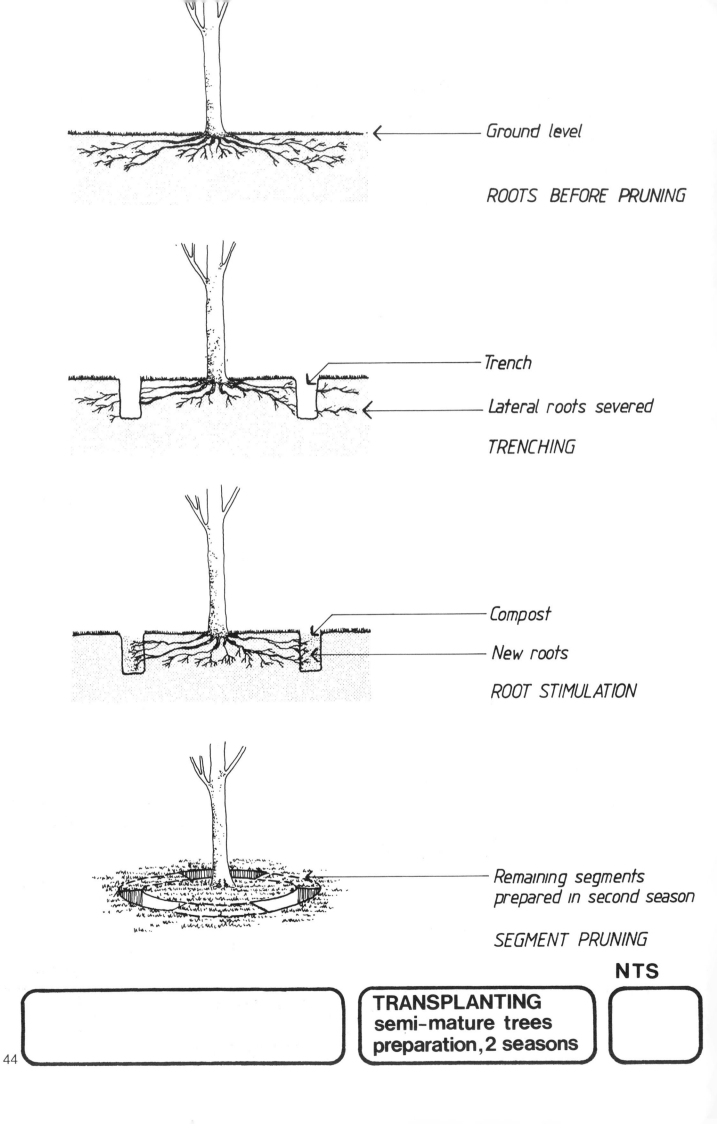

Ground level

ROOTS BEFORE PRUNING

Trench

Lateral roots severed

TRENCHING

Compost

New roots

ROOT STIMULATION

Remaining segments
prepared in second season

SEGMENT PRUNING

NTS

TRANSPLANTING
semi-mature trees
preparation, 2 seasons

44

Stock type	Minimum pit depth	Minimum pit width
Transplant	250	200
Whip	300	250
Feather	300	350

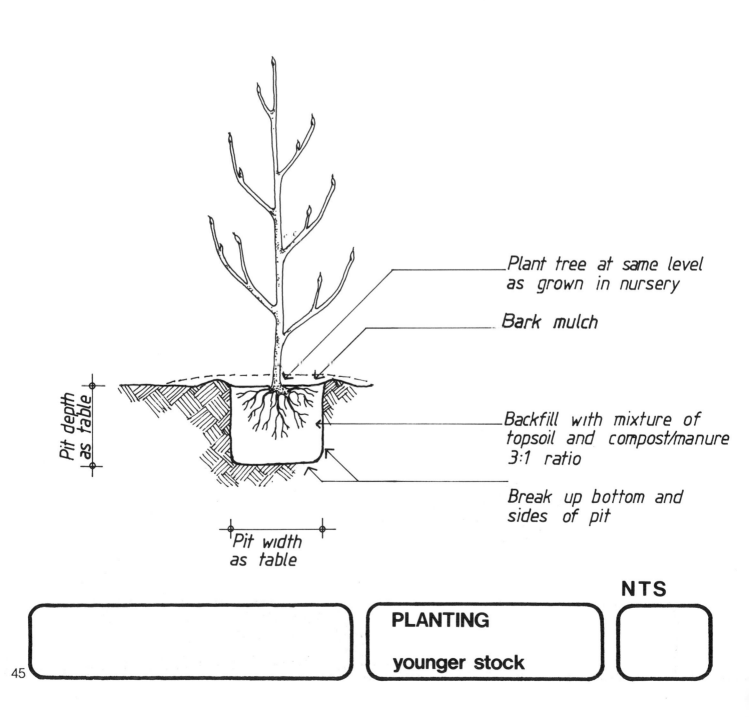

Plant tree at same level as grown in nursery

Bark mulch

Pit depth as table

Backfill with mixture of topsoil and compost/manure 3:1 ratio

Break up bottom and sides of pit

Pit width as table

NTS

PLANTING

younger stock

Stock type	Minimum pit depth	Minimum pit width
Half standard	300	400
Three-quarter standard	350	550
Light standard	400	600
Standard	400	650

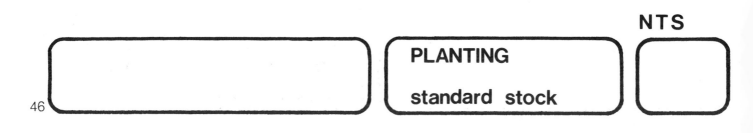

Plant tree at same level as grown in nursery

Bark mulch

Backfill with mixture of topsoil and compost/manur 3:1 ratio

Break up bottom and sides of pit

Pit depth as table

Pit width as table

NTS

PLANTING

standard stock

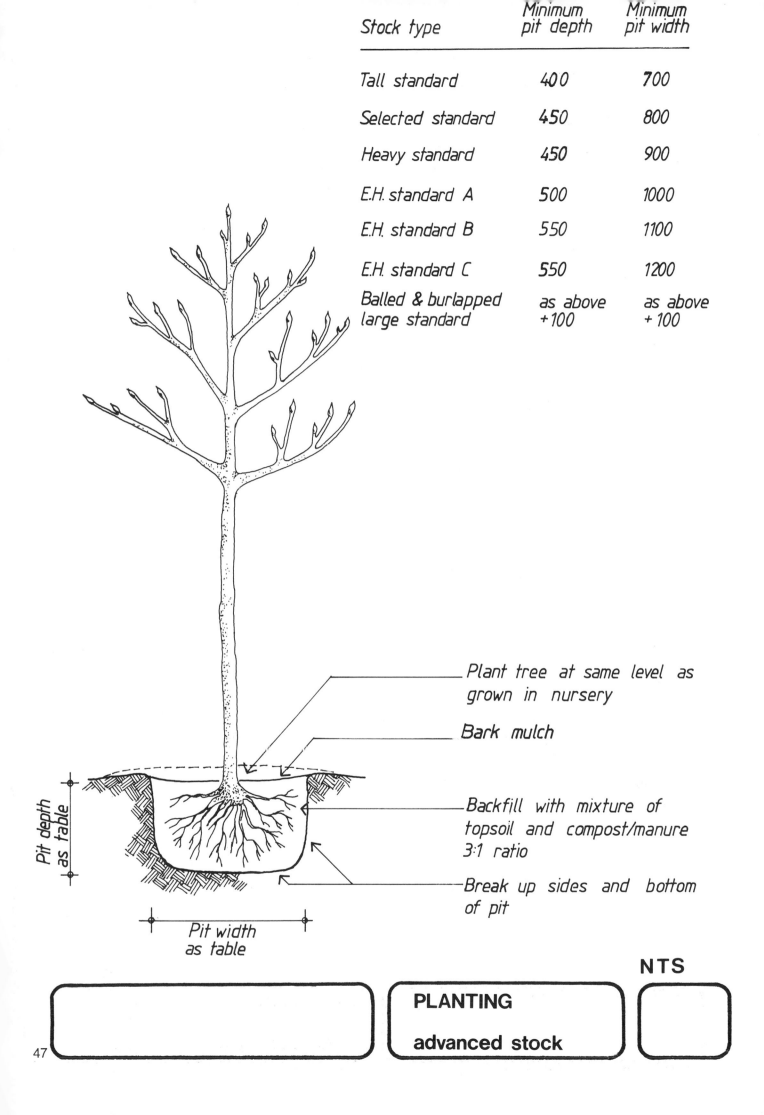

Stock type	Minimum pit depth	Minimum pit width
Tall standard	400	700
Selected standard	450	800
Heavy standard	450	900
E.H. standard A	500	1000
E.H. standard B	550	1100
E.H. standard C	550	1200
Balled & burlapped large standard	as above +100	as above +100

Plant tree at same level as grown in nursery

Bark mulch

Backfill with mixture of topsoil and compost/manure 3:1 ratio

Break up sides and bottom of pit

Pit depth as table

Pit width as table

NTS

PLANTING

advanced stock

47

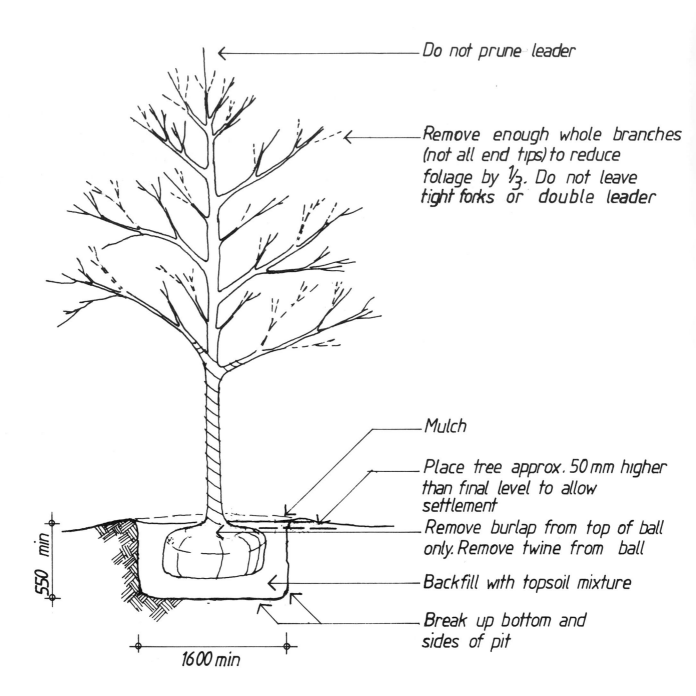

Do not prune leader

Remove enough whole branches (not all end tips) to reduce foliage by 1/3. Do not leave tight forks or double leader

Mulch

Place tree approx. 50 mm higher than final level to allow settlement

Remove burlap from top of ball only. Remove twine from ball

Backfill with topsoil mixture

Break up bottom and sides of pit

550 min

1600 min

Scale 1:50

PLANTING

semi-mature A

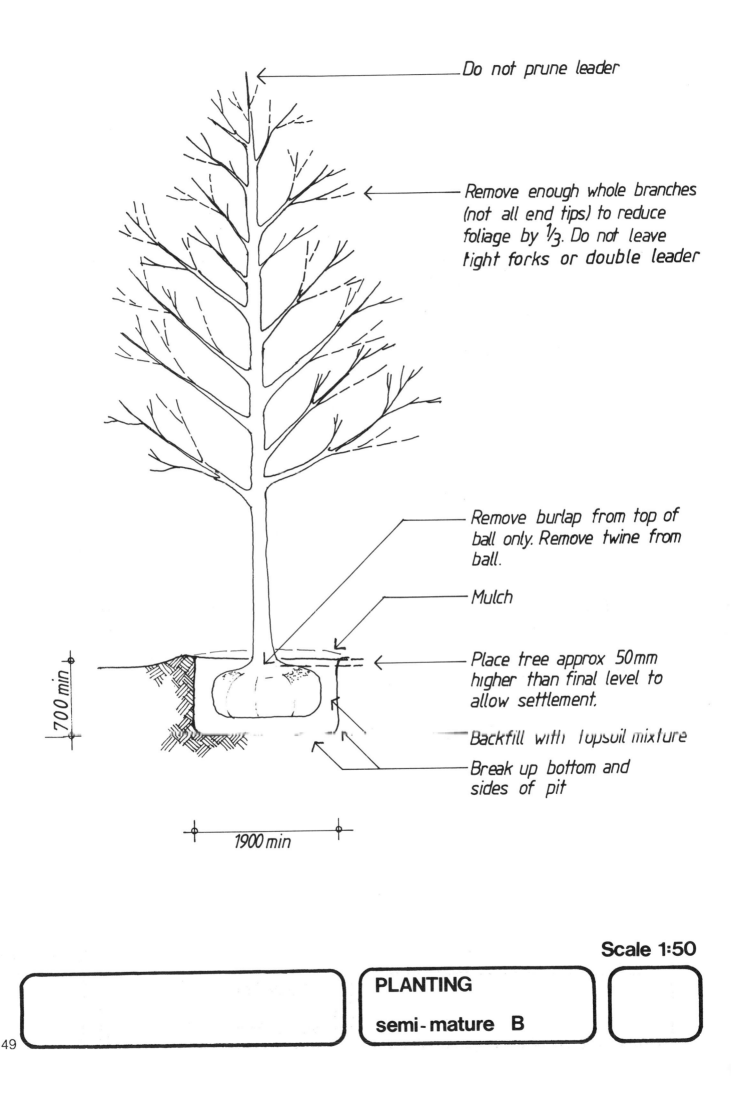

Do not prune leader

Remove enough whole branches (not all end tips) to reduce foliage by 1/3. Do not leave tight forks or double leader

Remove burlap from top of ball only. Remove twine from ball.

Mulch

Place tree approx 50mm higher than final level to allow settlement.

Backfill with topsoil mixture

Break up bottom and sides of pit

700 min

1900 min

Scale 1:50

PLANTING

semi-mature B

Stock height	Minimum pit depth	Minimum pit width
750	325	700
1000	375	750
1250	400	800
1500	450	900
2000	500	950

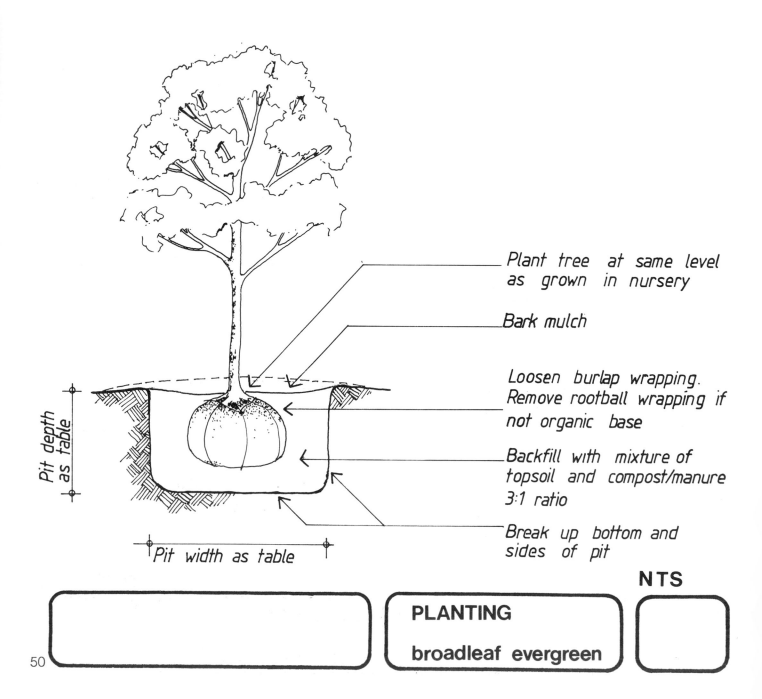

Plant tree at same level as grown in nursery

Bark mulch

Loosen burlap wrapping. Remove rootball wrapping if not organic base

Backfill with mixture of topsoil and compost/manure 3:1 ratio

Break up bottom and sides of pit

Pit depth as table

Pit width as table

NTS

PLANTING

broadleaf evergreen

50

Stock height	Minimum pit depth	Minimum pit width
300-375	300	400
375-450	300	400
450-600	300	450
600-750	325	500
750-900	325	500
900-1200	350	550
1200-1500	350	550
1500-1800	400	600
1800-2100	450	650

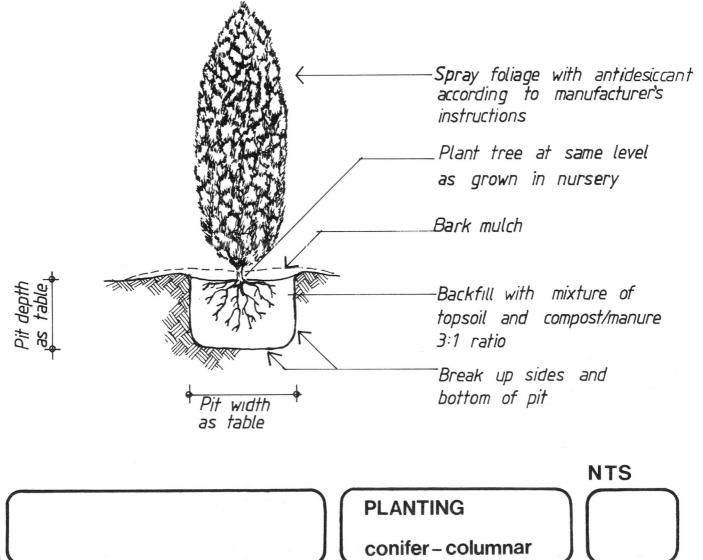

Spray foliage with antidesiccant according to manufacturer's instructions

Plant tree at same level as grown in nursery

Bark mulch

Backfill with mixture of topsoil and compost/manure 3:1 ratio

Break up sides and bottom of pit

Pit depth as table

Pit width as table

NTS

PLANTING

conifer – columnar

51

Stock height	Minimum pit depth	Minimum pit width
300-375	300	400
375-450	300	400
450-600	350	400
600-750	400	450
750-900	400	500
900-1200	450	550
1200-1500	450	600
1500-1800	450	700
1800-2100	500	800

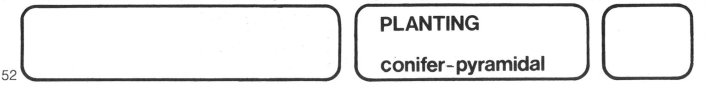

Spray foliage with anti-desiccant according to manufacturer's instructions

Plant tree at same level as grown in nursery

Bark mulch

Backfill with mixture of topsoil and compost/manure 3:1 ratio

Break up sides and bottom of pit

Pit depth as table

Pit width as table

NTS

PLANTING

conifer-pyramidal

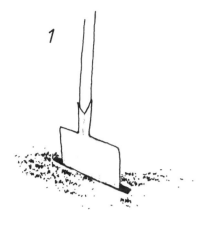

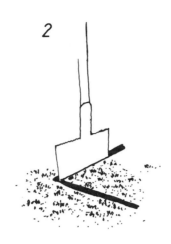

Make an L shaped cut, 150mm deep or more according to length of tree roots

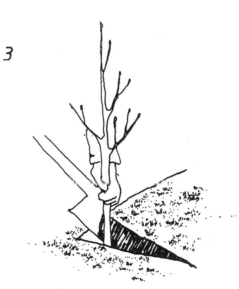

Lever the turf up with the spade to create a notch

Insert tree in notch slightly deeper than required. Ensure roots are well in then pull upward to bring root collar level with soil surface

Tread in around stem to firm the roots

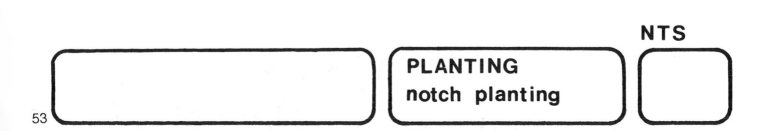

NTS

PLANTING
notch planting

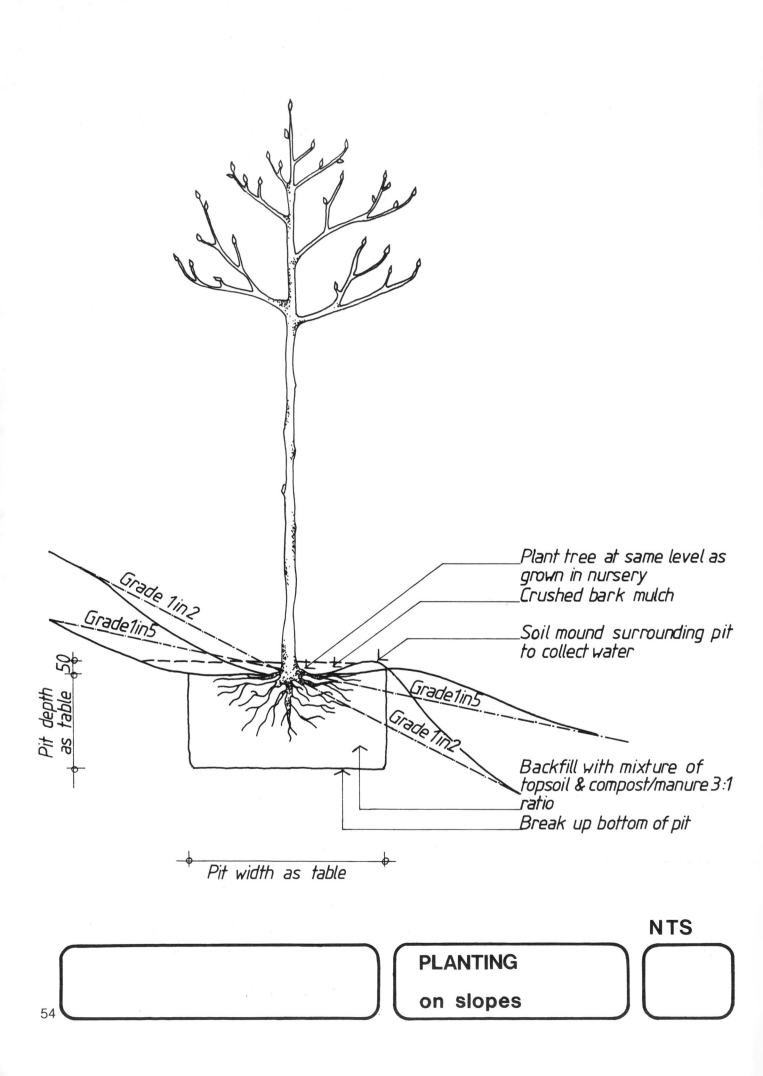

Plant tree at same level as grown in nursery

Crushed bark mulch

Soil mound surrounding pit to collect water

Grade 1in2

Grade1in5

Grade 1in5

Grade 1in2

Backfill with mixture of topsoil & compost/manure 3:1 ratio

Break up bottom of pit

Pit depth as table 50

Pit width as table

NTS

PLANTING

on slopes

54

3 PRUNING AND SURGERY

Pruning may be needed to control the growth of trees or to enhance their performance or function in the landscape. In mature, established trees, pruning is often only necessary to remove dead, diseased or damaged wood.

Some trees will grow in the desired form without any pruning. Others may need pruning for a variety of reasons. Wherever possible this should be carried out while the tree is young, when the branches are less than, say, 50 mm thick and when cut will leave only a small wound which will soon be overgrown by callus and is unlikely to allow rot to enter the tree. The cutting of large branches is much more likely to result in the tree becoming rotten.

Pruning young trees

The main purposes of pruning are:

i
to maintain a single main stem, in those species where this is appropriate (e.g. oak, beech, lime, ash), thus avoiding the risk of the tree splitting down the middle. Some trees, such as crab apple and ornamental cherries, do not normally grow with a single main stem.

ii
to remove lower branches where these are not required, e.g. in parkland or streets.

iii
to remove potential sources of trouble, such as crossing branches which rub against each other, or excessively long branches which may break in gales or heavy snow.
Attention should be given to any necessary pruning at the time of planting and at intervals of 2-5 years until the tree has reached about half its ultimate height, and thereafter at intervals of 5-10 years.

As a general rule, a tree should not have branches removed from more than the lower third of the stem; e.g. if a tree is only 9 m tall, do not remove branches to a height of more than 3 m. If a longer clean stem is required, wait until the tree is taller before carrying out further branch removal.

At the time of planting, it is often beneficial to reduce the crown by up to a third in order to improve the root/shoot ratio as an aid to successful establishment.

Root pruning

This is carried out in the nursery as part of the process of producing a tree with a compact root system, ready for sale. When a tree is planted in its final position, however, it needs all the root it has, and any pruning of them should be restricted to any which are badly damaged. If the roots are too long to fit into the planting hole, dig a larger hole! If the site is such that a large hole cannot be dug, plant a smaller tree. Root pruning in such circumstances can only be considered as a last resort, to be avoided if possible.

Mature fruit trees are sometimes root-pruned, to reduce their vigour and increase the amount of fruit. Root pruning of other types of mature tree is not recommended. There are better ways of reducing the size of a tree, and root pruning may result in instability of the tree and/or rot entering the system. Root pruning may be carried out to prepare a semi-mature tree for

55

transplanting, as described in Chapter 2.

Pruning of mature trees

Pruning of mature trees may be needed to:

i
remove dead, diseased or damaged branches, to eliminate the risk of their falling and causing damage to people or property.

ii
admit more daylight beneath or around the crown of the tree.

iii
provide greater headroom for pedestrians or vehicles.

iv
permit buildings to be erected near to trees.

v
remove rotten, split or otherwise unsafe branches.

Removal of branches

Remove large branches in sections. Make the final cut just outside the branch 'collar' or a line where this would be. Always cut back to a fork or the main stem. Do not leave a long stub; but it is better to err on the side of leaving too long a stub than to cut too close to the main stem. Making a cut flush with the main stem results in the severing of stem tissues as well as branch tissue and is much more likely to result in rot entering the main stem, as well as creating a larger wound which will take longer to callus over. When removing dead branches do not cut into the live tissue around the base of the branch.

Crown lifting

Crown lifting consists of raising the level of the crown to a specified height by removing lower branches. It may be carried out to allow uninterrupted movement underneath the tree and/or to increase light to buildings and surrounding plants. Retention of the tree's natural habit is essential; it is therefore recommended that only the minimum number of branches should be removed (see the detail sheet).

Crown reduction

This is the most difficult type of pruning to do correctly and effectively. Where it is necessary to reduce the overall size of a tree crown, the retention of the natural tree shape is essential. Outer branches of the tree should be cut back to a suitable outward- or upward-pointing bud or small branch; or to a convenient fork.

Crown thinning

This operation, which reduces the density of the foliage, is carried out to make the tree look tidier or reduce the wind resistance and the amount of light obscured by the tree. Crown thinning should only be done if there are clear benefits.

Remove dead, weakened and badly placed limbs, and crossing or rubbing branches. Cut back the major branches moderately, removing about one quarter to one third of their total yearly growth. About 20 per cent of the inner bushy growths, especially water sprouts, may be thinned to control the next year's growth. Less and less pruning is required each year.

Surgery

Recent studies indicate that it is better not to clean out pockets of rot or to drain pockets containing water; such treatment is likely to do more harm than good. Cavities can be filled with polyurethane foam and the surface painted for purely cosmetic purposes, but filling is not recommended for any other reason.

Branches can be rendered less likely to break in some instances by bracing them with cables. Bracing should be carried out with cables of galvanised steel wire rope of appropriate lengths and diameters (BS 3998). Each cable should be secured by not less than two V clips at each end or by splicing to eyebolts passing through the branches. Thimbles should be inserted in all eyes formed in the cable. All cables should be tightened to prevent independent movement of branches and so placed as not to rub against branches.

Bolts and cables should form a straight line at the point of attachment, which should be about one half to two thirds of the distance from crotch to branch end. Bolts, nuts and washers should be of galvanised steel and the diameter of the washer not less than three times the diameter of the bolt. Round or oval-shaped washers are recommended to reduce the risk of bark splitting. The washers should be countersunk below the bark, with surplus bolt thread cut off. Clamps, bonds and unprotected wire wrappings should never be used.

Branches or forks which are likely to split can be strengthened by placing rod bracing. This consists of using solid bolts with screwed ends, washers and nuts or, in suitable cases, threaded rod.

Countersinks should be provided for nuts and washers, as with brace bolts.

Wound sealants

These do not prevent wood-rotting fungi entering the wound. On large wounds and pruning cuts, apply wound sealant around the edge of the wound to prevent bark drying out. Leave the centre of the wound untreated.

Where silver-leaf disease or Nectria canker are likely to be a problem use appropriate fungicidal paint. Elsewhere, leave small wounds untreated.

Workmanship

All pruning operations should be carried out so as to leave a well-balanced tree of normal growth and pleasing appearance. Pruning or surgery of large trees requires a high degree of skill and training and must be carried out by operatives with such skill and adequate public liability insurance.

Adequate precautions should be taken to protect the tree being treated and the surrounding trees from damage by machinery, building materials and fires. Detailed recommendations on safety and workmanship are outlined in BS 3998: *Recommendations for tree work* (1966).

57

Checklist

Pruning young trees

Prune only when necessary to maintain desired form.
Restrict root pruning to badly damaged roots.

Pruning of mature trees

Remove large branches in sections as detailed.

Remove only minimum number of branches in crown lifting operation.

When crown thinning, remove dead, weakened or badly placed limbs, up to one quarter or one third of one season's growth.

Cut back outer branches to suitable outward- or upward-pointing bud or branch.

Surgery

Do not fill or drain cavities, unless for cosmetic reasons. Carry out bracing with cables or rods as detailed.

Workmanship

All pruning and surgery work to be carried out by operatives with a high degree of skill and adequate public liability insurance.

Provisions for safety and workmanship should be as according to recommendations in BS 3998:
.Recommendations for tree work (1966).

Bibliography

BRITISH STANDARDS INSTITUTION (1966) BS 3998: Recommendations for tree work

HARRIS, R. W. (1983) Arboriculture, Prentice-Hall

LANSDALE, D. (1983) Pruning: a rule of thumb, *GC and HTJ*, July 8

SMITH, A. (1983) To paint or not to paint, *GC and HTJ*, May 6

Detail sheets

3.1
Pruning - branch removal
3.2
Pruning - crown lifting
3.3
Pruning - crown reduction
3.4
Pruning - crown thinning
3.5
Tree surgery - bracing with cables
3.6
Tree surgery - bracing with bolts
3.7
Tree surgery - feeding

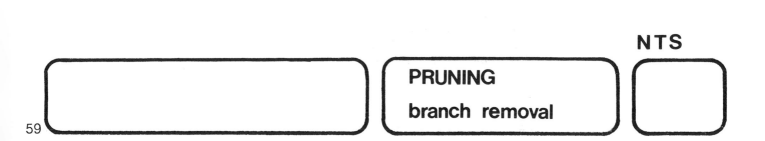

Second cut

First cut

Final cut

Branch "collar"

NOTE
Positions of first and second cuts may be reversed in some cases, particularly when cutting a large branch with a chainsaw

NTS

PRUNING

branch removal

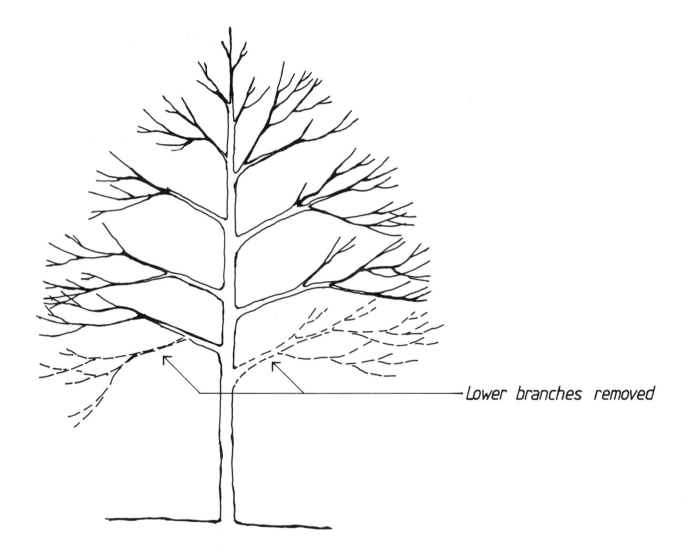

Lower branches removed

PRUNING

crown lifting

NTS

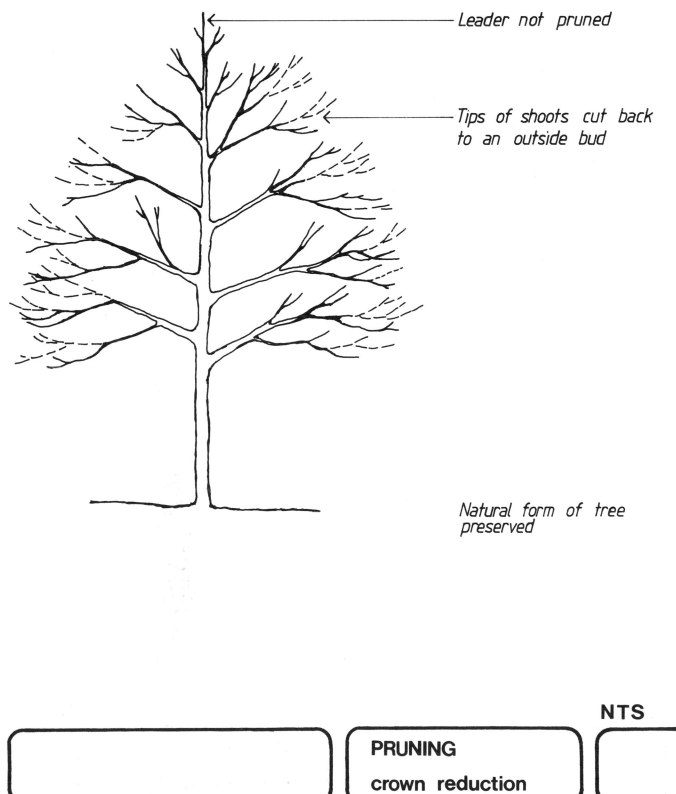

Leader not pruned

Tips of shoots cut back
to an outside bud

Natural form of tree
preserved

NTS

PRUNING

crown reduction

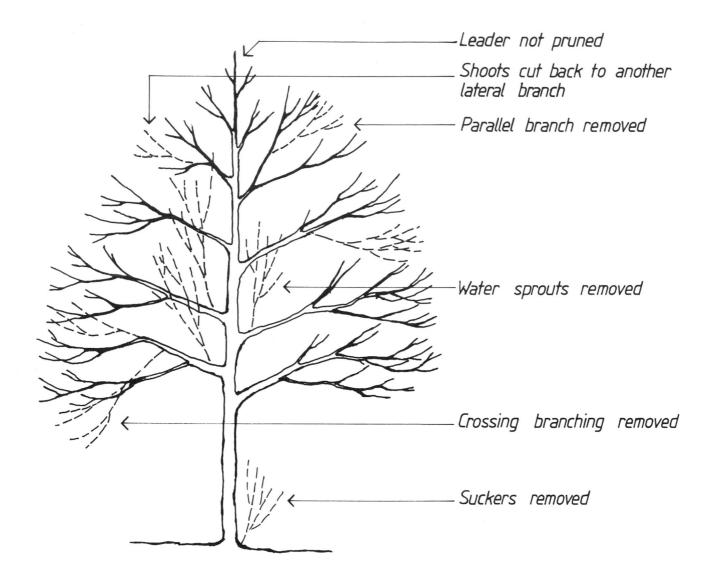

Leader not pruned

Shoots cut back to another lateral branch

Parallel branch removed

Water sprouts removed

Crossing branching removed

Suckers removed

PRUNING

crown thinning

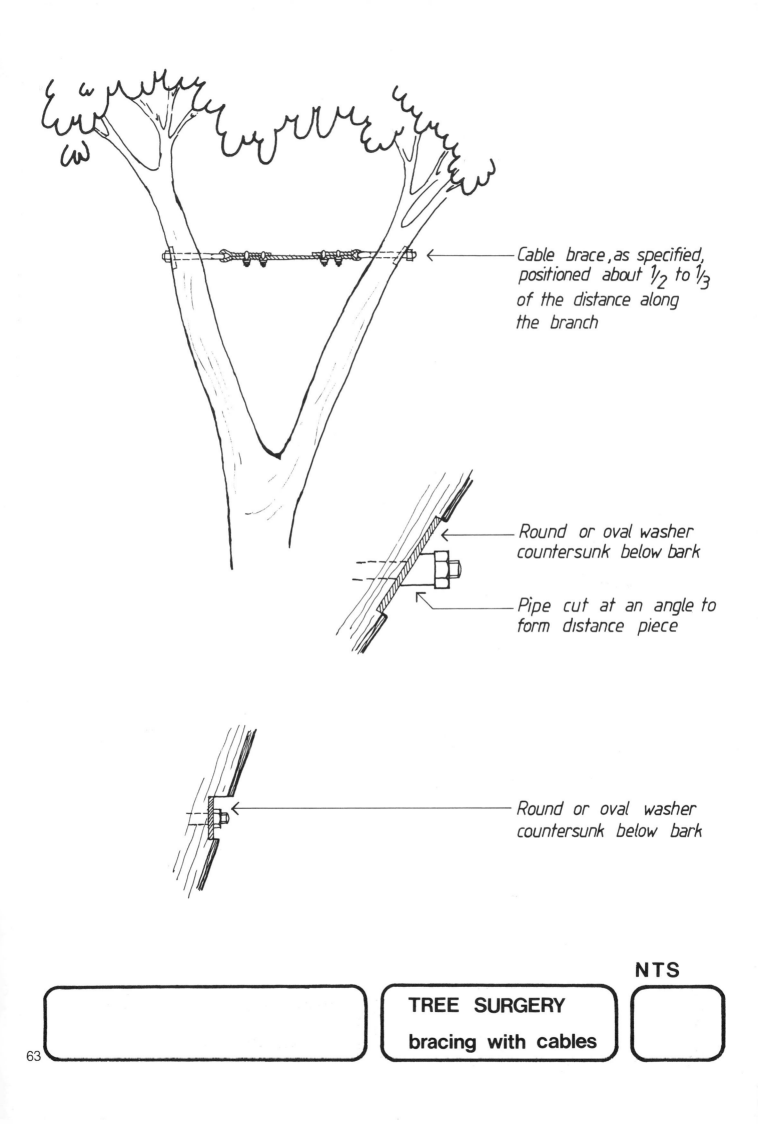

Cable brace, as specified, positioned about $\frac{1}{2}$ to $\frac{1}{3}$ of the distance along the branch

Round or oval washer countersunk below bark

Pipe cut at an angle to form distance piece

Round or oval washer countersunk below bark

NTS

TREE SURGERY

bracing with cables

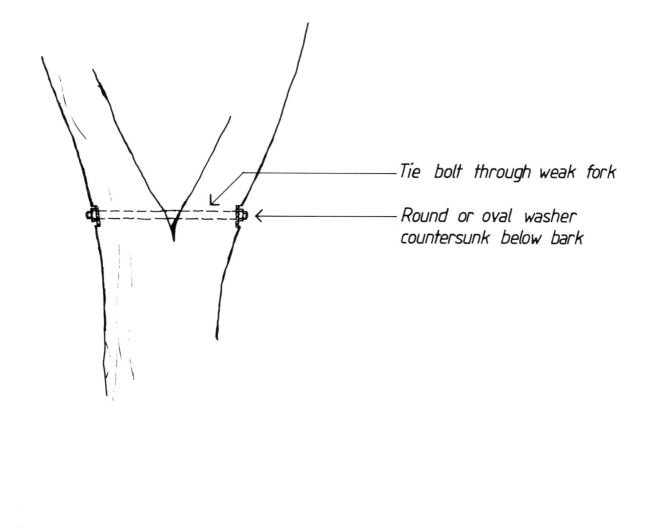

Tie bolt through weak fork

Round or oval washer
countersunk below bark

NTS

TREE SURGERY

bracing with bolts

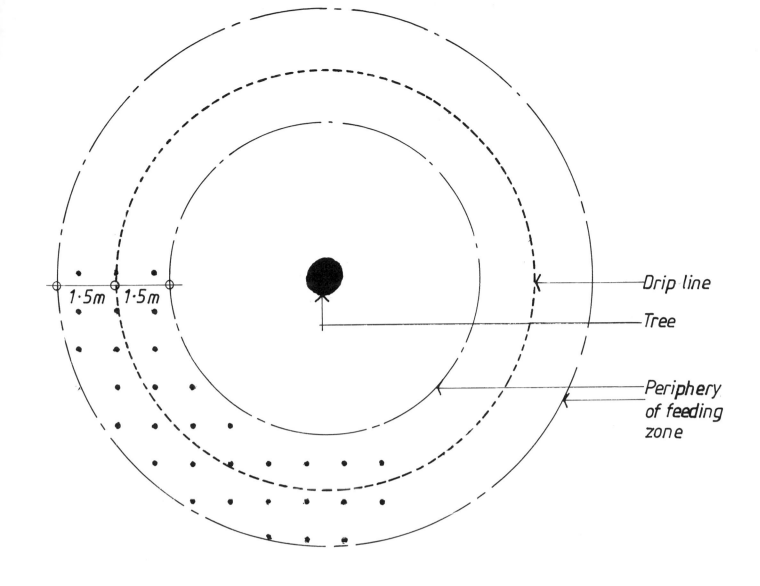

1·5m 1·5m

Drip line

Tree

Periphery
of feeding
zone

PLAN

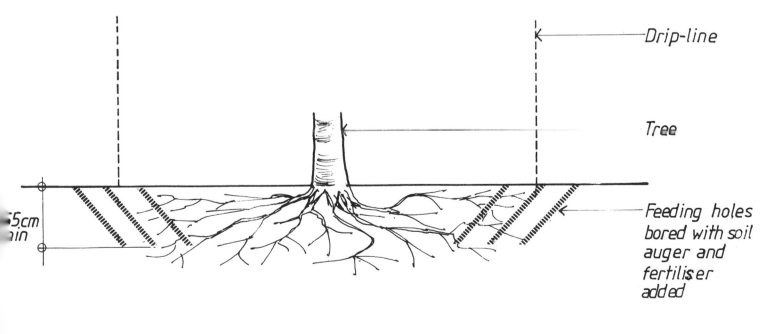

Drip-line

Tree

 5cm
min

Feeding holes
bored with soil
auger and
fertiliser
added

SECTION

NTS

**TREE SURGERY
feeding**

65

4 PROTECTION OF NEW TREES

This chapter outlines various methods of support for newly planted trees, including semi-mature trees. There are more variations in tree support than for any other aspect of planting, and traditional practice is now being re-examined. In the past, heavier staking was more common in Britain than on the continent, but recent research has shown that if staking is minimized, a stronger tree will develop quicker, providing that good stock has been planted.

Reasons for support systems

Support

Stakes and guys serve to maintain the tree in an upright position; this is particularly important in Britain because of the windy oceanic and cyclonic climate. Support can be provided by placing a single stake on the windward side of a tree, or by firmer methods such as double-stake in exposed situations.

Anchorage

Good anchorage is needed to encourage firm root development. Roots are initially inadequate because they are reduced during lifting or restricted by container growth. The stake must hold the roots firmly into the soil but still allow some rocking movement to stimulate thickening of the stem wood. If stakes are too tall or ties too firm, the stem remains weak and depends on the staking for support.

Protection

Stakes and other supports can contribute to the protection of trees from physical damage by, for example, mowers, children and vehicles. Three stakes, with or without crossbars, can form a protective "fence"; tree guards also perform this function.

Use of support systems

Support is required for almost all stock over 900 mm in height, but not for transplants or small whips. Staking is usual for standard categories of nursery stock. Above this size, guying and underground anchorage become feasible alternatives, and are vital for semi-mature trees.

In general, planting feathered trees rather than standards promotes development of a stronger stem, the growth of which is stimulated by lateral branches.

Guys or underground anchorage will usually be needed for semi-mature stock and should be fitted immediately after planting. Support is likely to be needed for two or three years. Protection of the tree stem is important for thin-barked species and where trees are planted in paved areas.

Staking

The traditional method was to stake up to the base of the crown. Recent studies have led to the current recommendation of using a stake supporting only one third of the height of the tree, to allow controlled movement.

Staking methods

Full height or low single stakes may be specified according to specific requirements. A tall stake may be necessary in some situations to deter vandals.

Two stakes with a crossbar provide improved anchorage and support, particularly useful for larger stock or in exposed situations, as the tree is supported on either side. This method is also a practical means of supporting rootballed stock, where the stake cannot be positioned near to the stem.

Three or more stakes may be used with or without cross-braces. Triple staking gives protection as a tree guard for all sizes of stock and support for advanced nursery stock.

For planting in exposed and/or hillside positions, a single stake driven in at an angle of 45 degrees and leaning towards the prevailing wind can be used. The stem is attached to the stake just below the lower branch. This method is suitable for small bare-rooted or rootballed trees and useful for feathered trees where it is difficult to position a vertical stake close to the stem.

Materials for staking

An adequate cross-section is required to reduce disturbance to the roots caused by rocking in the wind. Types of timber which are suitable for stakes include chestnut, larch and spruce. The latter will remain in better condition if pressure-treated with a non-toxic preservative, at least on the lower 0.9-1.2 m However, in most cases the stake should only be required for two or three years. The base of the stake should be pointed for driving into the ground.

The stake should be straight, stout and free of projections. Snags or burrs which would cause chafing of trees should be removed. Split stakes should be replaced. Table 5 gives a guide for the minimum length and thickness of stakes.

Tree ties

The tie selected should be strong but not harsh; rubber and plastic ties generally meet these requirements. The tie acts as a buffer between the tree and stake and as a fixing device. It is vital to use an adjustable tie to allow for stem growth.
Nails or staples should be used to secure the tree tie to the stake. A useful sizing for nails is: 10 mm diameter heads, minimum 25 mm long; Staples 40 mm long x 85WG.

Workmanship

Staking and tying should be completed at the time of planting. Stakes for bare-root trees should be driven into the hole before the tree is planted.

Table 5		
Length + of stake above ground	*Length of stake below ground*	*Diameter (round timber)*
Standard nursery stock:		
1/3 + height of tree	900 mm (2'11")	75 mm (3") (100 mm for tall standards)
Advanced nursery stock:		
1200mm + (4'0")	1500 mm (5'0")	100 mm (4")

Single staking

Position the stake close to the tree on the windward side and drive it vertically into the bottom of the pit until the top of the stake is at the specified height. Secure the tree to the stake firmly but not rigidly with a single tie. Position the tie within 25 mm of the top of the stake.

Double staking

Drive stakes vertically into the bottom of the pit on either side of the tree position until the tops of the stakes are at the specified height. Fix firmly but not rigidly to the crossbar with a tree tie.

Triple staking

Drive stakes vertically into the bottom of the pit at equal distances from the tree stem. Secure the tree firmly but not rigidly to the stakes, one tree tie and spacer for each stake. See the detail sheet.

Guying

The various guying details can be used for larger stock, semi-mature trees and multi-stemmed trees. Generally guys are fixed to eyelets at ground level, which in turn are fixed to cables secured underground by deadmen or proprietary anchors, or to some kind of stake or pin concealed in the soil.

Guys should not be too tight and must allow some movement, which stimulates stem thickening. Turnbuckle fittings allow adjustment of tension, and compression springs in the guys may be used to relieve the stress caused to the tree by wind-jerking.

Method

1
Use three guys of galvanised wire passed through crotch of lowest branch and stem.

2
Protect the tree with rubber hose sleeves threaded on to wire.

3
Secure wire at each end with two U-bolts.

4
Position stakes equidistant from the tree and from each other, and to give an angle of approximately 60 degrees between wire and ground.

5
Stakes should be driven 1.05 m into the ground, or deadmen should be sunk into the ground at least 900 mm deep and placed horizontally at right angles to the line of pull.

6
Incorporate a galvanised turnbuckle in each guy and adjust until wires are just taut. Turnbuckles should be at a height of 450 to 900 mm from the ground to allow easy adjustment.

Materials

The following list gives a guide to materials used in guying and underground anchorage.

Cables

Galvanised mild steel, 7 strands, 6-10 mm diameter, according to height and size of tree.

Deadmen

Logs, railway sleepers or stone; length 1.80 m or according to the size of tree and planting pit; diameter approximately 150 mm.

Turnbuckle

One 150-200 mm galvanised turnbuckle in each wire.

Metal stakes

Angle iron fencing standards: 40 x 40 x 5 mm with 10 mm diameter hole at 50-75 mm from top and pointed at the other end.

Wooden frame or boards

Any sound timber will serve, size according to size of rootball.

Staples

40 mm galvanised wire.

Underground anchorage

This method of tree support is most suitable for the largest stock categories, including semi-mature, and where pedestrian traffic makes above-ground guying dangerous. Concealed anchorage may also be visually preferable. The usual arrangement is for cables to be held over a frame fitted to the tree's rootball, the cables being secured by deadmen.

Method

Two methods of underground anchorage, with stakes or deadmen, are outlined below.

Anchorage with stakes

1
Position the tree and partly backfill.

2
Place stakes in position and partly drive.

3
Place boards of frame across rootball.

4
Cut to length and whip wires to stakes and turnbuckles. Join on crosswires. Lightly cover the turnbuckles with oil or grease before mulching.

5
Drive the stakes until all wires are taut.
6
Adjust turnbuckles as necessary.

With deadmen

1
Position the tree, then dig in deadmen on either side of the rootball.

2
Fix four lengths of wire securely to logs by both whipping and stapling, and firmly ram earth over deadmen. The lengths of wire should be long enough to meet and join on the turnbuckles over the rootball.

3
Place wooden frame over rootball.

4
Whip the turnbuckles on to wires and tighten.

5
Lightly cover the turnbuckles with oil or grease before mulching.

Tree guards

Trees which are liable to be damaged can be protected by tree guards. Guards are generally used in conjunction with a stake. Some proprietary brands also have the useful facility that they can be used in combination with paving support frames for the tree surround.

Protective sleeves, usually known as rabbit guards, are necessary where whips and feathers are planted in locations frequented by rabbits and not protected by general rabbit proof fences. The two main types of small rabbit guards are as follows:

1
plastic spiral guard, made from perforated PVC strips coiled spirally into a 30 mm diameter tube 600 mm to 750 mm long, wound around the stem of the branch, used without a stake

2
split plastic tube guard, a rigid perforated plastic tube 50-70 mm diameter in a range of lengths from 600 mm to 760 mm, split vertically and used without a stake

Larger, stronger guards which need support from a stake are available in plastic or galvanised mesh. Two types of plastic mesh guard are: 75 mm diameter, 15 mm square mesh guards, and 150 mm diameter 25 mm x 35 mm rectangular mesh guards. These guards are slit from end to end and formed into a tube around the tree, secured to a stake with staples.

Welded wire mesh guards are available in a range of stock sizes and used in the same way as plastic mesh guards.

Ornate tree guards, such as metal strip guards, illustrated in the detail sheet, vary considerably in size and shape.

Tree shelters

Tree shelters are often used with transplants to create a sheltered microclimate and provide rapid establishment. The shelters are composed of plastic tubes, made from corrugated polypropylene, reinforced PVC, or extruded cylindrical tube. Various patterns are available, none of which has been adopted as a trade standard. A sawn preserved timber stake, 25 x 25 mm (or 50 x 50 mm on exposed sites), is used to support the shelter.

Advantages

Protection from herbicide spraying, browsing animals, harsh weather and vandalism.

Details

The shelter should remain intact for at least five years, after which time disintegration of the plastic will occur. For aesthetic reasons the fragments must be removed. The tree will be self-supporting when the shelter disintegrates.

Tree shelters are available in various colours, styles and types of plastic, e.g. green, clear, brown; round, square and reinforced with wire mesh.

Checklist

Staking

Specify staking method according to tree size and site requirements.

71

Use a round stake of suitable thickness, straight and stout, in conjunction with a strong flexible tree tie.

Drive stake vertically into bottom of pit, secure tree firmly to stake(s) or crossbar with suitable tree tie, according to the details.

Guying

Used for larger stock and semi-mature trees.

Fix guys around tree with wire in rubber sleeve, secure wires to turnbuckles and to stakes or deadmen at bottom end. Position stakes or deadmen equidistant from tree. Ensure guys are taut but not rigid.

Underground anchorage

Used for larger stock and semi-mature trees.

Fix wires with turnbuckle over timber frame over rootball, attach to stakes or deadmen at ends. Ensure wires are taut.

Tree guards

Select guard according to the size of the tree and specific site requirements. Use smaller spiral or split plastic guards without a stake, supported by the tree.

Use larger mesh guards in conjunction with a stake, for very small trees.

Larger ornate guards to be constructed to details or manufacturers' instructions.

Tree shelters

Supply tree shelters for small transplants only. Construct and erect according to manufacturers' directions and/or detail sheets.

Bibliography

BRITISH STANDARDS INSTITUTION (1969) BS 4428: Recommendations for general landscape operations

BROWN, OLIVER and LANG (1985) Tree Shelters

EVANS, J., and SHANKS, C. W. - Tree shelters, Arboriculture Research Note 63/85/SILS

PATCH, D. (1983) In support of trees, *GC and HTJ* Arb. Research Note 40/82/ARB, March 25

PATCH, D. - Tree Staking, Arboricultural Research Note, DOE Arboricultural Advisory and Information Service

PEPPER, H. W. Plastic Net Tree Guards, Arboricultural Research Note, DOE Arboricultural Advisory and Information Service

PEPPER, H. W., RAVE, J. J., TEE, L. A. (1985) Individual Tree Protection, DOE Arboricultural Leaflet 10

TULEY, G. (1983) A sheltered start, *GC and HTJ*, October 7

TULEY, G. Shelters Improve the Growth of Young Trees, Arboricultural Research Notes 49/84/SILS

WALSHE, P. and WESTLAKE, C. (1977) Tree Guards, Management and Design Note 6, Countryside Commission supplement to Countryside Recreation Review No. 2

Detail sheets

Conversion Table			
mm	*ft. in*	*mm*	*ft. in*
6	¼"	550	1' 9½"
20	¾"	600	1' 11½"
25	1"	667	2' 2"
35	1½"	700	2' 3½"
50	2"	750	2' 5½"
75	3"	800	2' 7"
100	4"	900	2' 11"
125	5"	1000	3' 3"
250	10"	1175	3' 10"
300	11¾"	1270	4' 2"
333	1' 1"	1350	4' 5"
400	1' 3¾"	1800	6' 0"
450	1' 5¾"	1950	6' 5"
500	1' 7¾"	2000	6' 9"

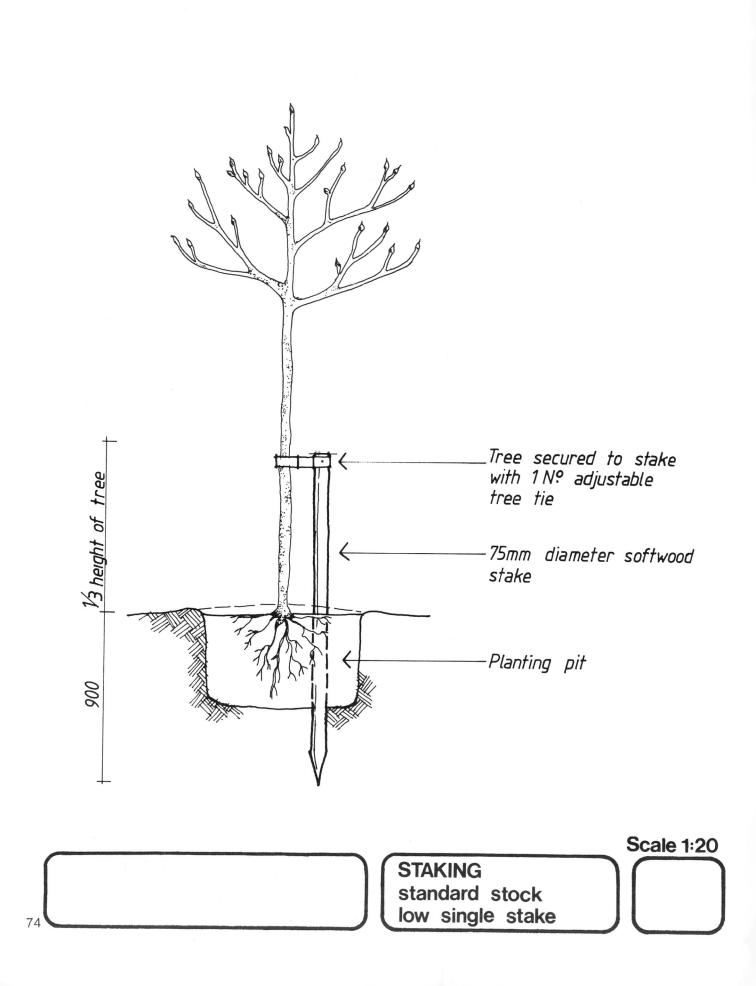

⅓ height of tree

900

Tree secured to stake
with 1 Nº adjustable
tree tie

75mm diameter softwood
stake

Planting pit

Scale 1:20

STAKING
standard stock
low single stake

74

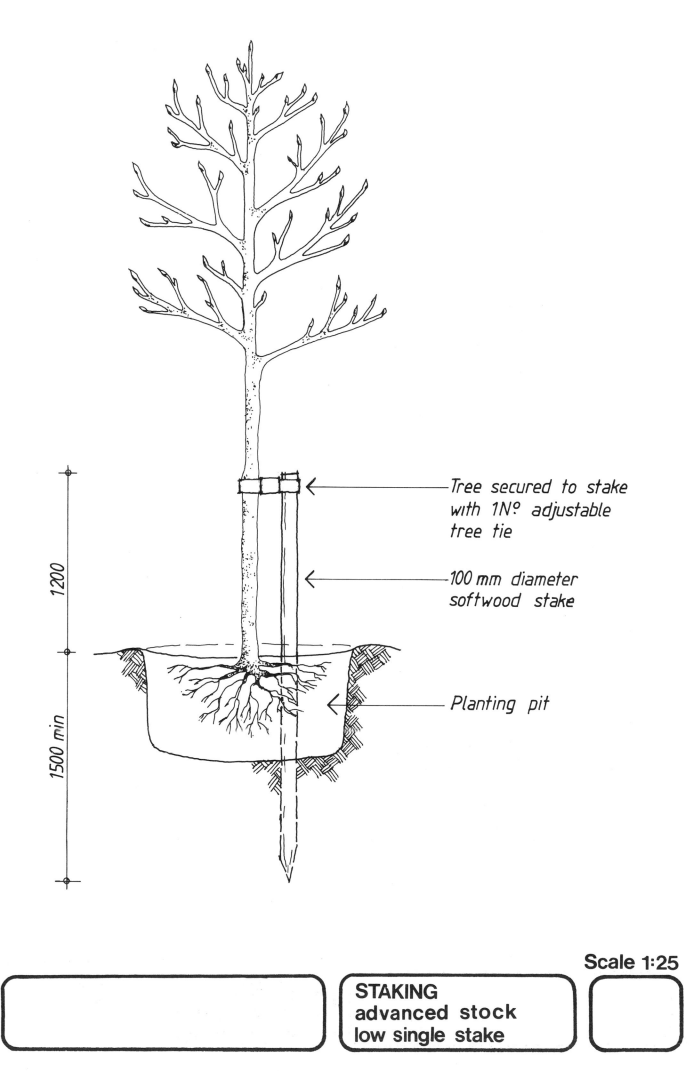

Tree secured to stake
with 1N° adjustable
tree tie

100 mm diameter
softwood stake

Planting pit

1200

1500 min

Scale 1:25

STAKING
advanced stock
low single stake

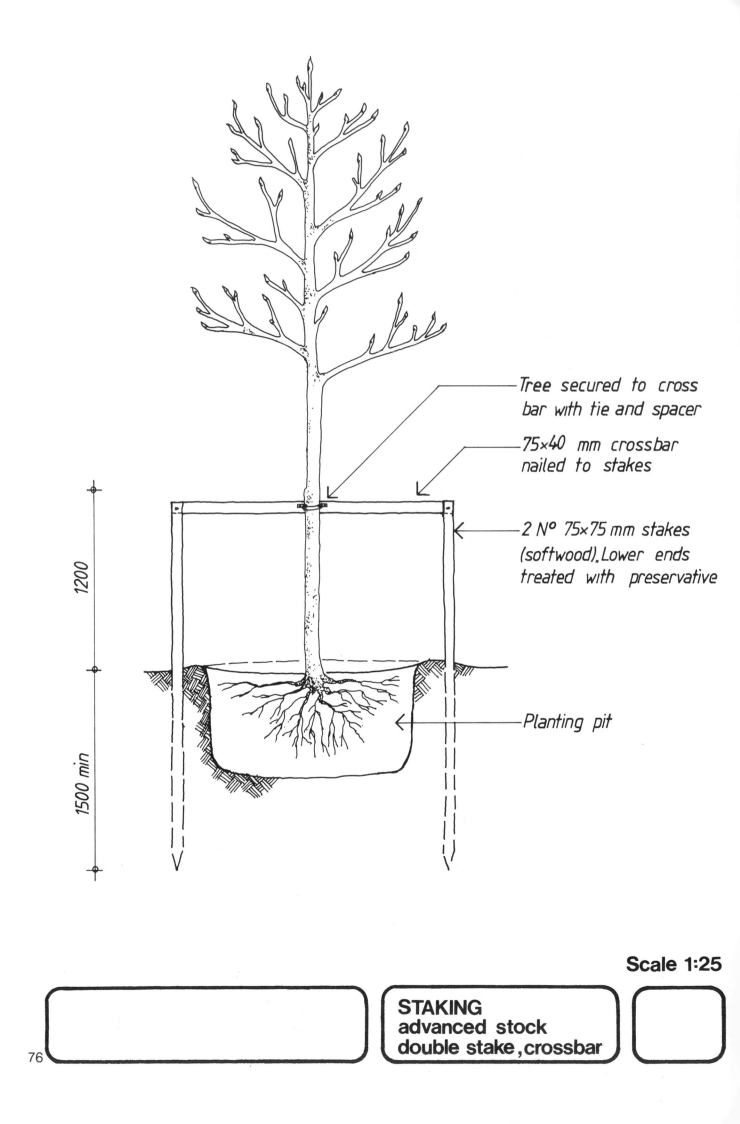

Tree secured to cross bar with tie and spacer

75×40 mm crossbar nailed to stakes

2 Nº 75×75 mm stakes (softwood). Lower ends treated with preservative

Planting pit

1200

1500 min

Scale 1:25

STAKING
advanced stock
double stake, crossbar

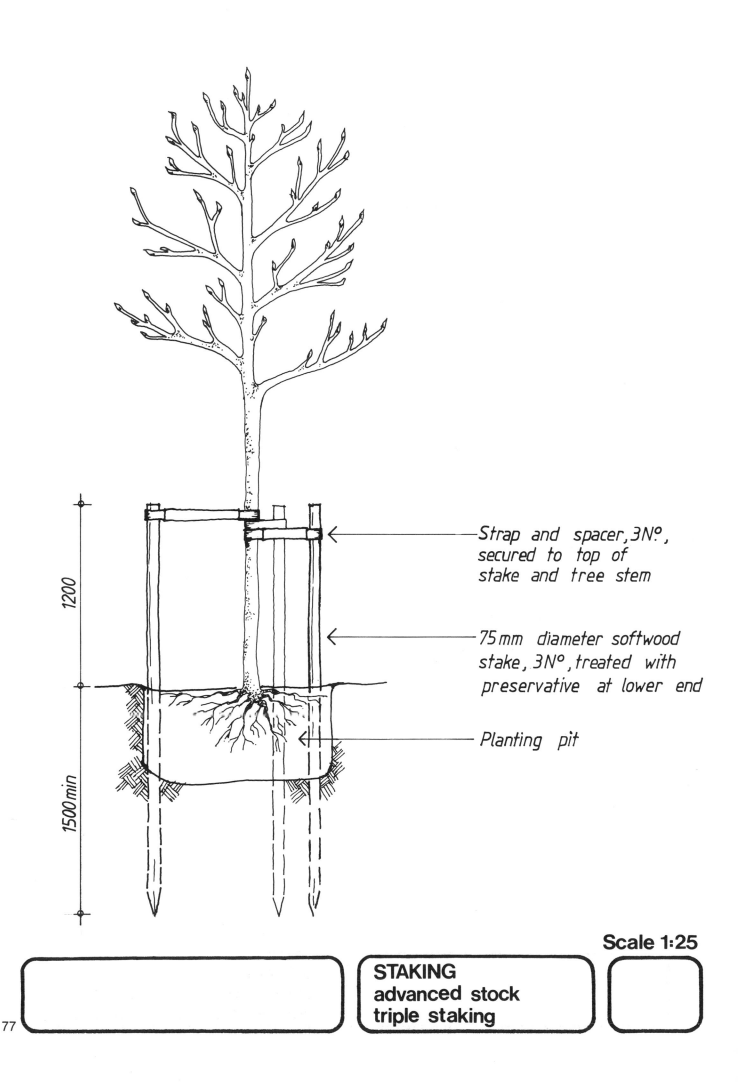

Strap and spacer, 3 N°,
secured to top of
stake and tree stem

75 mm diameter softwood
stake, 3 N°, treated with
preservative at lower end

Planting pit

1200

1500 min

Scale 1:25

STAKING
advanced stock
triple staking

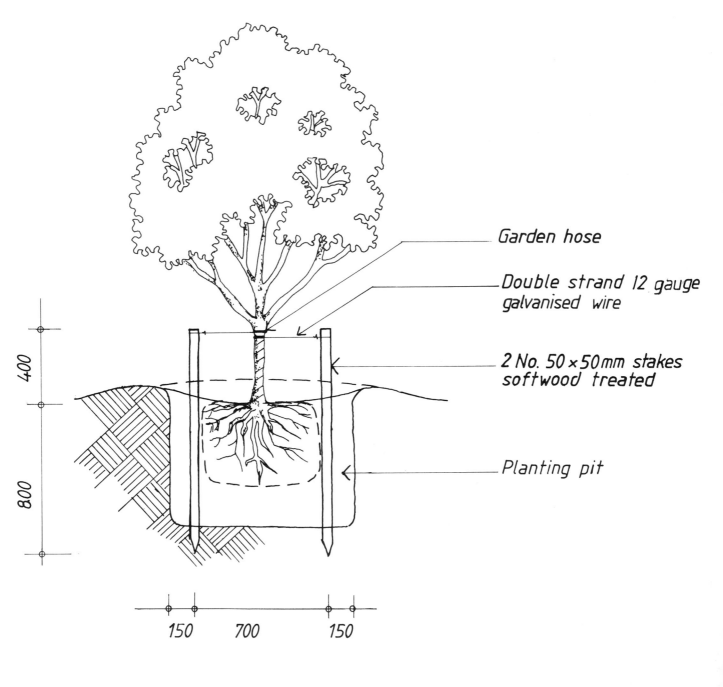

Garden hose

Double strand 12 gauge
galvanised wire

2 No. 50 x 50mm stakes
softwood treated

Planting pit

400

800

150   700   150

Scale 1:20

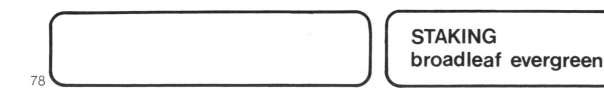

**STAKING
broadleaf evergreen**

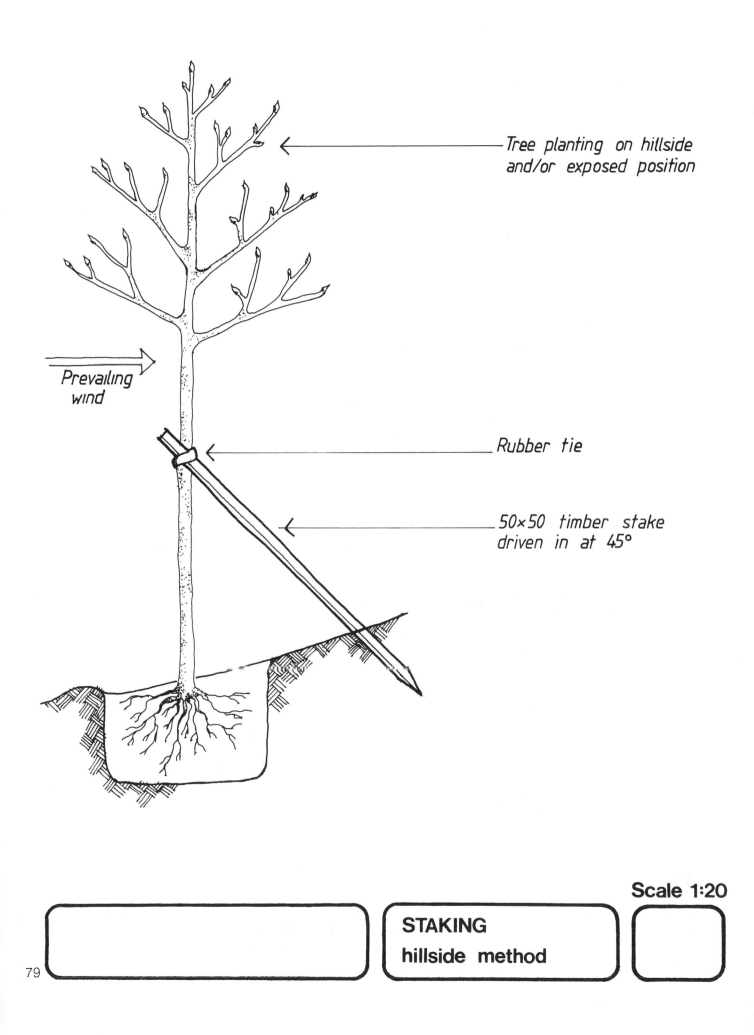

Tree planting on hillside
and/or exposed position

Prevailing
wind

Rubber tie

50×50 timber stake
driven in at 45°

Scale 1:20

STAKING
hillside method

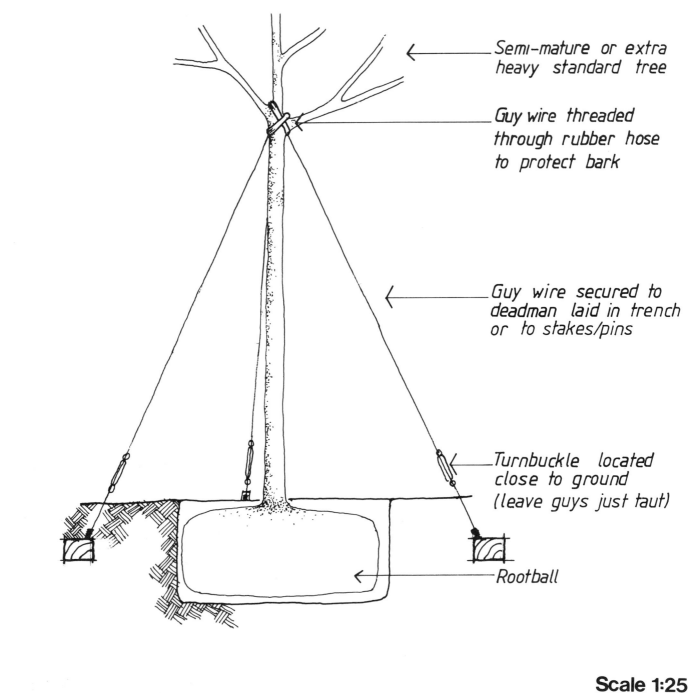

Semi-mature or extra heavy standard tree

Guy wire threaded through rubber hose to protect bark

Guy wire secured to deadman laid in trench or to stakes/pins

Turnbuckle located close to ground (leave guys just taut)

Rootball

Scale 1:25

GUYING
advanced stock

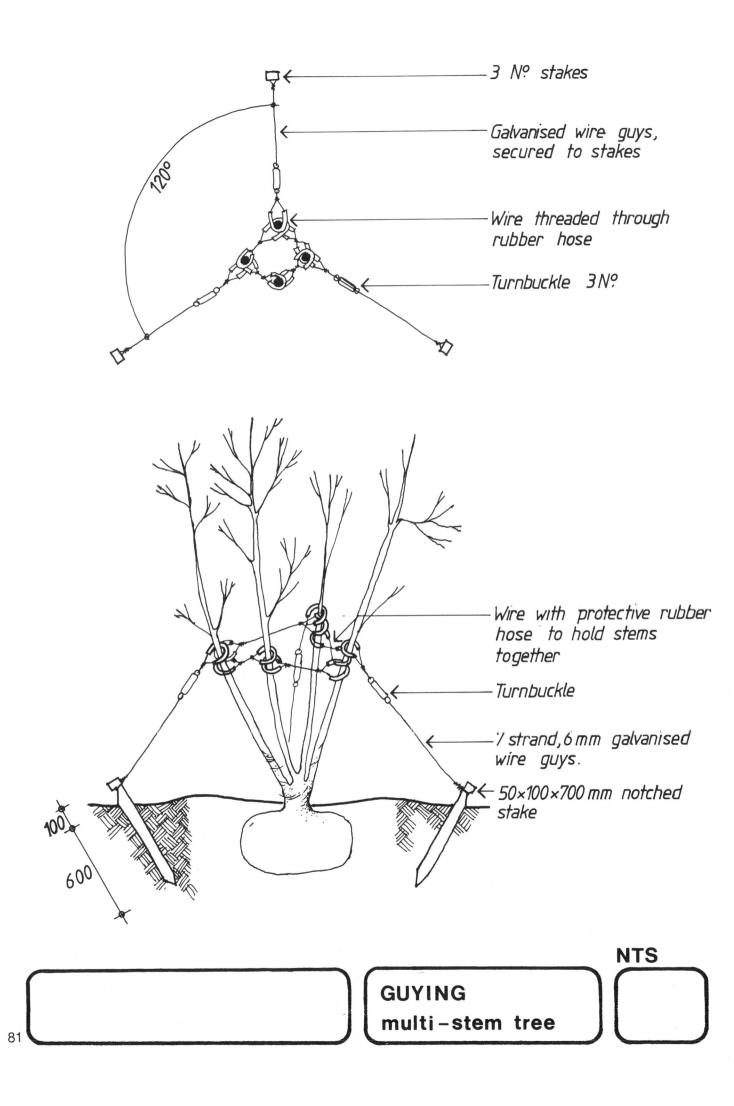

3 N° stakes

Galvanised wire guys, secured to stakes

Wire threaded through rubber hose

Turnbuckle 3 N°

120°

Wire with protective rubber hose to hold stems together

Turnbuckle

7 strand, 6 mm galvanised wire guys.

50 × 100 × 700 mm notched stake

100

600

NTS

GUYING
multi-stem tree

81

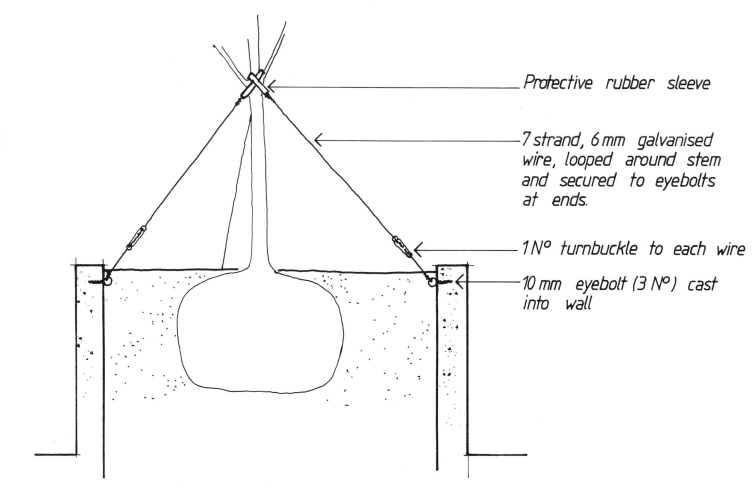

Protective rubber sleeve

7 strand, 6 mm galvanised wire, looped around stem and secured to eyebolts at ends.

1 N° turnbuckle to each wire

10 mm eyebolt (3 N°) cast into wall

GUYING

in planter

NTS

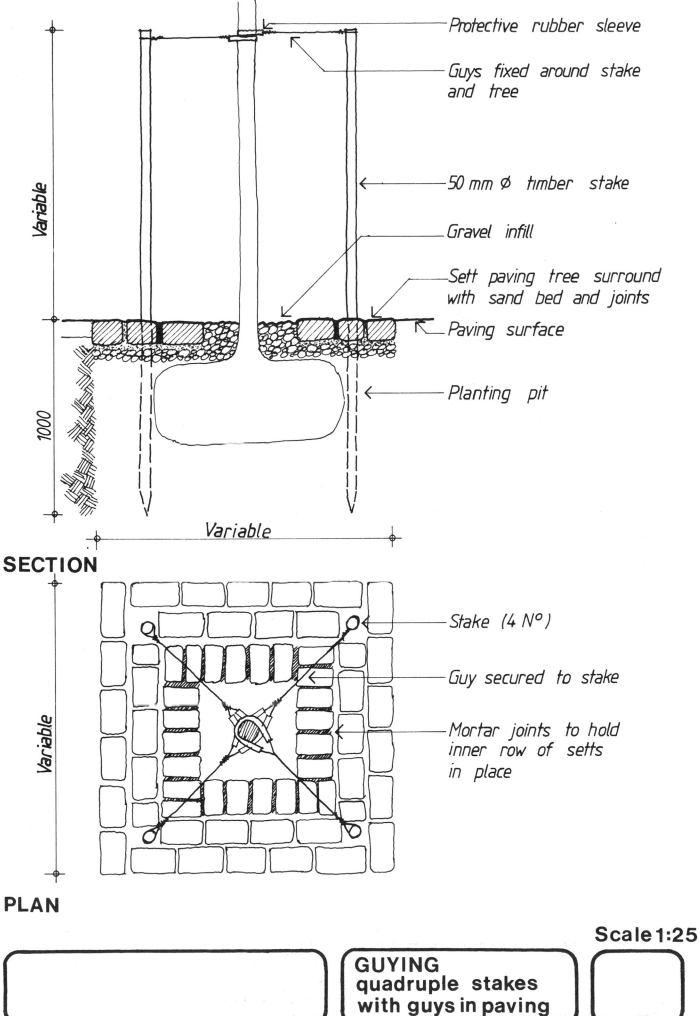

Protective rubber sleeve

Guys fixed around stake and tree

50 mm ∅ timber stake

Gravel infill

Sett paving tree surround with sand bed and joints

Paving surface

Planting pit

Variable

1000

Variable

SECTION

Stake (4 N°)

Guy secured to stake

Mortar joints to hold inner row of setts in place

Variable

PLAN

Scale 1:25

GUYING quadruple stakes with guys in paving

83

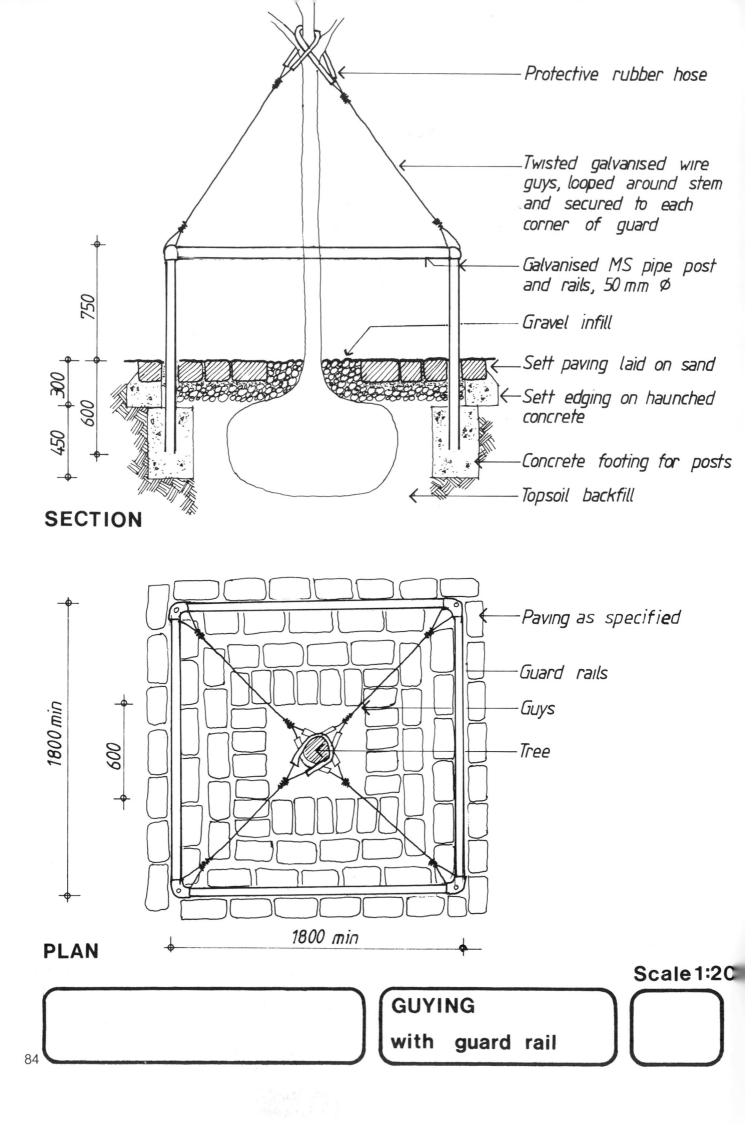

Protective rubber hose

Twisted galvanised wire guys, looped around stem and secured to each corner of guard

Galvanised MS pipe post and rails, 50 mm ∅

Gravel infill

Sett paving laid on sand

Sett edging on haunched concrete

Concrete footing for posts

Topsoil backfill

SECTION

750

300

600

450

Paving as specified

Guard rails

Guys

Tree

1800 min

600

1800 min

PLAN

Scale 1:20

GUYING

with guard rail

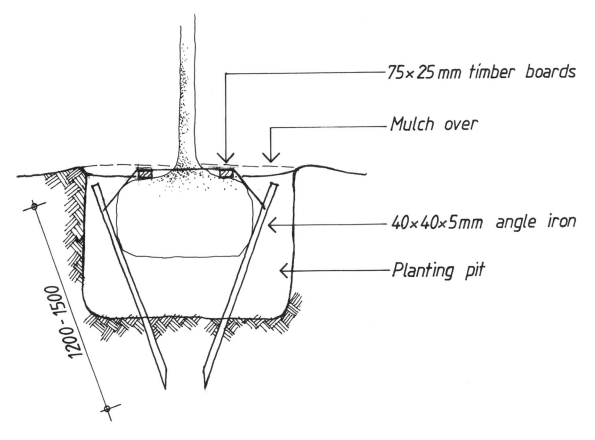

SECTION

75×25 mm timber boards

Mulch over

40×40×5mm angle iron

Planting pit

1200 - 1500

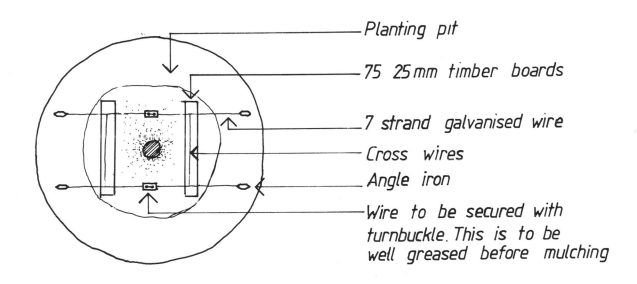

Planting pit

75 25 mm timber boards

7 strand galvanised wire

Cross wires

Angle iron

Wire to be secured with turnbuckle. This is to be well greased before mulching

PLAN

Scale 1:20

ANCHORAGE
advanced stock
metal stakes

85

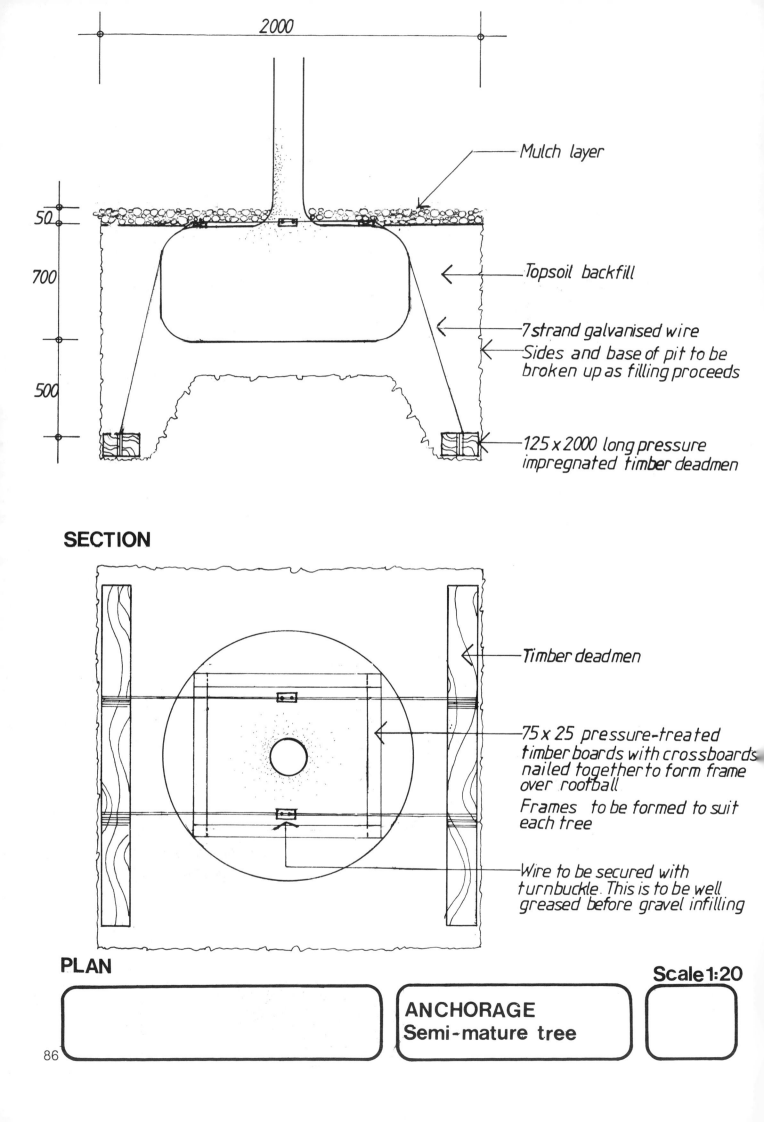

2000

Mulch layer

50

700

Topsoil backfill

7 strand galvanised wire

Sides and base of pit to be broken up as filling proceeds

500

125 x 2000 long pressure impregnated timber deadmen

SECTION

Timber deadmen

75 x 25 pressure-treated timber boards with crossboards nailed together to form frame over rootball

Frames to be formed to suit each tree

Wire to be secured with turnbuckle. This is to be well greased before gravel infilling

PLAN

Scale 1:20

ANCHORAGE
Semi-mature tree

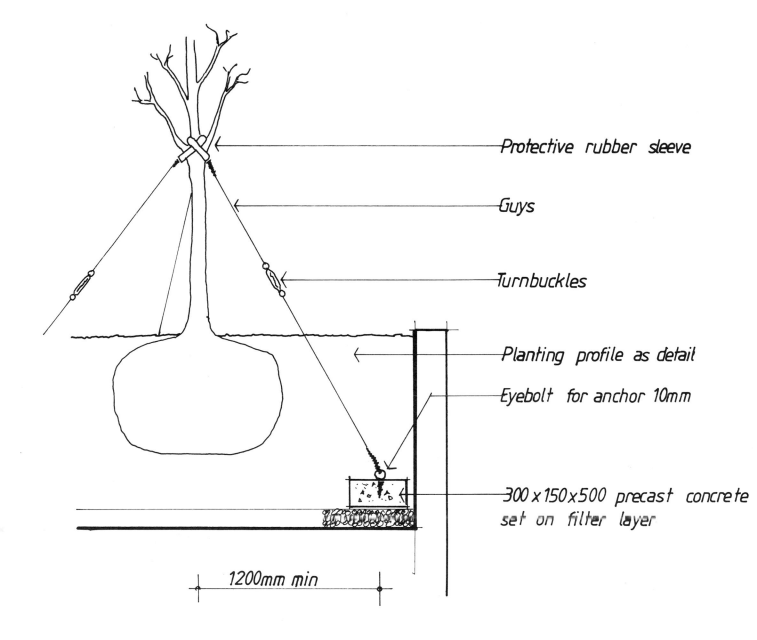

Protective rubber sleeve

Guys

Turnbuckles

Planting profile as detail

Eyebolt for anchor 10mm

300 x 150 x 500 precast concrete set on filter layer

1200mm min

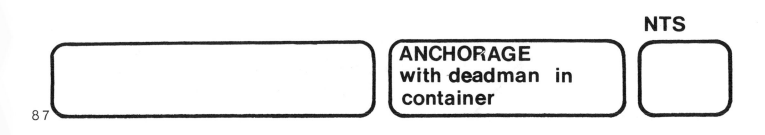

ANCHORAGE
with deadman in
container

NTS

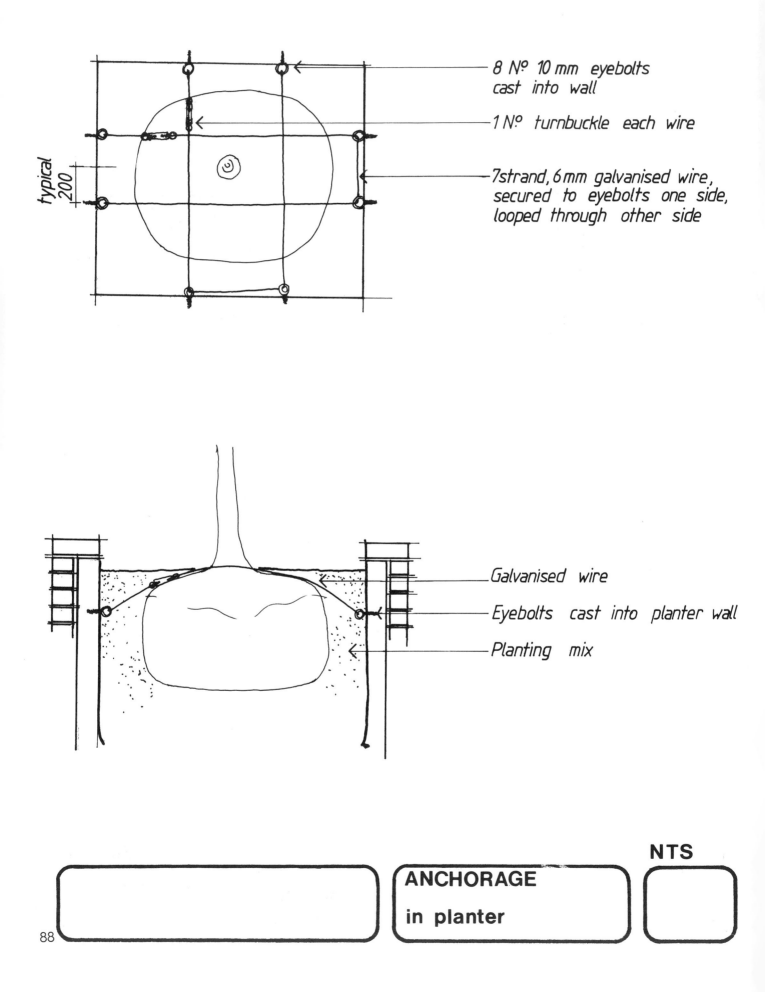

8 Nº 10 mm eyebolts
cast into wall

1 Nº turnbuckle each wire

7strand, 6mm galvanised wire,
secured to eyebolts one side,
looped through other side

typical 200

Galvanised wire

Eyebolts cast into planter wall

Planting mix

NTS

ANCHORAGE

in planter

Tree strap with buckle
to allow adjustment

PLAN

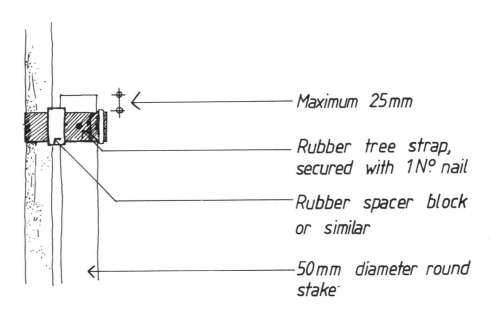

Maximum 25mm

Rubber tree strap,
secured with 1 Nº nail

Rubber spacer block
or similar

50mm diameter round
stake

SECTION

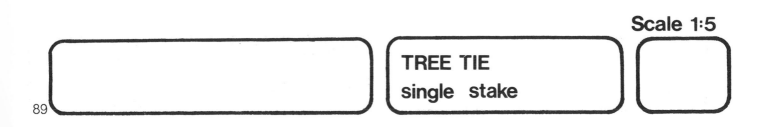

Scale 1:5

TREE TIE
single stake

89

PLAN

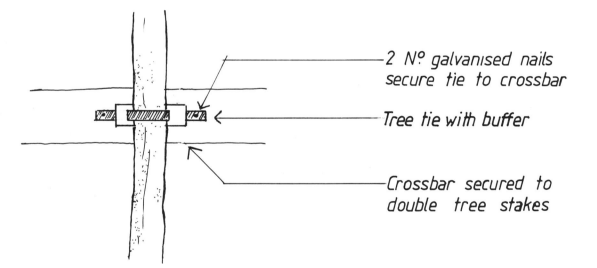

Tree tie secured to crossbar with buffer

SECTION

2 Nº galvanised nails secure tie to crossbar

Tree tie with buffer

Crossbar secured to double tree stakes

Scale 1:5

TREE TIE
double stake
& crossbar

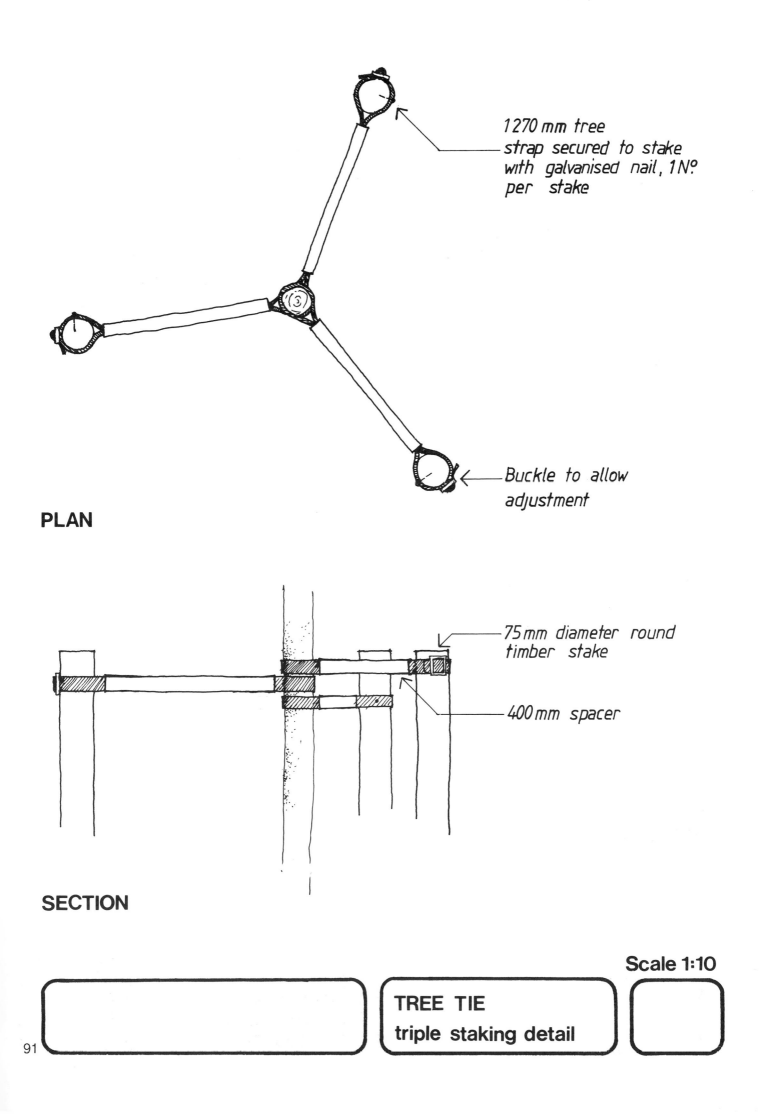

PLAN

1270 mm tree
strap secured to stake
with galvanised nail, 1 N°
per stake

Buckle to allow
adjustment

75 mm diameter round
timber stake

400 mm spacer

SECTION

Scale 1:10

TREE TIE
triple staking detail

91

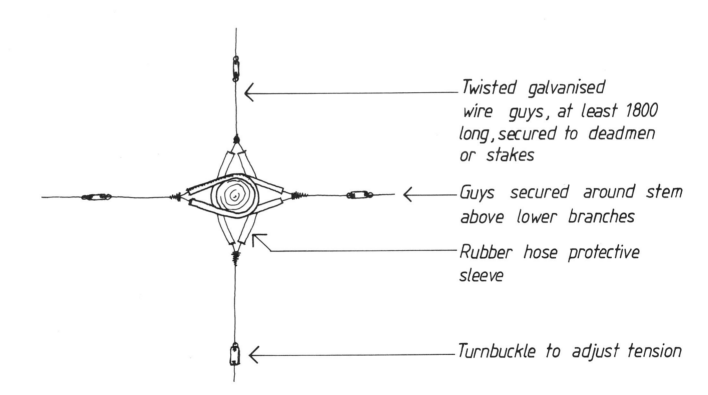

Twisted galvanised
wire guys, at least 1800
long, secured to deadmen
or stakes

Guys secured around stem
above lower branches

Rubber hose protective
sleeve

Turnbuckle to adjust tension

Scale 1:5

TREE TIE
guying detail

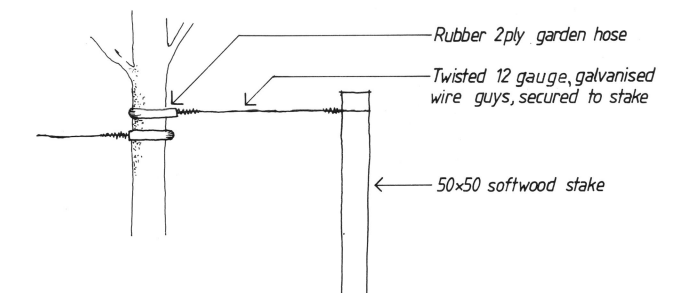

Rubber 2ply garden hose

Twisted 12 gauge, galvanised wire guys, secured to stake

50×50 softwood stake

Scale 1:5

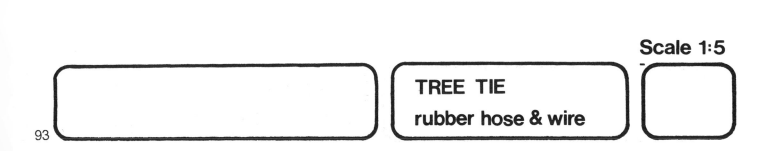

TREE TIE
rubber hose & wire

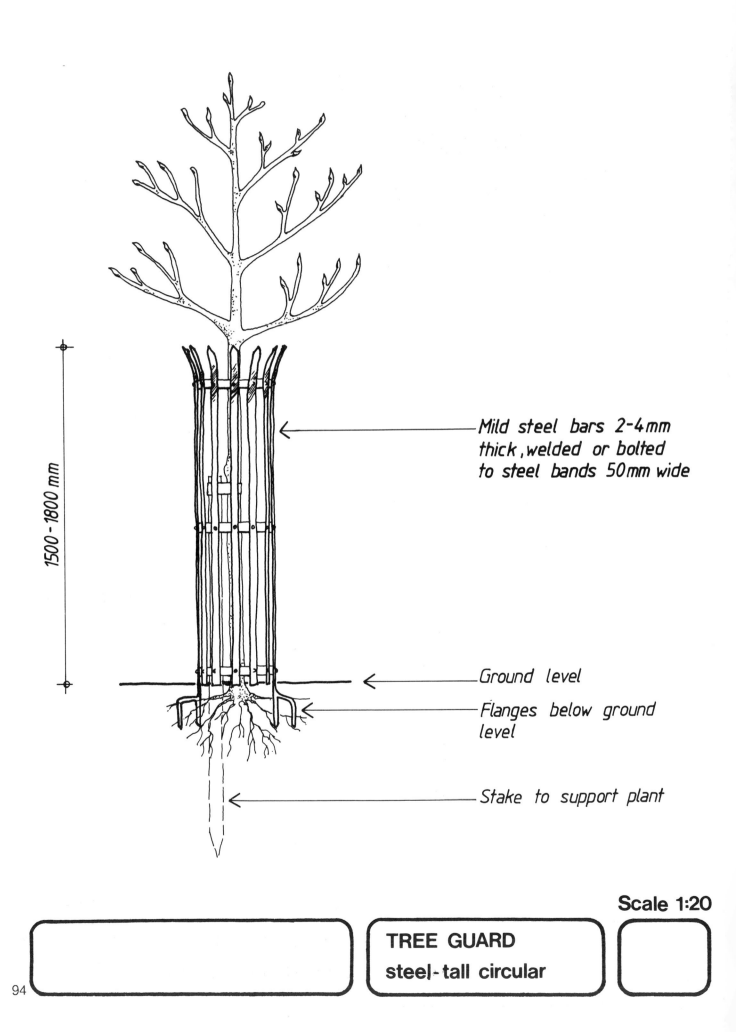

1500 - 1800 mm

Mild steel bars 2-4mm
thick, welded or bolted
to steel bands 50mm wide

Ground level

Flanges below ground
level

Stake to support plant

Scale 1:20

TREE GUARD
steel-tall circular

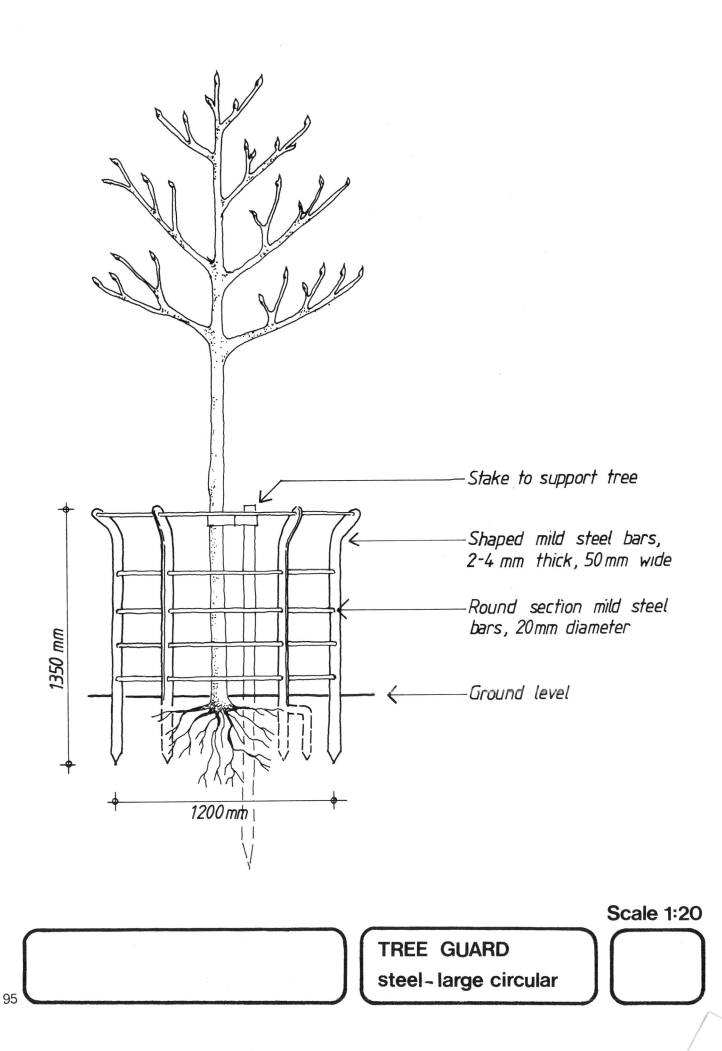

Stake to support tree

Shaped mild steel bars,
2-4 mm thick, 50 mm wide

Round section mild steel
bars, 20mm diameter

Ground level

1350 mm

1200 mm

Scale 1:20

TREE GUARD
steel - large circular

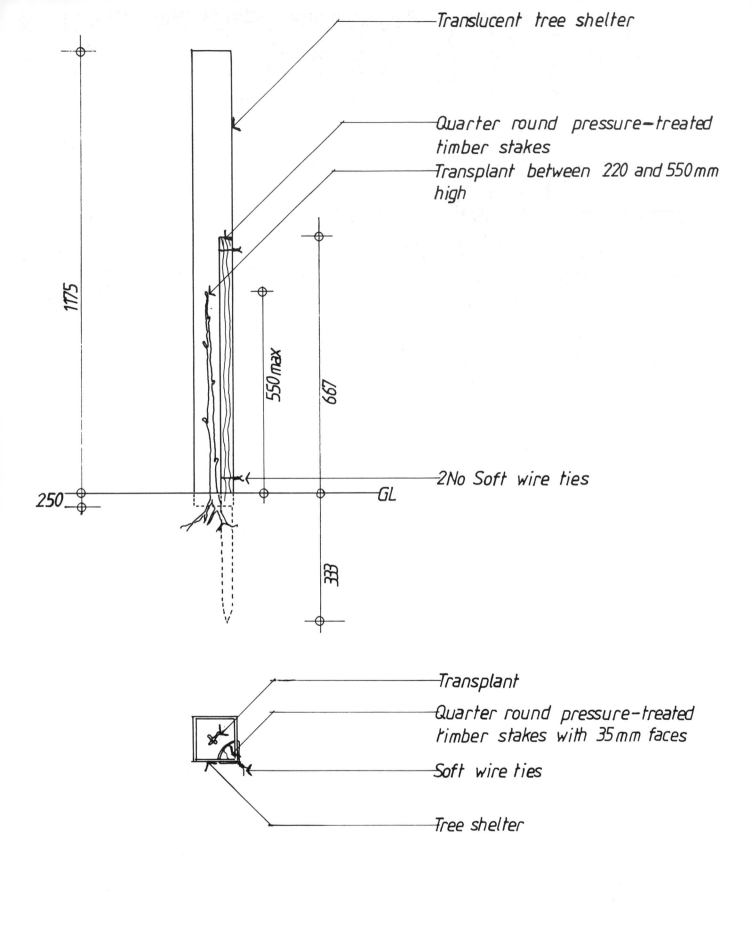

Translucent tree shelter

Quarter round pressure-treated timber stakes

Transplant between 220 and 550mm high

550 max

667

1175

2No Soft wire ties

GL

250

333

Transplant

Quarter round pressure-treated timber stakes with 35mm faces

Soft wire ties

Tree shelter

Scale 1:10

TREE PROTECTION
tree shelter

5 PROTECTION OF EXISTING TREES

In many development schemes it may be necessary or desirable to retain existing trees. Some trees may be a significant site feature; some may be covered by statutory protection such as a Tree Preservation Order or Conservation Area designation. Local authority approval is required for any work to protected trees. Any measures to preserve trees should be preceded by a thorough evaluation, as it can be costly to retain trees (especially in terms of inconvenience). In general this is a complex subject on which the advice of an arboriculturist should be sought. This chapter provides brief guidelines for tree protection.

Threats of development

An evaluation of the desirability of tree protection needs to consider the effects and side effects of development from the outset. Environmental changes may be physiologically damaging to trees, and attempting to preserve any trees affected could be wasted effort.

Any permanent changes in the root run of a tree will affect its viability. The root spread is often as much as the height of the tree plus one third. Removal of roots can cause significant die-back, and changing the surface or levels within the root area can prevent adequate water penetration and aeration (cf. Chapter 6 on trees in paved areas and car parks). Procedures for limiting such problems are considered in more detail below.

Protection of trees

Tree marking

Before any work commences the trees to be retained must be clearly marked with numbers corresponding to a tree schedule and plan.

Similarly trees in poor condition requiring removal for reasons of safety etc. must be suitably marked.

The clerk of works and all sub-contractors must be told the significance of the marks, and informed of the penalties for damage to or destruction of trees marked to be retained.

Fencing

Before work commences all trees to be retained should be protected by fences, enclosing a minimum area equal to the spread of the tree canopy overhead (greater in the case of trees of an upright habit). If branches are less than 5 m above ground, the fence line should be at least 0.5 m outside the branch spread to avoid interference by machinery. Fences should be at least 1.20 m high, and stoutly constructed, as shown in the detail sheets.

Maintaining protection

Felling

Experienced contractors, with full insurance cover and capable of working to BS 3998 (1966), should be used for the work to reduce the risk of damage to retained trees. When a tree to be removed is in close proximity to retained trees, it may be necessary to cut its roots close to its trunk, to avoid disturbing the other trees.

Burning

Areas for burning must be clearly defined so that there is no damage to retained trees. Bonfires must be at least

97

10 m clear of the canopy spread of the nearest tree.

Excavations

Where construction work of necessity on services is within the root spread, any essential excavation should be carried out by hand.

Any roots over 25 mm in diameter should be left, undamaged, across the trench until it is backfilled. Smaller roots should be cut cleanly.

No spoil from excavations should be dumped over the root spread, and adequate fences will help in this respect.

Branch thinning may be carried out to balance any reduction of the root system, and it may be helpful to water the tree in dry periods for the following four years.

Soil compaction

The effect of even small plant and machinery passing over the soil is to damage its structure; consequently no machinery should be allowed over the root spread of retained trees. Site buildings and temporary access routes should be sited outside the branch spread; but if this is not possible, access routes should be constructed of timber sleepers to spread the weight of vehicles.

Plant and machinery

As well as soil compaction, plant and equipment, particularly cranes and the arms of mechanical equipment, can cause damage in other ways. Branches likely to interfere with the working of such equipment should be tied back or removed at an early stage, with local authority approval if required. All tree work should be carried out to BS 3998.

No machinery or vehicles should be parked over the root spread of preserved trees, because of the risk of fuel leakage etc.

Materials storage

No materials should be stored and no liquids spilt over the root spread of trees.

Weedkillers

The effects of the above hazards can be minimised by the provision of adequate fences. However, such enclosed areas are likely to become weed-infested unless treated with weedkillers. Only non-residual weedkillers should be used for this purpose.

Excavation of tree roots

As tree root systems vary a great deal it is difficult to lay down general rules on excavation. Digging exploratory soil pits will give information on an individual tree's roots, particularly with an arboriculturist to interpret findings.

Mature trees cannot withstand very much root loss. A vigorous, young, healthy tree may be able to cope with the loss of up to 30 per cent of its root system without obvious ill-effects, whereas a loss of 5-10 per cent to a fully grown tree is likely to result in some die-back in the crown (Helliwell, 1985).

Ideally no roots should be severed, so where construction work on services of necessity is within the root spread, damage must be minimised by careful routing of services and excavation by hand to allow larger roots (greater than about 25 mm diameter) to remain undamaged. They can be left bridging a trench while pipes or cables are laid. If drains cannot be routed clear of trees they can be laid below the root run level, at about 1.2 m or greater depth.

Changes in drainage and water table

Drainage patterns will change as a result of development work such as earth moving, surface compaction and foundation building. If the water table is lowered, for example because of structures reducing infiltration into the ground, mature trees may have difficulty adapting. On the other hand, a fall in water table can be stimulating in the long run as the potential well-drained zone for rooting is increased; again expert advice is required. A rise in water table near the surface is likely to kill tree roots as the soil around them becomes saturated.

The installation of impermeable paving over the rooting zone (cf. Chapter 6) will reduce moisture reaching the roots. Ideally a fully permeable paving or ground-cover planting should be used around existing trees. In practice it is advisable to approach this situation as nearly as possible. Special precautions may be employed to make up any moisture deficit under impermeable paving, including irrigation pipes. Another solution to a deficit is to redirect some of the rain water from buildings into soakaways adjacent to the tree (except in heavy soils where the water cannot drain away). Ground falls around existing trees need careful detailing; water falling towards the bole will cause it to be permanently moist, encouraging

pathogen activity and waterlogging of the soil.

Changes in level

The best advice is not to change site levels within the root spread of existing trees. However, changes may be unavoidable for design or technical reasons. A change of level on one side of a tree is usually feasible with care. Reducing the crown may help compensate for lost roots. Technical issues involved are discussed at length by Harris (1983).

Vigorously growing trees are more likely to withstand upward changes of level, whereas just 150 mm of fill can in time kill a mature tree; so operations need extreme care.

Any fill should be of light texture, as the addition of heavy clay or silty material over the roots will impair aeration.

One design solution to raise the level is to build a retaining wall level with the edge of the canopy, leaving the ground in the rooting zone at its original height. Adequate drainage must be provided. Alternatively levels can be raised by constructing a retaining structure around the tree, which is filled, partially or completely, with a coarse material such as gravel or clinker, flush with adjoining made-up ground (see the detail sheet). The coarse material will allow aeration and drainage to continue.

It may be possible for levels to be made up with soil of similar or coarser texture to that existing, providing it is added gradually over several years. Roots can grow into the new fill material, the response being better in species such as poplar, willow and maples.

Lowering the ground level around an existing tree is possible providing that its stability is not threatened and damage to surface roots is limited. The soil level may be lowered in a limited area to one side of a vigorous tree (see the detail sheet), removing up to 30 per cent of the shallow roots. Any excavation downward within the root zone should be by hand and must avoid cutting the sinker roots essential to anchorage. Building a retaining structure part or the whole way around a tree is a preferable solution if a greater reduction in adjacent levels is needed, as roots are disrupted less (see the Chapter 4 detail sheets 4.9 and 4.15). Constructing a retaining wall at no more than one third of the distance from the drip-line to the trunk may leave an adequate root system intact.

Checklist

Marking trees

Trees to be retained or removed should be marked appropriately and all relevant persons informed of the significance of the marks.

Fencing

Construct stout fences, 1.20 m minimum, around trees or groups of trees to be retained, enclosing adequate area.

Felling

Avoid damage to retained trees when felling trees to be removed.

Burning

Clearly define areas for burning. Such areas should be clear of canopy spread of retained trees.

Plant and machinery

Restrict use of plant and machinery in the root area of protected trees to avoid soil compaction or material damage.

Materials storage

No materials to be stored or spilt in tree protection area.

Weedkillers

Use non-residual weedkillers for weed control inside tree protection area.

Excavation of tree roots

Excavation around tree roots by hand, leaving larger roots to bridge trenches. No spoil to be dumped over root spread. Thin branches appropriately.

Drainage

Install permeable paving over tree root area. Take necessary steps to provide adequate drainage to or away from tree roots.

Change in level

Avoid changes of level wherever possible. Follow the detail sheets for changes in level, such as retaining walls or tree wells. Excavate near trees by hand, restrict excavation to one third of distance from drip line to trunk wherever possible.

Bibliography

ARBORICULTURAL ASSOCIATION (1970) Advisory Leaflet No 1, Tree Preservation Orders

BRITISH STANDARDS INSTITUTION (1966) BS 3889: Recommendations for Tree Work.

BRITISH STANDARDS INSTITUTION (1980) BS 5837: Trees in relation to construction

HARRIS, R. W. (1983) Arboriculture, Prentice-Hall

HELLIWELL, D. R. (1985) Trees on Development Sites, Arboricultural Association

HICKS, P., The Care of Trees on Development Sites

LA DELL, W. T. (1986) Retaining Trees on Development Sites, AJ Database CI/SfB 998, 19 February

Detail sheets

5.1
Tree protection - example of fencing
5.2
Tree protection - fencing
5.3
Tree protection - fencing tree groups
5.4
Tree protection - trunk barrier
5.5
Tree protection - service trenches
5.6
Tree protection - fill on level ground
5.7
Tree protection - raised level: organic method
5.8
Tree protection - tree well
5.9
Tree protection - cut level ground: grass bank
5.10
Tree protection - cut slope: retaining wall
5.11
Tree protection - cut on sloping ground

Conversion Table			
mm	*ft. in*	*mm*	*ft. in*
10	⁵⁄₁₆"	1.5	4' 11¼"
25	1"	4	13' 2"
50	2"		
75	3"		
100	4"		
150	6"		
200	8"		
300	11¾"		
600	1' 11½"		
1200	3' 11¾"		

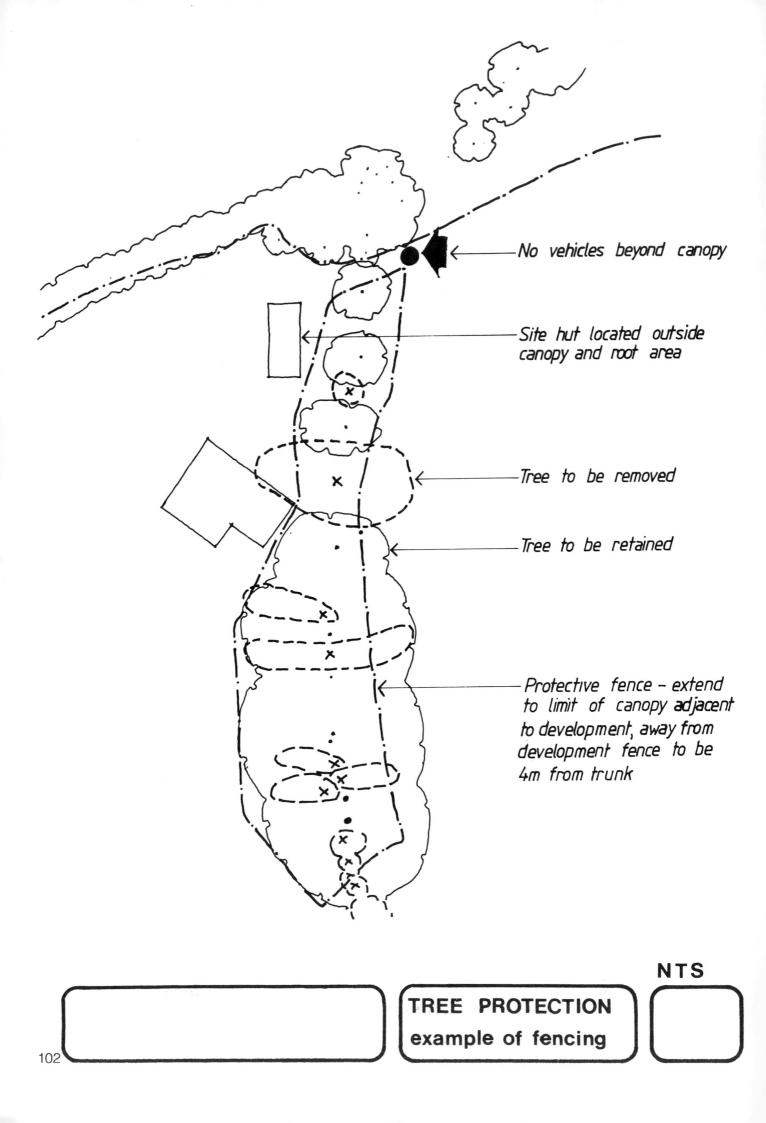

No vehicles beyond canopy

Site hut located outside canopy and root area

Tree to be removed

Tree to be retained

Protective fence – extend to limit of canopy adjacent to development, away from development fence to be 4m from trunk

NTS

TREE PROTECTION
example of fencing

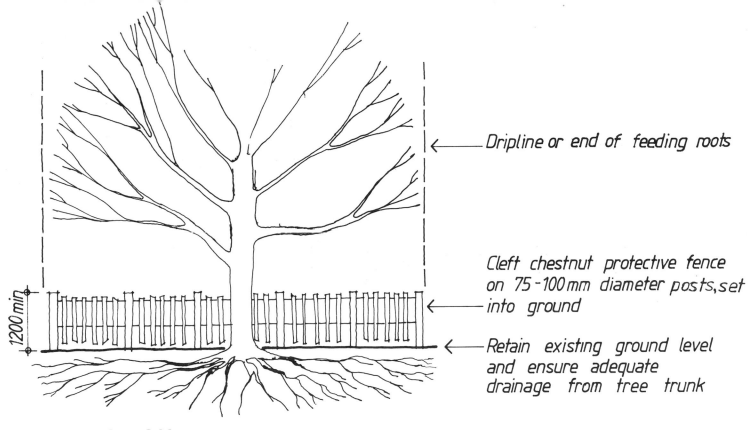

← Dripline or end of feeding roots

← Cleft chestnut protective fence on 75-100 mm diameter posts, set into ground

← Retain existing ground level and ensure adequate drainage from tree trunk

1200 min

ELEVATION

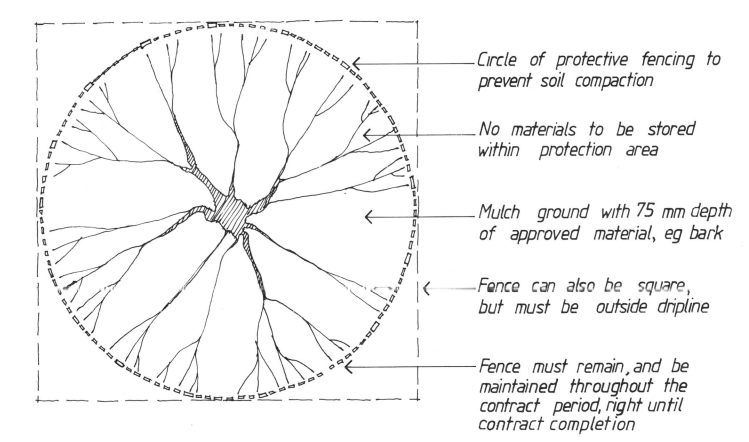

← Circle of protective fencing to prevent soil compaction

← No materials to be stored within protection area

← Mulch ground with 75 mm depth of approved material, eg bark

← Fence can also be square, but must be outside dripline

← Fence must remain, and be maintained throughout the contract period, right until contract completion

PLAN

Scale 1:75

TREE PROTECTION
fencing

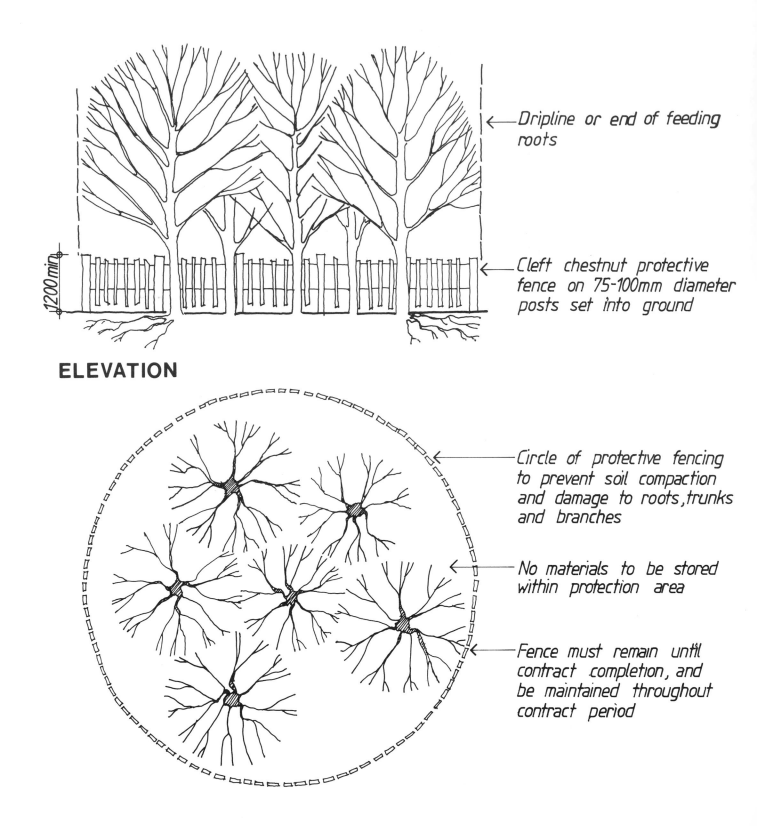

ELEVATION

← Dripline or end of feeding roots

← Cleft chestnut protective fence on 75-100mm diameter posts set into ground

1200 min

← Circle of protective fencing to prevent soil compaction and damage to roots, trunks and branches

← No materials to be stored within protection area

← Fence must remain until contract completion, and be maintained throughout contract period

PLAN

Scale 1:7:

TREE PROTECTION
fencing tree groups

104

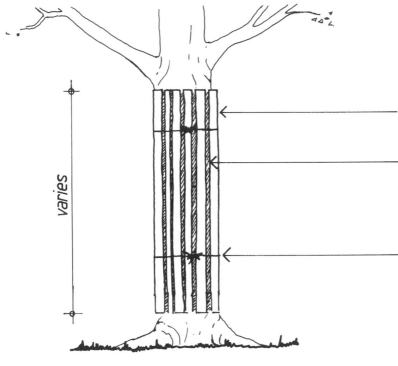

ELEVATION 1:50

50 × 150 mm timber boards

Hessian between boards and timber

12 gauge wire stapled to boards and tied together

NOTE
To be used only where space prohibits fence.

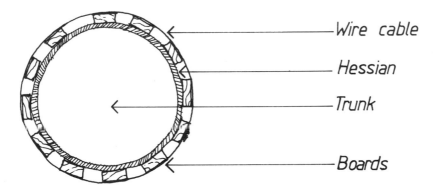

Wire cable

Hessian

Trunk

Boards

PLAN 1:25

NTS

TREE PROTECTION
trunk barrier

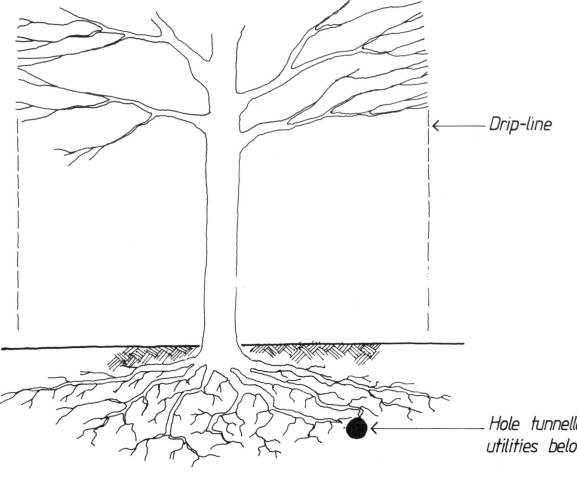

Drip-line

*Hole tunnelled for services/
utilities below rootzone*

*Finish open trenches
outside dripline*

TREE PROTECTION
service trenches

NTS

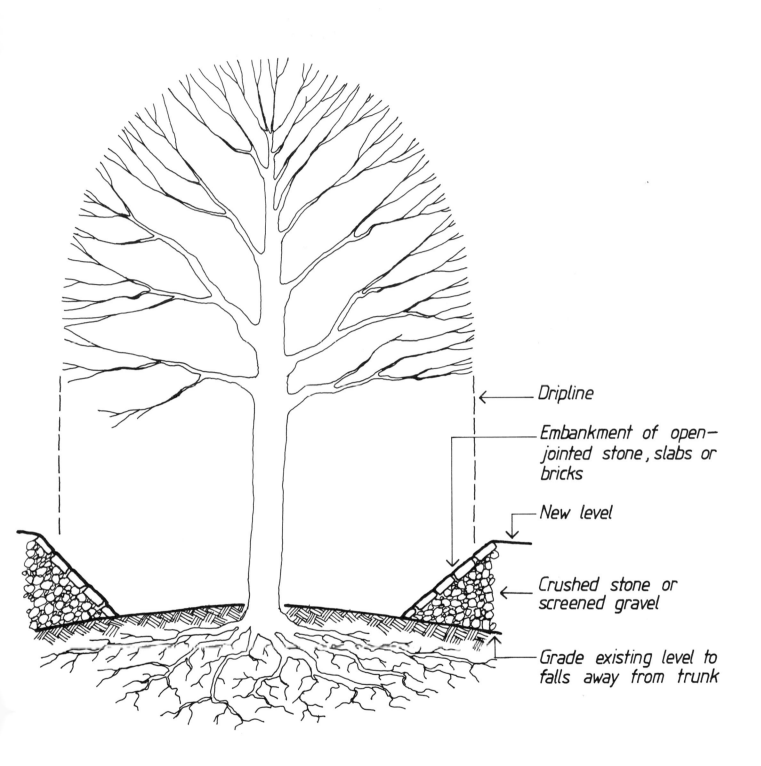

Dripline

Embankment of open-jointed stone, slabs or bricks

New level

Crushed stone or screened gravel

Grade existing level to falls away from trunk

NTS

TREE PROTECTION
fill on level ground

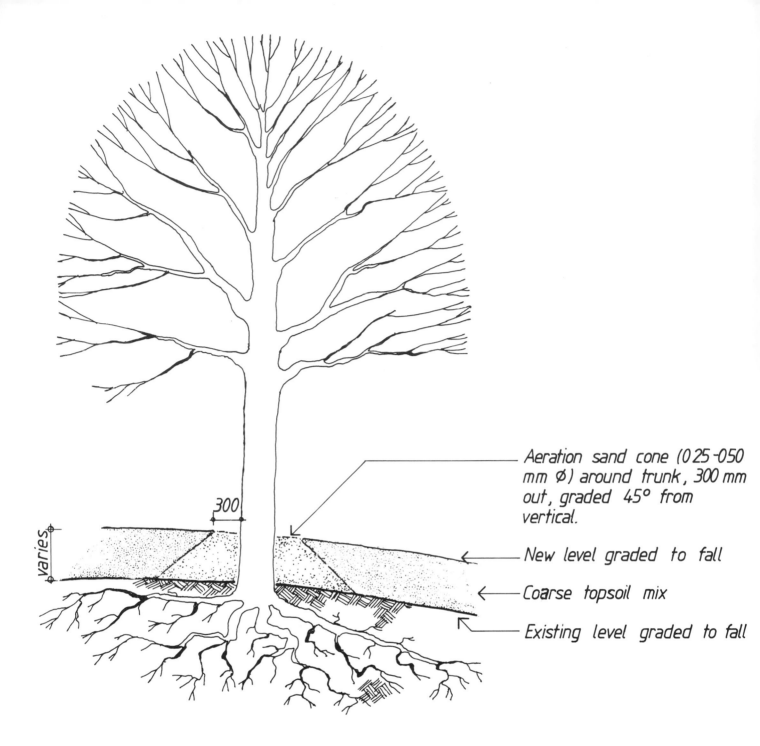

Aeration sand cone (025-050 mm Ø) around trunk, 300 mm out, graded 45° from vertical.

New level graded to fall

Coarse topsoil mix

Existing level graded to fall

300

varies

NTS

TREE PROTECTION
raised level
organic method

108

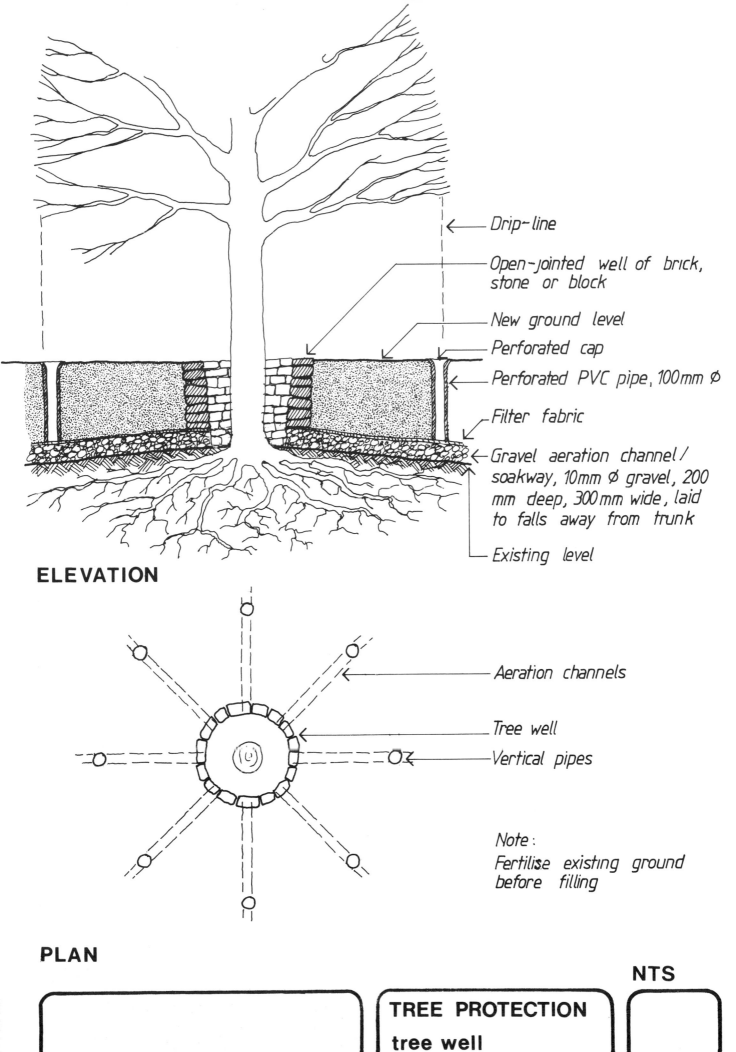

← Drip-line

Open-jointed well of brick, stone or block

New ground level

Perforated cap

Perforated PVC pipe, 100mm ⌀

Filter fabric

Gravel aeration channel / soakway, 10mm ⌀ gravel, 200 mm deep, 300 mm wide, laid to falls away from trunk

Existing level

ELEVATION

Aeration channels

Tree well

Vertical pipes

Note:
Fertilise existing ground before filling

PLAN

109

TREE PROTECTION
tree well

NTS

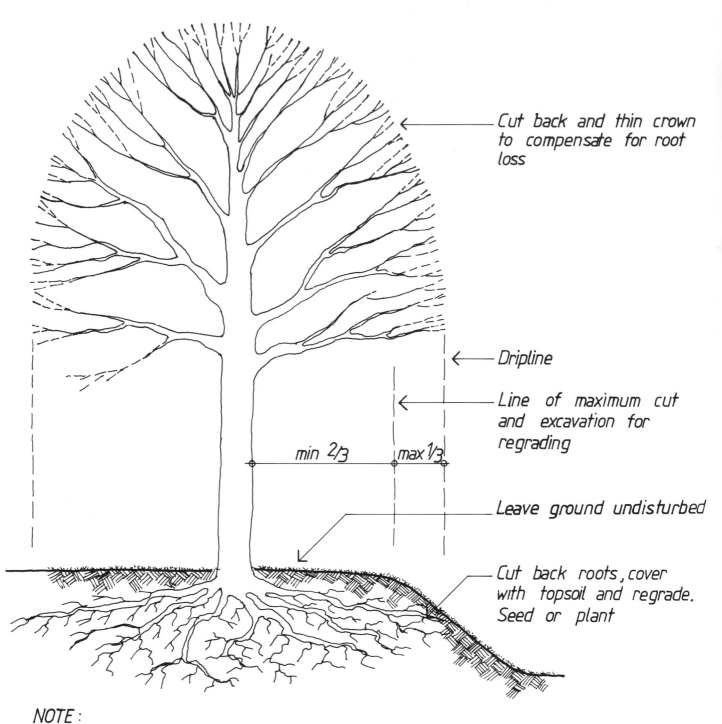

Cut back and thin crown
to compensate for root
loss

Dripline

Line of maximum cut
and excavation for
regrading

min 2/3   max 1/3

Leave ground undisturbed

Cut back roots, cover
with topsoil and regrade.
Seed or plant

NOTE:
Start excavation as far out from
crown spread as possible

Water tree and apply general fertilizer if necessary
during following years

Remove soil and cut any roots
to leave a clean wound

TREE PROTECTION
cut level ground
grass bank

NTS

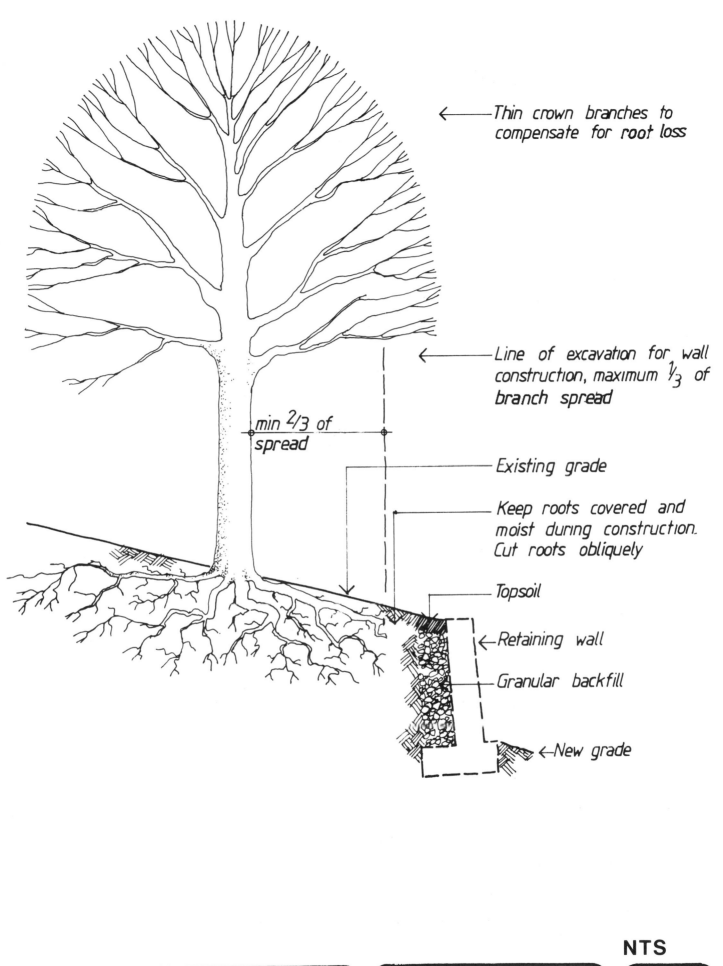

Thin crown branches to compensate for root loss

Line of excavation for wall construction, maximum $\frac{1}{3}$ of branch spread

min $\frac{2}{3}$ of spread

Existing grade

Keep roots covered and moist during construction. Cut roots obliquely

Topsoil

Retaining wall

Granular backfill

New grade

NTS

TREE PROTECTION
cut slope retaining wall

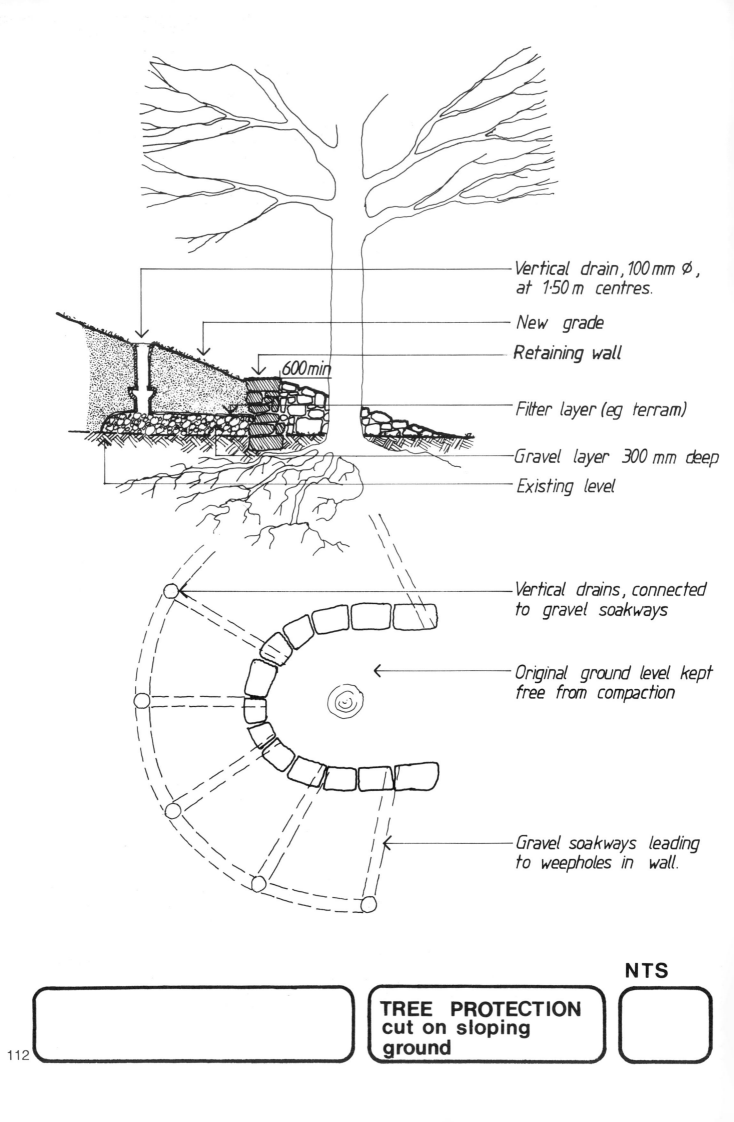

Vertical drain, 100 mm ∅, at 1·50 m centres.

New grade

Retaining wall

600 min

Filter layer (eg terram)

Gravel layer 300 mm deep

Existing level

Vertical drains, connected to gravel soakways

Original ground level kept free from compaction

Gravel soakways leading to weepholes in wall.

NTS

TREE PROTECTION
cut on sloping
ground

6 TREE SURROUNDS

Trees planted in paving are a vital part of many landscape schemes, but it is important to bear in mind that such a situation for plants is unnatural.

The success of such planting depends heavily on attention to details and the satisfaction of the basic needs of the tree: adequate supplies of water and nutrients, a well-drained growing medium and aeration of roots, sufficient root space for root anchorage and feeding, support for establishing trees and protection from vehicles, vandalism etc. Regular maintenance is particularly important to maintain good growing conditions (cf Chapter 8).

Selection of stock

Tree species are known to vary in their suitability for planting in paved areas. Differences are found in rates and forms of growth as compared to trees grown in normal conditions. In general, as growing conditions are less than ideal, trees attain a smaller ultimate size. If a full-size tree is required, provision of a gravel sub-base under surrounding paving may be considered. Where smaller species are being planted, growing them in free-standing containers may be a viable alternative to planting pits.

In selection of stock the tree form should be considered. Branching of the crown starting at about 2.5 m in pedestrian zones and 5.0 m beside a carriageway is likely to give adequate clearance, and a strong central leader is needed to maintain dominance and promote early height growth. Deeper rooting species are to be preferred, as less damage to paving is likely.

Planting pits

No universal tree pit design can be applied in all situations, so the problems involved need to be investigated. Trees in paved areas may be dependent almost exclusively on soil within the planting pit - this varies with the nature of the ground beneath adjacent paving. The opportunity for roots to take up moisture, air and nutrients is therefore limited, so aeration, irrigation and feeding may be needed, especially if the roots are covered by impermeable materials. Facilities such as watering pipes and drilled irrigation holes make irrigation possible (see the detail sheet).

As tree roots spread mainly in a lateral direction the width of the pit is more important than the depth. Shallow root development may damage paving foundations and surfaces. Various measures may minimise this problem: choice of deeper-rooted species, keeping the soil level around the stem well below the paving level (making up the depth with a coarse gravel infill; see the detail sheet), choice of small or medium-sized trees rather than larger types, and encouraging roots to grow downwards rather than laterally. The use of large concrete or sheet metal cylindrical pipes to contain roots may lead to spiral growth resulting in root girdling, whereas diagonal barriers, sloping inwards at the top, train roots downwards as well as outwards in their formative years (specially designed polyethylene tree planters have been developed in the United States for this purpose). Use of a honeycomb wall construction for the pit's sides should allow roots to extend outwards while maintaining stability of the sub-grade so that the paving surface is not damaged.

Avoidance of surface rooting is dependent, in the long term, on creating suitable conditions for rooting at a lower depth (say 150-450 mm) and, if possible, avoidance of viable rooting conditions in the upper 100 mm.

This may be possible by the use of very coarse gravel in the upper 100 mm; but the sandy material in which most paving is bedded provides ideal rooting conditions.

Because trees are often dependent on the soil within the planting pit, use of a good-quality topsoil with organic ameliorants is normal practice. Growing conditions around the pit must allow effective drainage, otherwise field drainage of each pit, connected to a general outflow system, will be required (see the detail sheet). Poor drainage is common in compacted urban soils where planting pits in paving are needed. Merely breaking up the base of the pit in such conditions has been found not to provide adequate drainage. If possible, the surrounding areas should be loosened and drained, to enable roots to spread beyond the planting pit.

When some trees in paving at Milton Keynes were removed it was found that the roots had completely clogged the drainage pipes supplied to each pit, thereby eliminating their effectiveness and killing the trees.

Paving details

Any paving constructed around the base of a tree will need to incorporate protective items such as stakes, tree guards and wheel stops in its design. This is most easily done in granular or small-unit materials, where, for example,

a stake may be driven into the ground, replacing a single stone sett in the paving pattern, until the tree can support itself.

As a general rule, the more permeable the paving material, the better for the aeration and watering of the tree. Open pits are a hazard to pedestrians, especially where space is limited; a compromise solution using a loose granular material, units with open joints, or a perforated grid supported firmly over the soil surface is often adopted. Where impermeable tree surrounds are unavoidable, an aeration and irrigation system becomes vital to good growth. Tree surround paving must be able to accommodate stem growth and soil movement and will possibly be relaid periodically to maintain safety standards and appearance. An opening of about 450 mm, depending on the ultimate size of the tree, is needed for the growing stem at the centre of a tree surrounded by paving of rigid units.

Paving designed with a fall past the planting pit rather than into or away from the tree allows some water infiltration and avoids problems of excess water and general increases in alkalinity. Falls towards tree pits adjacent to main roads should be avoided, as the road salts running into the tree pit may damage or kill the tree. Upstanding edge details around a pit impede free water movement and may create a rubbish trap, so a flush paving edge is preferable.

Edge materials set in large footings are likely to be unsuitable because they may easily be damaged by growing roots, and if they are constructed around existing trees, roots may be severed during groundworks.

114

Tree surrounds

A variety of paving methods and products is available for tree surrounds, including unit paving, precast tree pit covers and cast-iron tree grids. (see the detail sheets). The size of surrounds should be at least 1.2 m, to allow excavation of the tree pit after placing the edging.

The function of edging is to retain paving on the outside of the tree surround, and to support tree grids and pit covers. An edging should be chosen which will not damage any roots close to the surface. Edgings are usually flush with the surrounding paving surface, so as not to impede the general drainage flow.

Infill material should be porous to enable surface run-off to water the tree. The material should be lightly, compacted by hand. Unit paving as a tree surround should be bedded on sand, and joints should be unfilled or filled with sand. Cast-iron tree grids should be supported off the ground by the edging or can be bedded on sand as paving.

Checklist

General

If trees are incorporated in paved areas, a soil pocket is required round each trunk, and an adequate surface water supply should be able to pass through the soil to the tree roots. If the earth round the tree is sealed, the tree may dry up and die for lack of water and air. Another important point is to leave enough spare to allow for the tree's natural growth, including the expansion of the trunk.

There are three methods of detailing the tree surround. The first is a radial paving pattern of precast concrete units with drainage holes. The second is to have a panel of setts or bricks around the tree for a radius of approximately 2.0 m. The third is to lay tree grids or grills made by various manufacturers in concrete or cast iron.

A fourth method is to use an edging, its function being to retain the paving on the outside of the tree surround and infilled with granular material.

A kerb is sometimes misguidedly fitted around the tree to protect it and to edge the pavings. This should not be done. It breaks up the horizontal surface and forms a useless miniature flower bed for collecting litter, while offering only negligible protection to a hardy tree trunk.

Edging

Care is required when working around existing trees to choose an edging that will not damage any roots that may be close to the surface.

Edgings are usually flush with the surrounding pavings to allow surface run-off to drain into the tree surround.

Infill material

The infill material should be porous to enable surface run-off to water the tree. The material should be lightly compacted by hand.

When working around existing trees, the ground should not be excavated at all around the tree, the infill material being placed on the hand compacted topsoil.

Rigid Units

Rigid units should be bedded on sand, and joints should be unfilled or filled with sand.

When using rigid units as infill, a hole of about 450 mm square should be left free for the tree trunk.

Planting pits

Specify width and depth according to stock size and planting situation.

Incorporate root barriers only where necessary.

Specify good quality topsoil with organic ameliorants as infill.

Provide adequate drainage and irrigation.

Paving Details

Incorporate stakes, guys and tree guards as necessary.

Design falls in paving past pits.

Tree surround size should be at least 1.2 m outer diameter, with 450 mm opening in the centre.

Edgings should not be large or deep enough to damage roots and flush with surrounding paving.

Infill material should be porous to allow drainage and aeration.

Material around trees should be lightly compacted by hand.

Specify tree grids or pit covers according to manufacturers' description.

Bibliography

BRITISH STANDARDS INSTITUTION (1980) BS 5837 Trees in relation to construction

DEREK LOVEJOY AND PARTNERS, Spons Landscape Handbook, E. and F. N Spon Ltd

HARRIS, R. W. (1983) Arboriculture, Prentice-Hall

LANDSCAPE INSTITUTE (1977) Landscape Design with Plants, ed. Brian Clouston, Heinemann

PATCH, D. (1981) Broadleaved Trees for Amenity, *Q J Forestry* 75(1)

Detail sheets

6.1
Tree pit - paved area
6.2
Tree pit - in filled ground
6.3
Tree surround - cast iron
6.4
Tree surround - cast iron
6.5
Tree surround - mild steel
6.6
Tree surround - precast concrete
6.7
Tree surround - precast concrete
6.8
Tree surround - precast concrete
6.9
Tree surround - unit paving
6.10
Tree surround - concrete block
6.11
Tree surround - perforated brick
6.12
Tree surround - brick

6.13
Tree surround - brick and drainage channel
6.14
Tree surround - brick/gravel
6.15
Tree surround - railway sleepers
6.16
Tree surround - log rool
6.17
Tree Irrigation - system for pit

Conversion Table			
mm	*ft. in*	*mm*	*ft. in*
10	5/16"	800	2' 7"
12	½"	900	2' 11"
25	1"	1000	3' 3"
50	2"	1140	3' 9"
60	2½	1200	3' 11¾"
75	3"	1210	3' 11¾"
100	4"	1500	4' 9"
150	6"	1520	5' 0"
200	8"	1600	5' 3"
215	8½"	1800	6' 0"
225	8¾"	2000	6' 9"
440	1' 5½"	2500	7' 2½"
450	1' 5¾"		

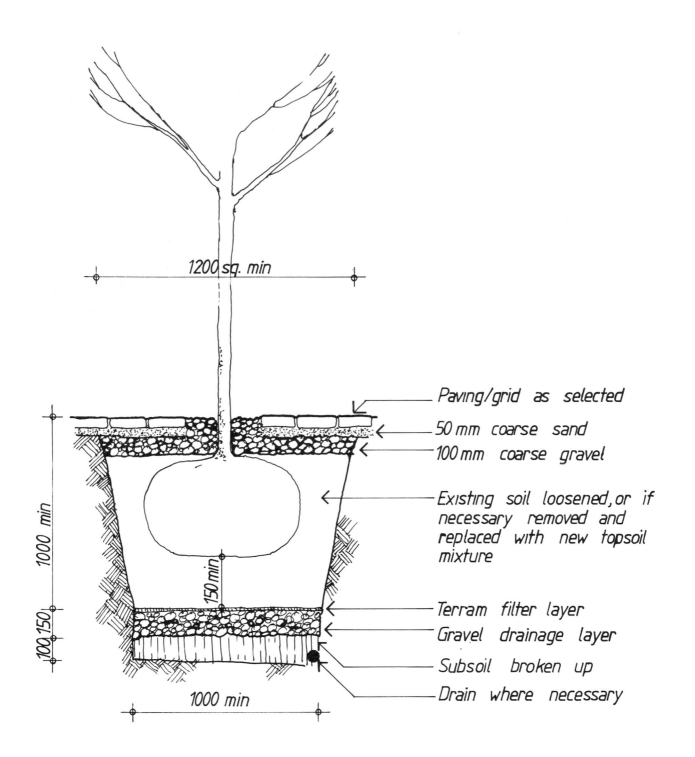

1200 sq. min

Paving/grid as selected

50 mm coarse sand

100 mm coarse gravel

Existing soil loosened, or if necessary removed and replaced with new topsoil mixture

1000 min

150 min

100 150

Terram filter layer

Gravel drainage layer

Subsoil broken up

Drain where necessary

1000 min

Scale 1:2

TREE PIT

paved area

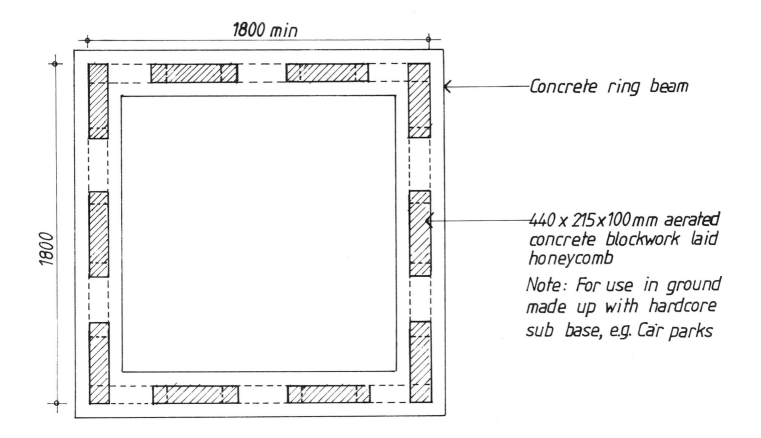

1800 min

1800

Concrete ring beam

440 x 215 x 100 mm aerated
concrete blockwork laid
honeycomb

Note: For use in ground
made up with hardcore
sub base, e.g. Car parks

PLAN

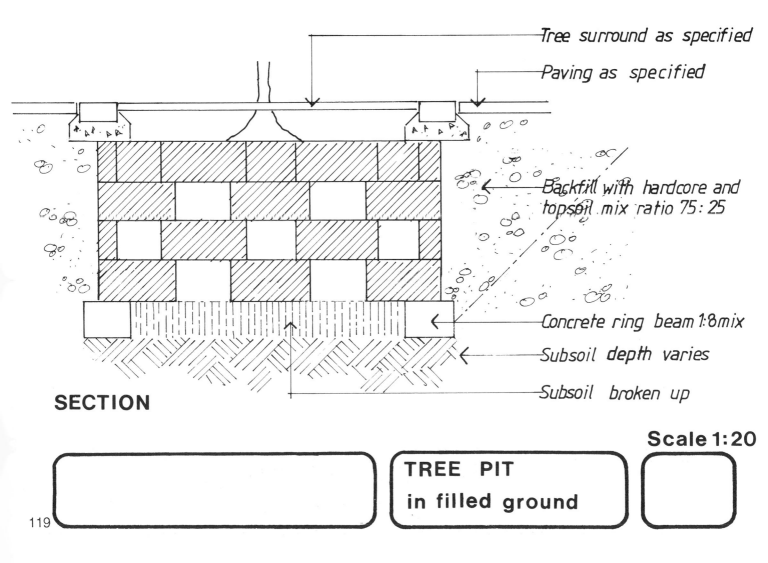

Tree surround as specified

Paving as specified

Backfill with hardcore and
topsoil mix ratio 75 : 25

Concrete ring beam 1:8 mix

Subsoil depth varies

Subsoil broken up

SECTION

Scale 1:20

TREE PIT
in filled ground

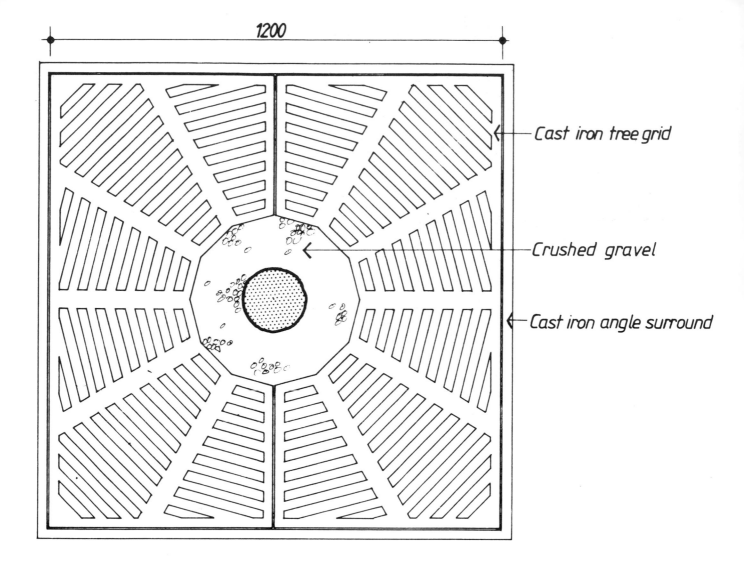

1200

Cast iron tree grid

Crushed gravel

Cast iron angle surround

PLAN

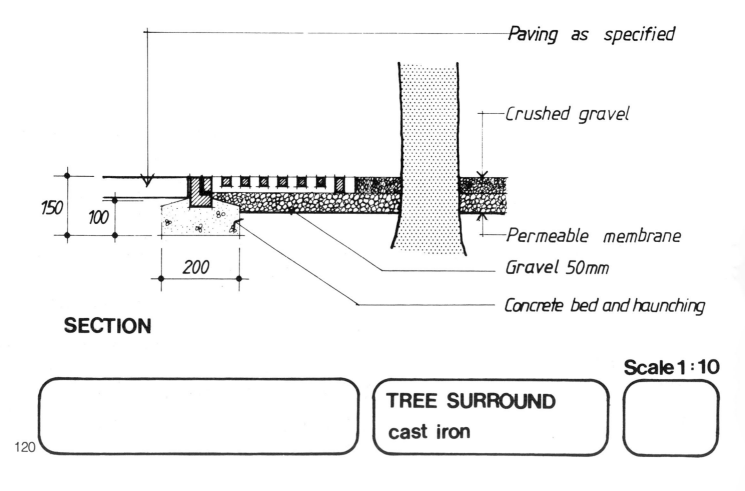

Paving as specified

Crushed gravel

150

100

200

Permeable membrane

Gravel 50mm

Concrete bed and haunching

SECTION

Scale 1:10

TREE SURROUND
cast iron

120

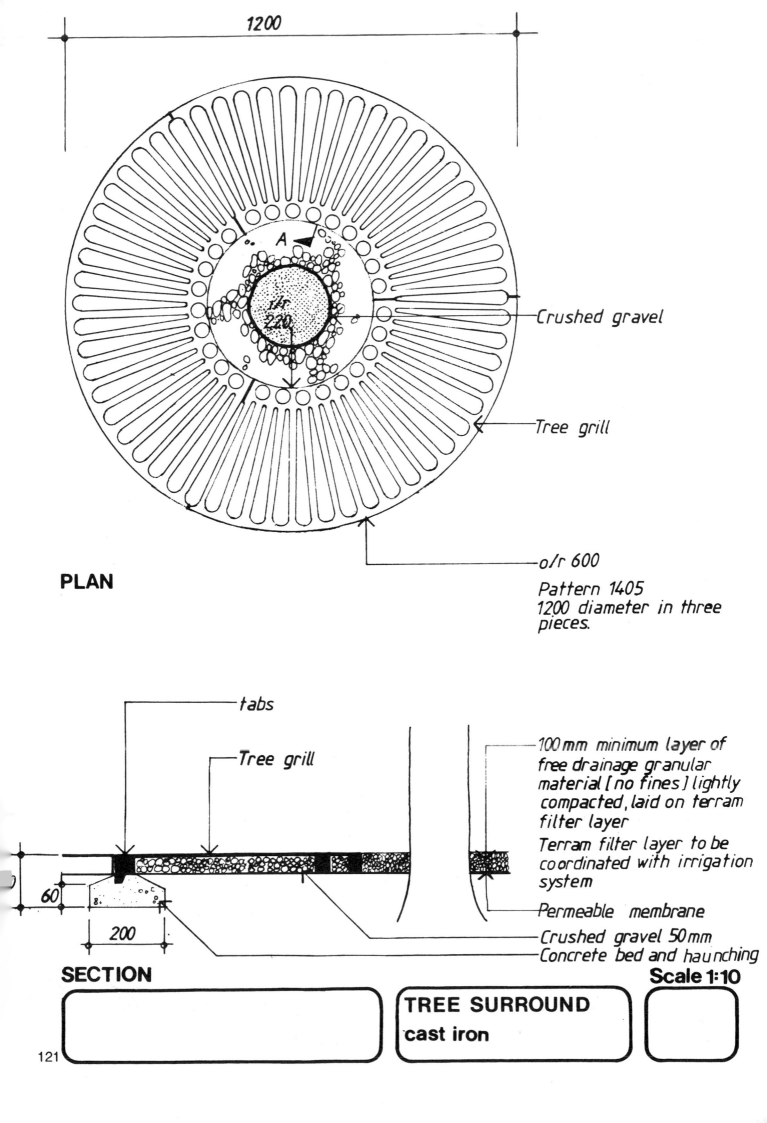

1200

PLAN

Crushed gravel

Tree grill

o/r 600

Pattern 1405
1200 diameter in three
pieces.

tabs

Tree grill

100 mm minimum layer of
free drainage granular
material [no fines] lightly
compacted, laid on terram
filter layer

Terram filter layer to be
coordinated with irrigation
system

Permeable membrane

Crushed gravel 50 mm

Concrete bed and haunching

60

200

SECTION

Scale 1:10

TREE SURROUND
cast iron

121

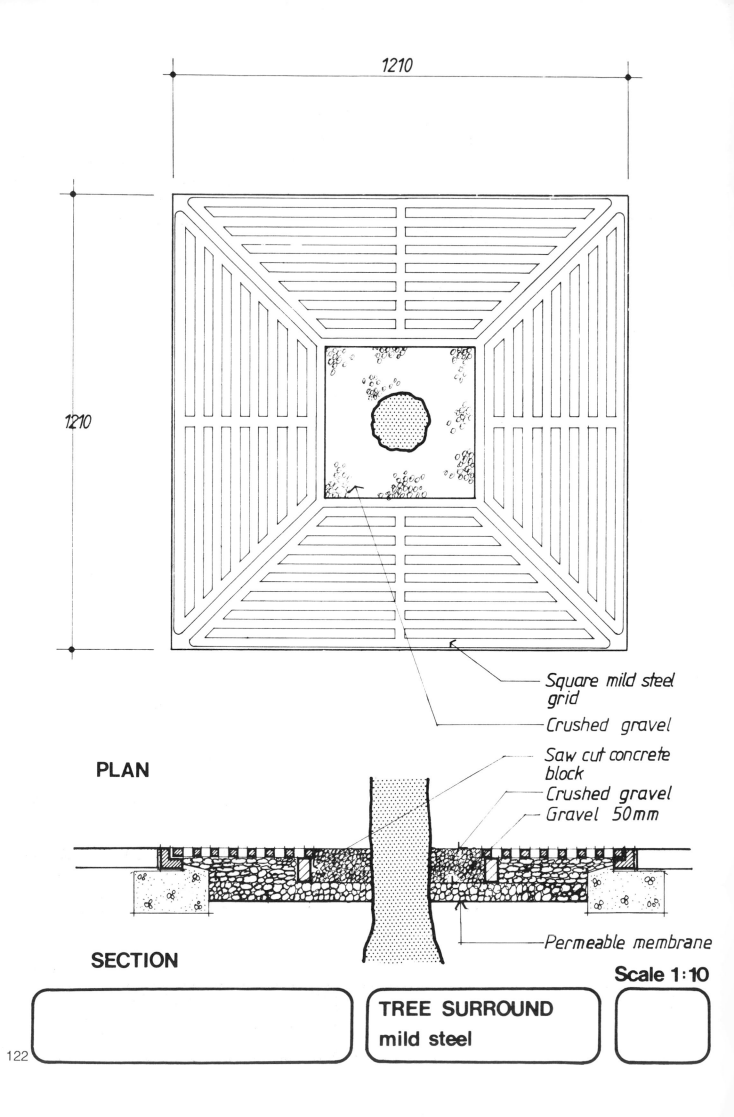

1210

1210

Square mild steel grid

Crushed gravel

Saw cut concrete block

Crushed gravel

Gravel 50mm

PLAN

Permeable membrane

SECTION

Scale 1:10

TREE SURROUND
mild steel

122

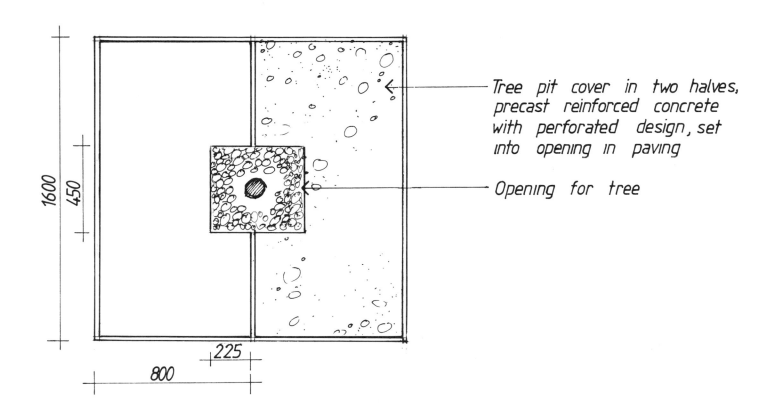

PLAN

Tree pit cover in two halves, precast reinforced concrete with perforated design, set into opening in paving

Opening for tree

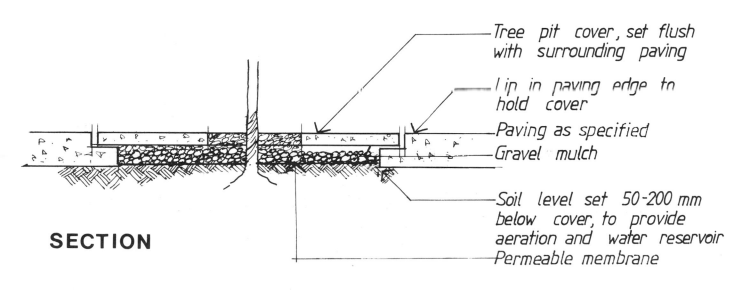

SECTION

Tree pit cover, set flush with surrounding paving

Lip in paving edge to hold cover

Paving as specified

Gravel mulch

Soil level set 50-200 mm below cover, to provide aeration and water reservoir

Permeable membrane

Scale 1:20

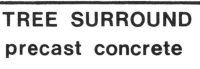

TREE SURROUND
precast concrete

123

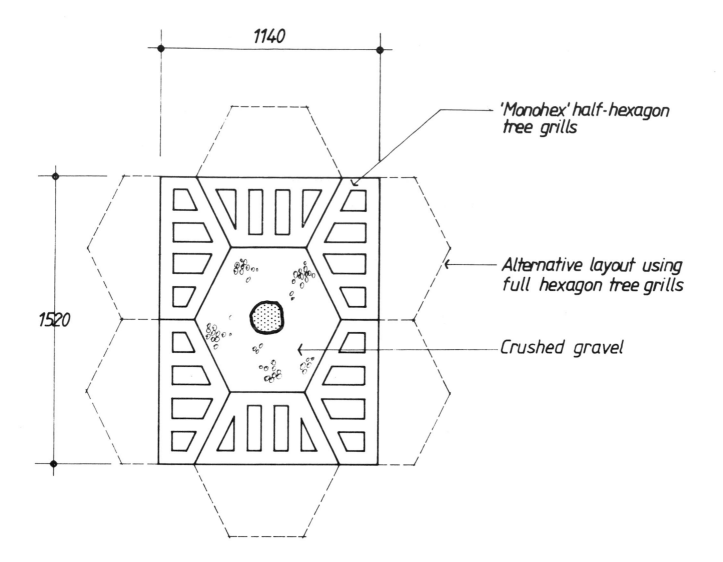

1140

1520

'Monohex' half-hexagon tree grills

Alternative layout using full hexagon tree grills

Crushed gravel

PLAN

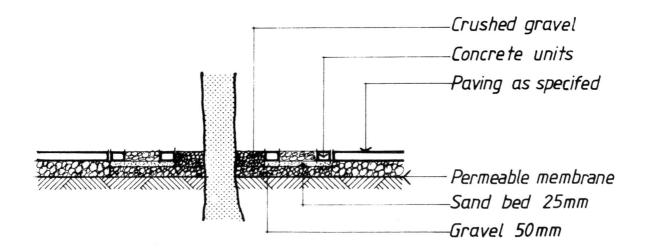

Crushed gravel
Concrete units
Paving as specifed

Permeable membrane
Sand bed 25mm
Gravel 50mm

SECTION

124

TREE SURROUND
precast concrete

Scale 1:20

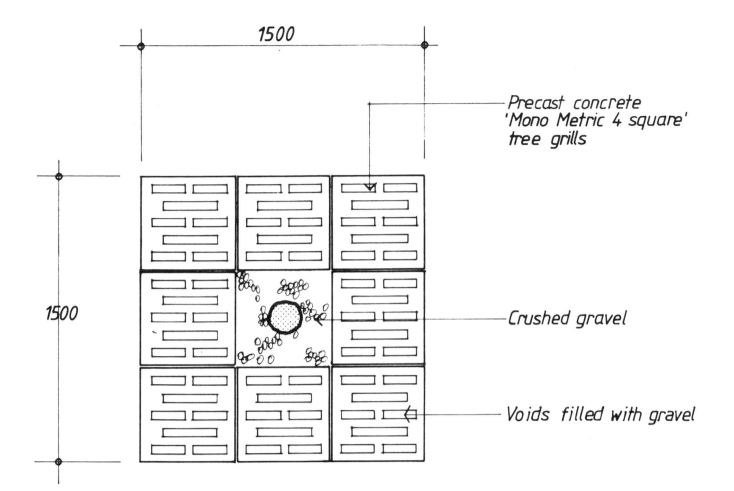

1500

1500

Precast concrete
'Mono Metric 4 square'
tree grills

Crushed gravel

Voids filled with gravel

PLAN

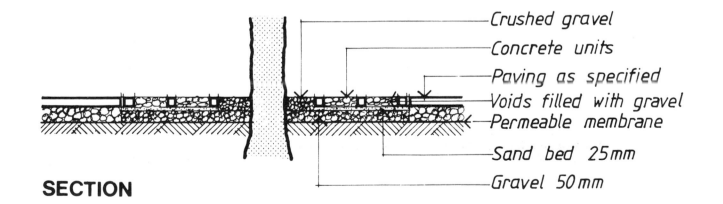

Crushed gravel

Concrete units

Paving as specified

Voids filled with gravel

Permeable membrane

Sand bed 25mm

Gravel 50mm

SECTION

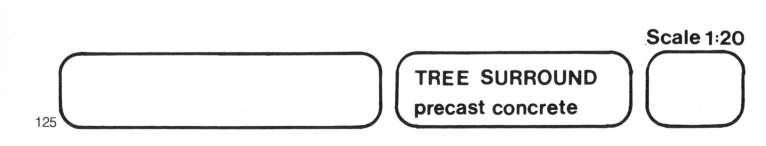

Scale 1:20

TREE SURROUND
precast concrete

125

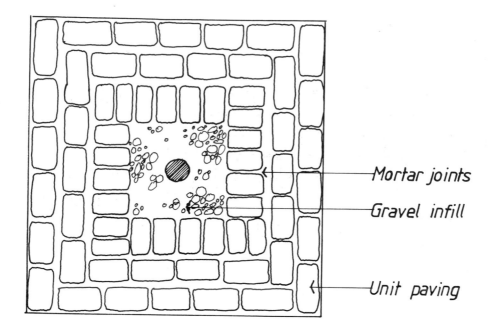

Mortar joints

Gravel infill

Unit paving

PLAN

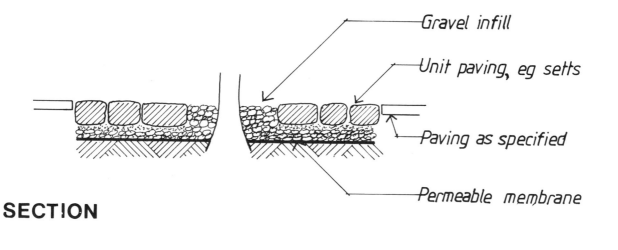

Gravel infill

Unit paving, eg setts

Paving as specified

Permeable membrane

SECTION

Scale 1:25

TREE SURROUND
unit paving

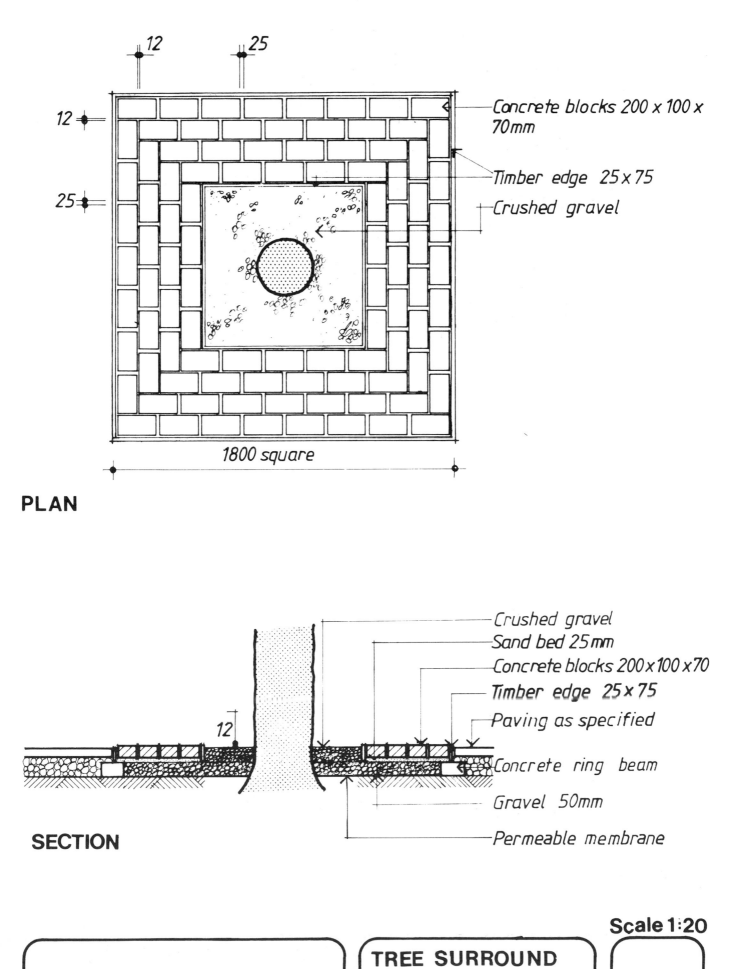

12 25

12

25

Concrete blocks 200 x 100 x 70mm

Timber edge 25 x 75

Crushed gravel

1800 square

PLAN

Crushed gravel
Sand bed 25 mm
Concrete blocks 200 x 100 x 70
Timber edge 25 x 75
Paving as specified
Concrete ring beam
Gravel 50mm
Permeable membrane

12

SECTION

Scale 1:20

TREE SURROUND
concrete block

127

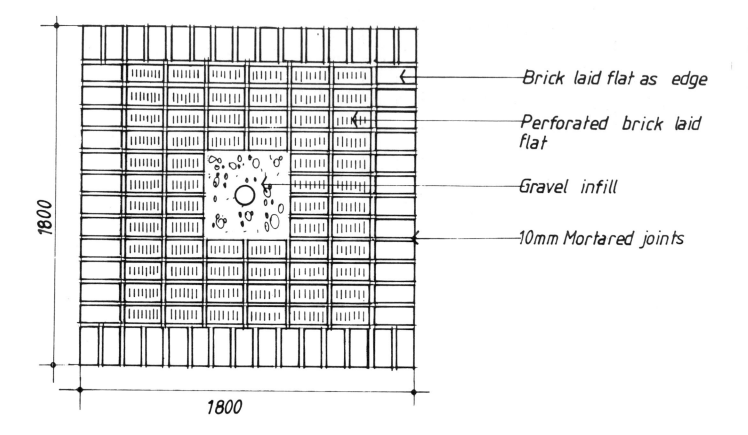

Brick laid flat as edge

Perforated brick laid flat

Gravel infill

10mm Mortared joints

PLAN

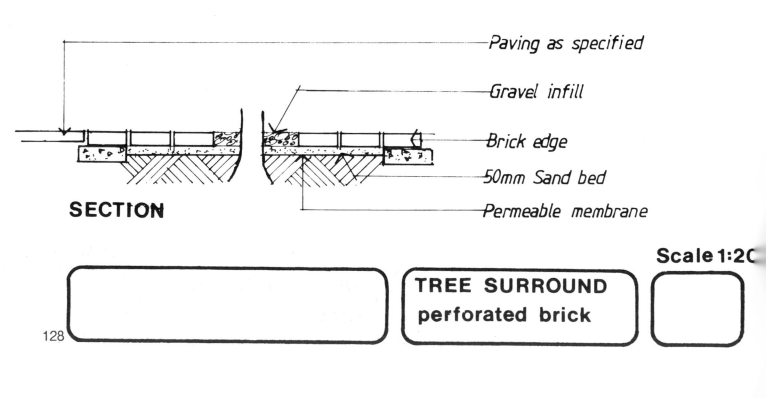

Paving as specified

Gravel infill

Brick edge

50mm Sand bed

Permeable membrane

SECTION

Scale 1:20

TREE SURROUND
perforated brick

128

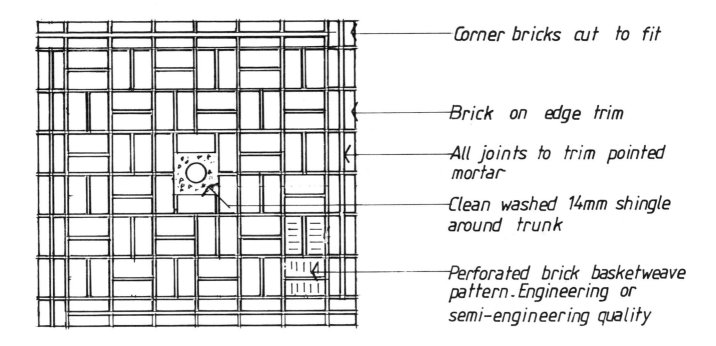

Corner bricks cut to fit

Brick on edge trim

All joints to trim pointed mortar

Clean washed 14mm shingle around trunk

Perforated brick basketweave pattern. Engineering or semi-engineering quality

PLAN

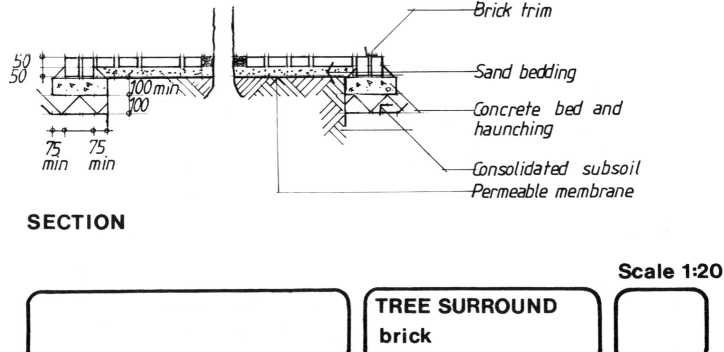

Brick trim

Sand bedding

Concrete bed and haunching

Consolidated subsoil

Permeable membrane

50
50

100 min
100

75 min   75 min

SECTION

Scale 1:20

TREE SURROUND
brick

129

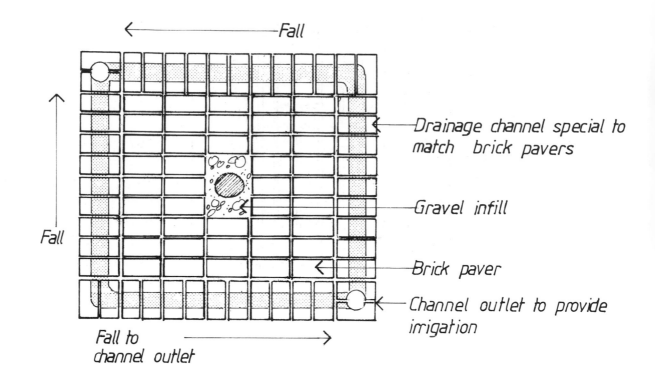

Fall

Drainage channel special to match brick pavers

Gravel infill

Brick paver

Channel outlet to provide irrigation

Fall

Fall to channel outlet

PLAN

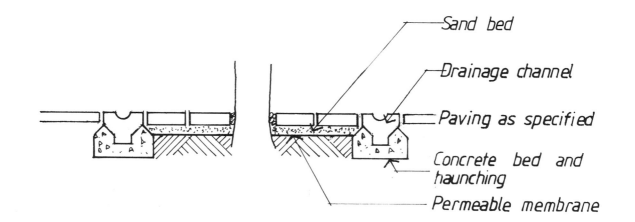

Sand bed

Drainage channel

Paving as specified

Concrete bed and haunching

Permeable membrane

SECTION

Scale 1:20

TREE SURROUND
brick and
drainage channel

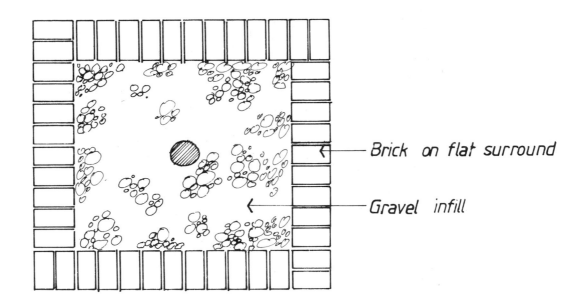

PLAN

- Brick on flat surround
- Gravel infill

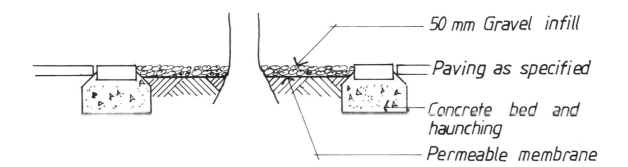

- 50 mm Gravel infill
- Paving as specified
- Concrete bed and haunching
- Permeable membrane

SECTION

Scale 1:20

TREE SURROUND
brick/gravel

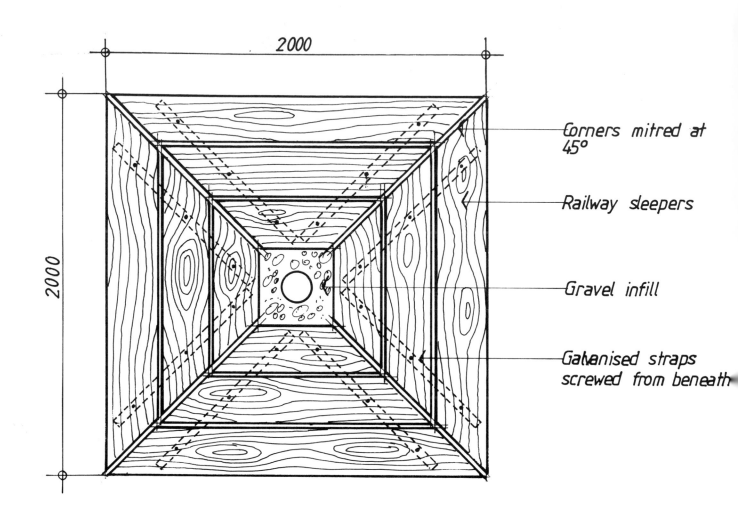

PLAN

Corners mitred at 45°

Railway sleepers

Gravel infill

Galvanised straps screwed from beneath

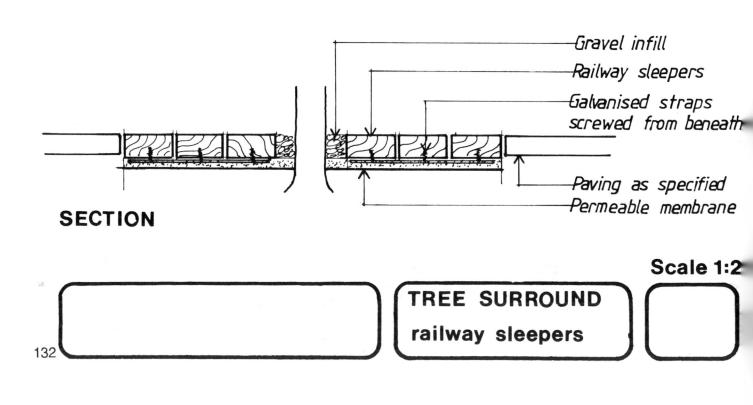

SECTION

Gravel infill

Railway sleepers

Galvanised straps screwed from beneath

Paving as specified

Permeable membrane

Scale 1:2

TREE SURROUND

railway sleepers

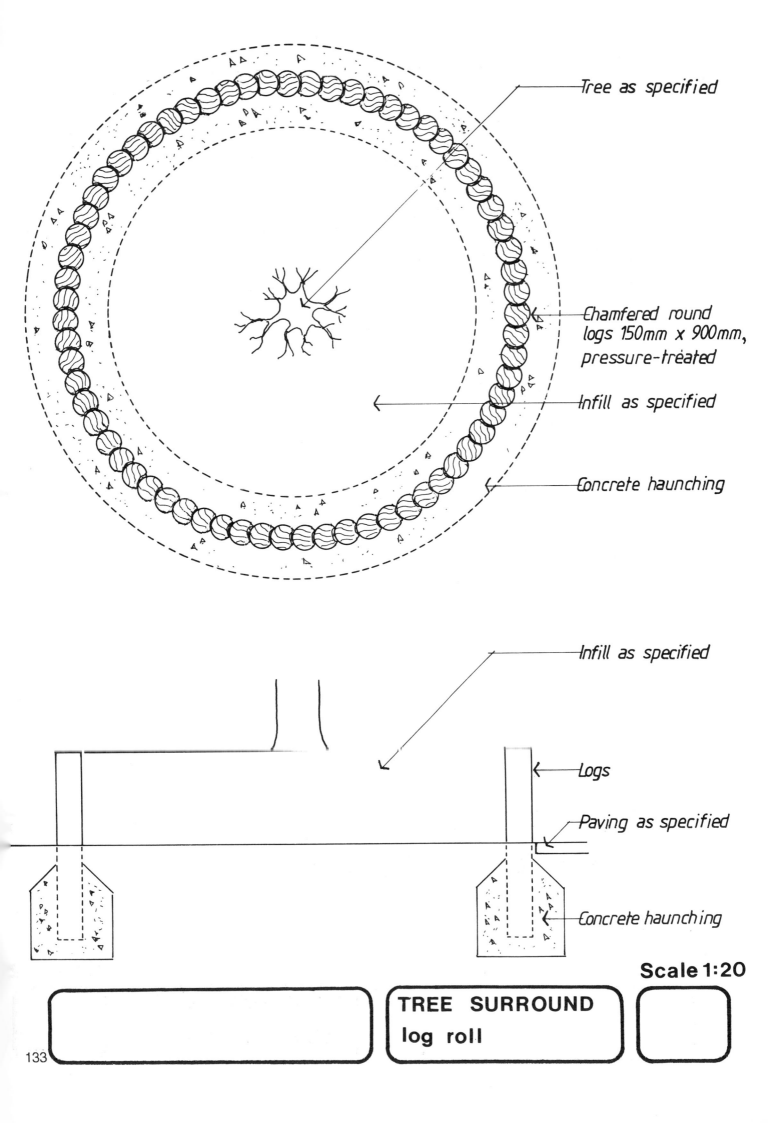

Tree as specified

Chamfered round
logs 150mm x 900mm,
pressure-treated

Infill as specified

Concrete haunching

Infill as specified

Logs

Paving as specified

Concrete haunching

Scale 1:20

**TREE SURROUND
log roll**

133

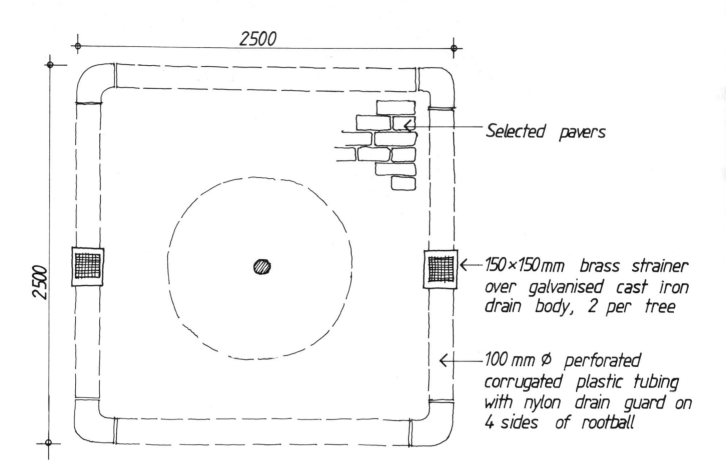

PLAN

Selected pavers

150×150mm brass strainer over galvanised cast iron drain body, 2 per tree

100 mm ⌀ perforated corrugated plastic tubing with nylon drain guard on 4 sides of rootball

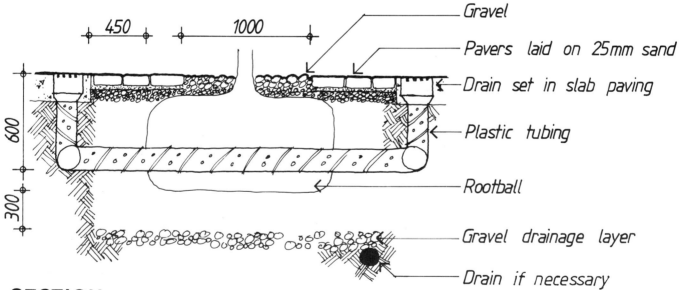

Gravel

Pavers laid on 25mm sand

Drain set in slab paving

Plastic tubing

Rootball

Gravel drainage layer

Drain if necessary

SECTION

TREE IRRIGATION
system for pit

Scale 1:25

7 TREES IN CONTAINERS AND ROOF GARDENS

The selection and detailing of tree planting in containers and for roof gardens should reflect the fact that an artificial plant support system is required for successful growth. The support system of containerised planting, including moisture, aeration, drainage, nutrition and anchorage, should be considered in detail in specification. Planting schemes, particularly on roof gardens, should consider the microclimatic effects caused by surrounding buildings.

Tree selection

Any analysis for tree selection in situations such as roof gardens, courtyards and building forecourts should emphasise exposure to wind and sun. The microclimate is a more critical selection factor at roof level than on the ground. A rooftop environment can be very harsh, affected by increased wind, direct and reflected radiation, prolonged and varying intensities of light, and low or high root temperatures.

Trees for planting in such situations should be selected on the basis of hardiness. The trees chosen should also reach a moderate size and grow slowly; and the weight of the mature tree should be considered in roof gardens.

Soil requirements

Drainage, weight and aeration are the most important characteristics of a soil mix. Weight of the soil may be particularly important on roof gardens or other supported containers. There is no ideal mix which may be universally applied in all situations. Although soil requirements will vary according to different situations, an optimum mix will be composed of materials which lighten the total weight, prevent long term filling of soil voids with water, yet retain some water long enough to be absorbed by the roots. Nutrients and anchorage can be artificially supplied.

Container soil mixes recommended by the University of California Manual 23 combine uniform coarse sand (0.5-1 mm) and organic matter in volume ratios from 50:50 to 75:25. Water and nutrient-holding capacities may be improved by the addition of a little silt or loam, but more than 5 per cent may hamper drainage and aeration. A 50:50 sand/organic mix weighs three to four times as much when wet as when dry. As bulk densities vary greatly with slight changes in formulation, wet weight should be estimated by sampling the soil mix. Each soil mix should be specified for compliance before it is put into place.

The introduction of lightweight materials into the mix can theoretically increase the amount of soil which can be used in limited weight situations. Lightweight soil additives which can be used instead of sand include perlite, vermiculite and plastic foam.

Certain minimum soil depths should be adhered to in order to ensure successful root establishment. Depending on the size of the tree, a recommended minimum is 800-1300 mm. Where possible greater soil depths should be used. Additional soil volume will encourage an increase in potential plant size, as well as reducing the need for watering and fertilising.

Drainage requirements

The drainage system must be designed

to remove excess water from the container or planting bed. The soil mix must allow water to drain rapidly to the bottom of the container. Drainage lines and outlets must be large enough to collect water rapidly from the container for discharge into building or street drainage systems. The maximum amounts of excess water should be considered in the design of drainage systems.

To assist the rapid collection and discharge of excess water, containers and large rooftop planting beds should have sloping bottoms (2 per cent minimum), with an outlet at the lowest point. Apart from this slope, the bottom of each bed with a common drainage system should be fairly level.

A commonly used drainage system combines the use of a layer of gravel on the container bottom, covered by a fibreglass filter layer, over which the soil mix is placed. The fibreglass layer filters fine soil and peat particles which may clog up the drainage layer below. A variation of this method uses 100 mm of gravel with a 15 mm fibreglass blanket over; above the filter is a 100 mm layer of granulated peat which compresses by half when the soil mix is laid on and which acts as a water reservoir (Clouston, 1977; see the detail sheet).

When a sandy soil is used over a gravel layer the extreme difference in pore sizes may cause drainage to cease when the soil above the gravel is near saturation, thereby creating an artificial water table (Harris, 1983). The commonly used gravel layer may also waste valuable space for the growing medium, especially where weight is a consideration. A system of drainage which avoids the use of gravel utilises

tile drains instead. Water moves into the drainage tile when soil reaches saturation point.

A 25 mm diameter plastic pipe, with four rows of holes spaced evenly around the pipe, is suitable for most containers or contained areas. Ten 25 mm lines, on 0.5-1.0 m centres, connected to larger 25-50 mm diameter pipes, will remove water rapidly from the bottom of planters. Such a system is easy to install and will help to reduce the weight load of plantings.

To keep lines from silting up, drainpipes should be wrapped with 12 mm fibreglass filter pads, or strips of filter pad laid directly over the drainpipe (see the detail sheets). A 25 mm layer of coarse sand should be placed on the bottom of the planter to assist water flow. Clean-out standpipes should be connected to any drainage system. One standpipe
is necessary for each container and several for a large container area.

Irrigation

Soil in containers or on roof decks does not have access to the water table, so moisture can be replenished only by rain or watering. Evaporation losses in these planting situations are increased by the presence of adjacent hard surfaces and the likelihood of windy conditions, thereby increasing watering needs.

Watering can be carried out by hand, automatic sprinkle or trickle irrigation, or by capillary action irrigators. A proper and efficient irrigation system will reduce maintenance costs and will help to ensure healthy plants. The type of system selected will depend on cost, available labour and the characteristics of the area to be served. A careful assessment of the likely soil water status should be made for each planting situation.

In general, the irrigation design should incorporate one waterline to serve each container or container area of any size. The irrigation system should also be an integral part of the structure which supports the containers.

Waterproofing

To prevent soil moisture from penetrating the walls and floor or porous containers, some form of waterproofing is necessary. This is particularly important for the floors of planters in roof gardens, where moisture must not penetrate into the structure of the building.

The most common method of waterproofing on rooftops is a full asphalt specification, laid to a fall of about 1:60, directly over the entire roof area to provide an impermeable base. In planted areas a protective screed over the main waterproof membrane, covered with a further membrane provides extra protection against invasive plant roots and forks. Various bituminous products are available, combined with milled glass fibres or yarns, which provide resilient water- and rot-proof membranes. Sheet linings such as butyl or polythene are suitable for use in smaller areas such as single containers. Care should be taken to ensure that the level of planting medium and mulch is below the top of the lining.

Fertilising

A combination of lightweight soil mix and frequent watering may result in a loss of nutrients available to the tree. Therefore the soil in containers or roof gardens should be fertilised more often than soil at grade.

The fertiliser should be mainly composed of organically derived nutrients, since these release their nourishment more slowly and are less easily leached than chemically derived nutrients. The type of fertiliser will vary according to tree and location. Testing of the soil mix should be carried out to allow for correction of any deficiencies prior to planting. Monitoring of the soil thereafter should be performed at regular intervals, and deficiencies corrected as part of a maintenance programme.

Anchorage

An anchorage system for trees in containers and roof gardens is of prime importance. The reduced volume of soil in containers and lightweight mixes and windy conditions on roof gardens reduce the soil's ability to anchor trees. The deeper and wider the soil volume, the better will be the anchorage for trees.

Where soil depth and weight are adequate, normal staking, guying or anchorage systems can be used (cf. Chapter 4). Permanent guying or anchorage may be necessary in high wind situations. In cases of reduced soil depth or where there is a danger of stakes penetrating membranes, a system of guying or anchorage to eyebolts secured in the walls of the container may be necessary (see the detail sheets in Chapter 4, *Guying*, 4.9, and *Anchorage*, 4.15).

Checklist

Soil requirements

The soil mix must have adequate drainage and aeration characteristics.

The weight of soil mix is important on roof decks.

Specify soil mix components and ratio, and in some cases desired wet/dry weight.

Adhere to mimimum soil depths and exceed them where possible.

Drainage requirements

Soil mix must allow rapid drainage.

Slope container bottoms a minimum 2 per cent.

Incorporate a system to remove excess water, including a filter for fine soil particles.

Irrigation

Irrigation system specified according to tree and soil water status.

One waterline to serve each container.

System should be part of supporting structure.

Waterproofing

An impermeable membrane to be specified for each container or rooftop area.

Double membrane on roof planting areas.

Ensure that membrane is above soil and mulch level.

Fertiliser

Specify fertiliser on the basis of results of soil testing.

Provide anchorage for all trees according to particular needs and site conditions.

Bibliography

GENERAL MORTGAGE AND HOUSING CORPORATION Roof Decks Design Guidelines

HARRIS, R. W. (1983) Arboriculture, Prentice-Hall.

ILA INFORMATION SHEET (1962) External Fixtures and Equipment, SFB 78, November

LANDSCAPE INSTITUTE (1977) Landscape Design with Plants, ed. Brian Clouston, Heinemann

Detail sheets

7.1
Planting profile - in container
7.2
Planting profile - in container
7.3
Planting profile - on roof deck

Conversion Table			
mm	*ft. in*	*mm*	*ft. in*
6	¼"	150	6"
10	⁵⁄₁₆"	200	8"
20	¾"	300	11¾"
25	1"	500	1' 7¾"
40	1½"	800	2' 7"
100	4"	1200	3' 11¼"

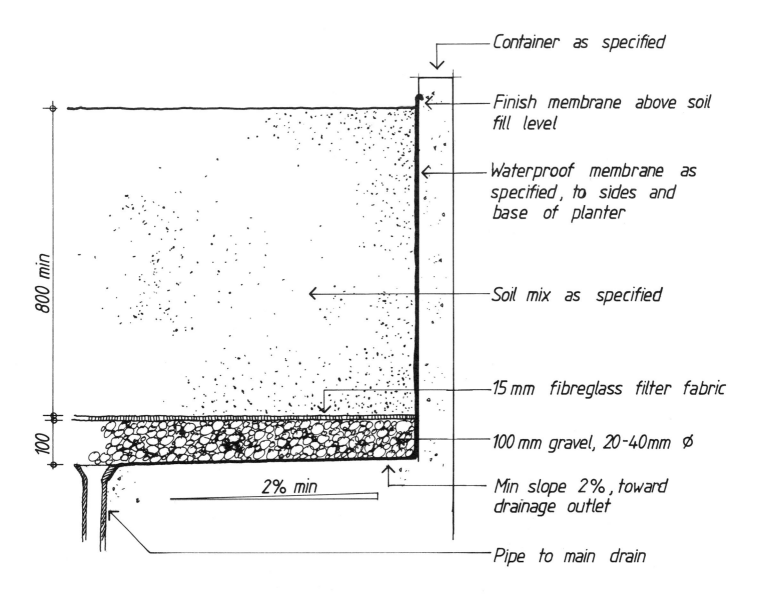

Container as specified

Finish membrane above soil fill level

Waterproof membrane as specified, to sides and base of planter

Soil mix as specified

800 min

100

15 mm fibreglass filter fabric

100 mm gravel, 20-40mm Ø

2% min

Min slope 2%, toward drainage outlet

Pipe to main drain

Scale 1:10

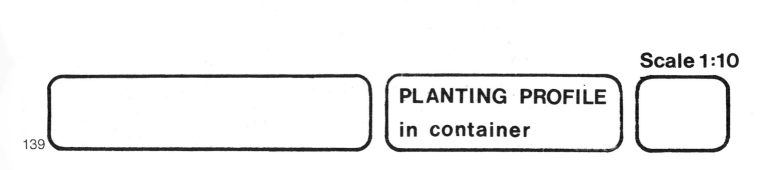

PLANTING PROFILE
in container

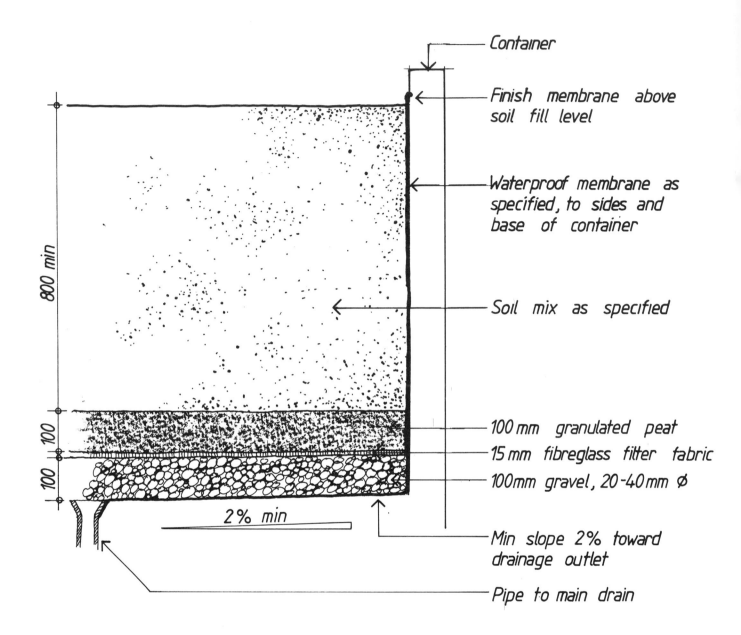

Container

Finish membrane above soil fill level

Waterproof membrane as specified, to sides and base of container

Soil mix as specified

800 min

100

100

100

100 mm granulated peat

15 mm fibreglass filter fabric

100mm gravel, 20-40mm ∅

2% min

Min slope 2% toward drainage outlet

Pipe to main drain

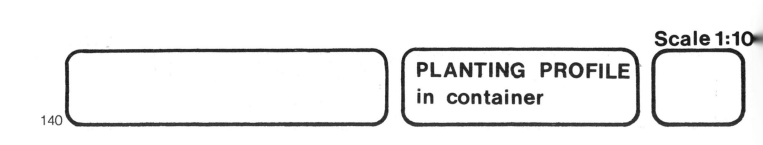

PLANTING PROFILE
in container

Scale 1:10

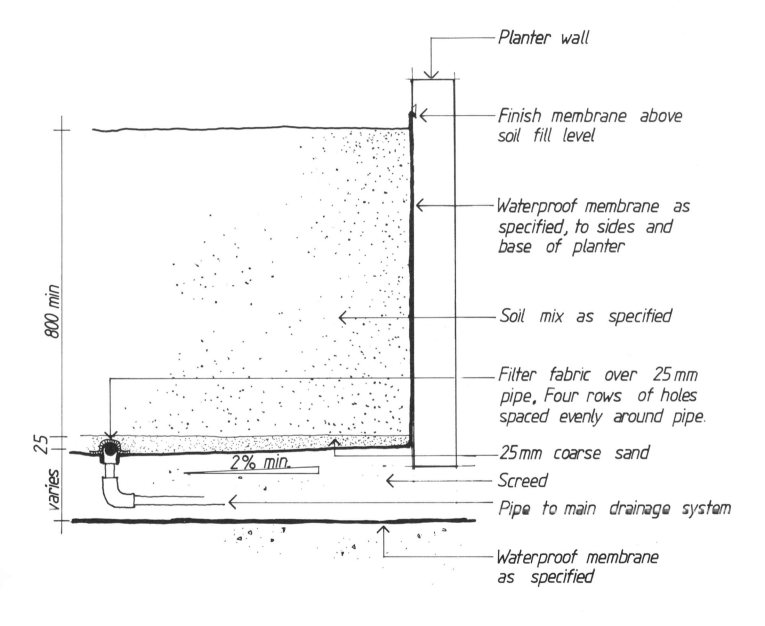

Planter wall

Finish membrane above
soil fill level

Waterproof membrane as
specified, to sides and
base of planter

Soil mix as specified

Filter fabric over 25 mm
pipe. Four rows of holes
spaced evenly around pipe.

25mm coarse sand

Screed

Pipe to main drainage system

Waterproof membrane
as specified

800 min

25

varies

2% min.

Scale 1:10

PLANTING PROFILE
on roof deck

141

8 MAINTENANCE AND MANAGEMENT

A management and maintenance programme should be drawn up for all planting. This will be in two parts:

,1.
The management programme should include a maintenance schedule showing the timing and frequency of maintenance operations (see the example on p. 147).

2.
The maintenance specification detailing the various operations and methods.

Initially, maintenance by the landscape contractor after planting is usually for 1-2 years. Management plans are related to the life-span of the plant materials, with maintenance being carried out by the original landscape contractor or others.

Maintenance of large stock

An intensive maintenance programme extending over several years is needed for semi-mature planting. This will include periodic watering and possibly testing of moisture in the soil, feeding with fertiliser and mulching for moisture retention. Where trees are planted in paving, nutrients and water need especially careful monitoring. Stem wrappings and support structures need to be checked to ensure a good fit and to see whether they are still required.

Watering

Watering is particularly important to tree establishment in the first spring and summer after planting. Varying with species and location, watering will be required for the first 1-4 years. In specification clauses instructing watering during 'dry periods' it is

advisable to define such a period, e.g. weeks in March-August with less than 10 mm of rain.

Furthermore, the water demand of trees becomes most critical during the spring droughts in April-June, and it is essential that trees are watered during this period to ensure successful establishment during the first season of growth.

The quantity of water to apply varies with the size of the tree. CCS advises 20-30 litres per standard or large feather tree, 50 litres for each advanced nursery stock tree. Over-watering is counter-productive, leaching light soils or saturating heavy soils. On the other hand under-watering will stimulate very shallow roots, making a tree less able to withstand dry weather.

The method of watering, whether by hand, hose, tanker or irrigation system, will necessarily vary with location, accessibility and soil conditions. An irrigation system may be considered for trees planted in paved areas and is indispensable for trees growing in containers. Watering basins are often used to aid infiltration but should not remain around young trees in heavy soil through the winter. If using a hand-held hose always have a rose or sprinkler on the end.

Mulching and weeding

The main purpose of a mulch is to control weed growth in the rooting zone of trees. Weeds, especially grasses, compete fiercely for moisture and nutrients; therefore their growth needs to be controlled for at least the first 2-3 years after planting to allow good initial tree growth. A mulch has the added benefit of reducing moisture loss by evaporation, which may be significant in some soils.

Materials used for mulching include organic materials such as bark, which may need replenishing annually; inert mulch such as gravel; and various types of tree spat including biodegradable types. Very fine materials such as fine bark grades should be avoided, because they may impede water infiltration and aeration. Granular materials should be laid to finished thicknesses of at least 50 mm.

It is common practice to keep at least 1 m diameter area weed free around the stem, by use of a mulch, hand weeding or chemical methods, or a combination of these. In hand weeding, pulling by hand is preferable to hoeing which can damage surface roots. Chemical weed control after the first year is usually by residual herbicide, until the tree is vigorous enough to withstand competition.

Checking support

Support mechanisms need maintenance to remain effective. They should be checked regularly, with special attention in autumn and after gales. Checks should include adjusting ties so as not to restrict stem growth, adjusting turnbuckles on guys, making sure the stem is not being chafed and replacements and/or removal of stakes and guys. It should be possible to remove or reduce support after two years but it may be needed longer; this can be determined only by individual inspection.

Pruning (cf Chapter 3)

Formative pruning will be part of the

regular maintenance programme in the first few years but should be minimised after this time, performed only to repair storm damage, remove obstructions etc.

Protection

Individual tree guards and general fencing against rabbits, stock and other animals will need regular inspection and renovation where necessary.

Pests and diseases

Planting should be examined for pests and diseases at least once each season and this followed by any necessary control measures.

Replacement planting

Replanting of dead or missing stock needs to be covered in any specification including clarification of time limits for replacements and seasons for planting, as well as arrangements for any costs incurred.

Management

Management plans

A management plan is a phased programme of inspection, pruning, thinning, felling and planting drawn up with professional advice for a population of trees in a defined area. One of the main aims is to distribute operations evenly through time, not waiting until all work is urgent. To be realistically related to the life-span of the trees, the period covered should be at least fifty years. Such a plan includes an outline of costs and manpower requirements. The actual aims of the plan will vary with the type of planting (e.g. park, woodland or commercial planting) and its situation.

144

Cost of management

The cost of planting and early maintenance of a tree is a very small proportion of the total outlay on management throughout its life. A large tree growing in an awkward position is very expensive to fell when the need arises; therefore such operations need to be spread through time.

Felling

Management plans allow for felling of trees which become unsafe or over-mature. The normal life span for trees ranges from about fifty years for willows and poplars to about 250 years for oak, sycamore and lime. However, the safe life-span may be considerably less, owing to various hazards, such as damage by grass-cutting machinery, grey squirrels, storms and heavy snow and problems in the root zone including road salt, oil pollution and soil compaction. A plan will allow for the progressive felling of a few selected trees per year within a population, to maintain a safely growing tree stock.

Replacement planting

A phased programme to replace trees with young stock should run in tandem with felling.

Thinning

Trees may be required to be felled earlier in their life-cycle to make room for others to develop. Most young trees are planted 2-5 m apart, whereas the spacing of mature trees is much greater: 5-15 m is usually desirable. In open situations, to avoid trees distorting each other's growth, thinning is needed when the branches of adjacent trees start to touch and overshadow each other. In other situations later thinning is more appropriate, although on exposed sites where trees need to be encouraged into sturdier growth, early thinning is to be recommended.

Checklist

Watering

Ensure that all trees are watered as frequently as necessary to provide satisfactory growth in all seasons.

Weeding and mulching

Keep a 1 m diameter area around trees weed-free by hand weeding or by chemical control. Remove weeds from the site. Maintain at least 50 mm depth of mulch around tree.

Checking support

Inspect each tree and refirm support as necessary, adjust or replace stakes and ties as necessary, and adjust turnbuckles on guys.

Pruning

Prune trees to remove broken branches, or remove obstructions such as crossing branches.

Protection

Inspect and renovate tree guards as necessary.

Pests and diseases

Inspect for pest and disease once each season and carry out necessary control measures.

145

Replacement

Replace dead or missing stock as necessary (state time limit in clause).

Management

Draw up a management plan where necessary and include a programme for felling, replacement planting and thinning.

Bibliography

ARBORICULTURAL ASSOCIATION (1987), Arboricultural Handout No. 4, Tree Management

COUNTRYSIDE COMMISSION FOR SCOTLAND INFORMATION SHEET (1980) Plants 3.6: Maintenance for establishment

HARRIS, R. W. (1983) Arboriculture, Prentice-Hall

HELLIWELL, D. R. (1983) Woodland Choice, *GC and HTJ*, October 7

Conversion Table			
litres	*Imp. gal.*	*mm*	*ft. in*
20	5¼	10	5/16"
30	6½	50	2"
50	11	2	6' 9"
		5	16' 5"
		15	49' 3"

Tree Maintenance Schedule

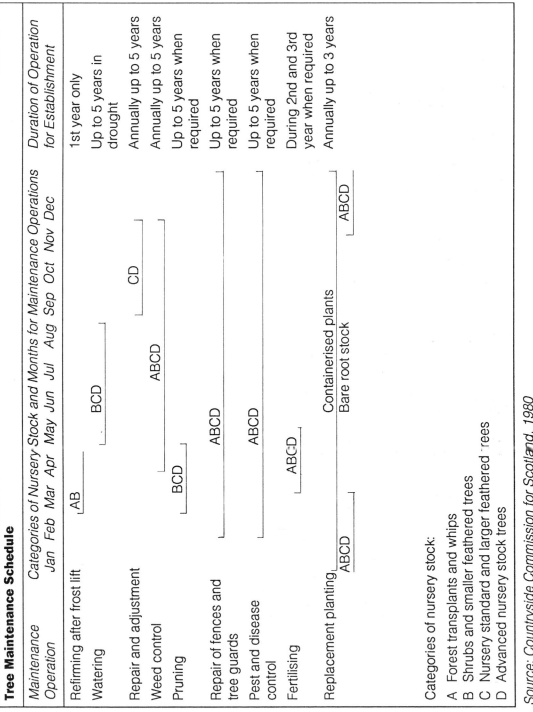

Maintenance Operation	Categories of Nursery Stock and Months for Maintenance Operations (Jan Feb Mar Apr May Jun Jul Aug Sep Oct Nov Dec)	Duration of Operation for Establishment
Refirming after frost lift	AB (Jan–Feb)	1st year only
Watering	BCD (May–Jun)	Up to 5 years in drought
Repair and adjustment	CD (Oct–Nov)	Annually up to 5 years
Weed control	ABCD (Jul–Sep)	Annually up to 5 years
Pruning	BCD (Mar–Apr)	Up to 5 years when required
Repair of fences and tree guards	ABCD (May–Jul)	Up to 5 years when required
Pest and disease control	ABCD (May–Jul)	Up to 5 years when required
Fertilising	ABCD (Apr–May)	During 2nd and 3rd year when required
Replacement planting	Containerised plants ABCD (Apr–Jun); Bare root stock ABCD (Oct–Dec)	Annually up to 3 years

Categories of nursery stock:

A Forest transplants and whips
B Shrubs and smaller feathered trees
C Nursery standard and larger feathered trees
D Advanced nursery stock trees

Source: Countryside Commission for Scotland, 1980

9 BUILDING, ENGINEERING AND TREES

Proximity to buildings

Trees on shrinkable soils present the greatest risk of damage to buildings, because roots extracting moisture from the soil cause it to shrink when dried and swell when rewetted, and the movement produced by shrinkage and swelling can damage foundations.

Shrinkable soils are classified as soils containing more than 35 per cent fine particles (silt and clay) and having a plasticity index of more than 10 per cent.

Planting a tree "too close" to an existing building entails some risk of damage when the tree reaches a sufficiently large size and particularly in the event of a drought. One way to avoid root problems is to maintain a "safe" distance between the tree and the building so that the tree cannot influence the soil beneath the building. A rule of thumb, which is based mainly on poplar, willow, elm and oak trees in highly shrinkable soils, is that a safe distance is slightly more than the expected maximum height of the tree.

This rule can be relaxed for soils of lower shrinkability. There appears to be no significant evidence for specifying a minimum distance of trees from buildings in non-shrinkable soils, other than adequate clearance for the stem and major root buttresses.

Provided there is sufficient room for trunks and roots to grow, there is little risk of pressure being exerted that will displace house foundations. The depth to which roots extract moisture varies with distance from the centre of the tree: the nearer to the trunk, the greater the depth and extent of moisture depletion.

Choice of species is also important, since species vary in their ability to extract moisture from a clay soil. Demand for water varies with species, rate of growth and size.

The inter-relationship of factors is complex, and distance and water demand, distance and climatic variations should be considered in evaluation of the combined effects of soil movements. High rainfall replaces moisture deficits caused by trees, and cool damp weather reduces the rate of water loss from the tree; these conditions therefore reduce the risks of undue movement. This consideration is most critical in the south-east of England, where temperatures are higher and rainfall is lower; these effects diminish with distance north and west.

Soil swelling can occur when a tree which was extracting moisture from the soil dies, is removed or has roots severed, and consequently the soil takes up moisture.

If a building suffers structural damage when there is a tree in the vicinity, the roots will usually be blamed. Careful investigation is needed. In some cases factual information can be used to disprove incorrect allegations and provide a measure of the amount of damage if the tree is partially to blame.

At present there is insufficient reliable data on the moisture deficiencies caused by different isolated species at different periods of growth and on the behaviour of trees subjected to various urban conditions. Practice Note 3 (1985) entitled *Building near trees*, rewritten and published in January 1986 by the National House Building Council (NHBC), offers recommendations on foundation depths in relation to the distance of trees from the foundations. It is not intended that this Practice Note should be "applied dogmatically" and the recommendations "should always be tempered by common sense and good judgement."

The age of the clay is also significant; London clay is younger than Gault clay and is more likely to be affected by root growth.

Building foundations

There is some evidence to support the proposition that trees are an important factor in causing building foundation failures, but only on shrinkable soils and when foundations are not deep enough. Even when trees are not present, shrinkable soils have a natural seasonal movement, swelling in winter and shrinking in summer.

The proximity of existing trees is an important factor in deciding the safe depth of foundations, and building near major trees on very shrinkable soils can be safely considered using suitable foundation solutions. Foundations must be constructed to a depth where the soil is stable. To establish this level it is necessary to consider the shrinkability of the soil, the moisture demand of trees and the depth to which roots will affect the soil when the trees reach maturity. Climatic factors must also be taken into account.

A stable depth for the foundation is not the only consideration. The design and construction of foundations must be able to accommodate ground movements, which in shrinkable soils can occur in all directions. Allowance for movement is particularly important

where trees have been removed or have had roots severed. Where shrinkable soils can recover moisture, the swelling effect can continue for many years after a tree has been removed. The position, height and species of trees which are to be removed or which have died should be recorded for determining foundation depths. It is extremely difficult to assess the depth at which soils have been desiccated by trees and whether after removal the moisture has been regained. If no details are available of what trees have been removed, a soil test should be carried out to decide the stable foundation level.

Branch pruning is a method that may be used to restrict the growth and water demand of trees which might otherwise affect foundations. Root pruning and root barriers are considered ineffective and impractical on the basis that they are unreliable and there is no guarantee that these methods will be well maintained.

It is debatable whether foundation design should attempt to prevent all movement, or to permit minor damage which might be acceptable. The recommendations in NHBC Practice Note 3 are aimed at preventing undue movement, taking account of climatic conditions likely to be experienced with a fifty-year weather pattern. Any building which is adequately founded to cope with the various problems normally associated with buildings in shrinkable or expansive clay soils should not present major problems when trees are planted.

Underground services and drainage

The effect of root damage on services is often exaggerated; nevertheless service runs should be designed taking into account the location of tree planting and the potential root spread.

Near trees it is important to ensure that joints are well sealed and that drain runs can tolerate movement without disruption of the joints. These joints should have flexible joints where root growth or soil movement is likely. Water from leaking drains can encourage root growth, which in turn can cause blockage of drains if roots gain entry; but sound drains will not normally be disturbed by roots unless very close to the tree. If drains run through the root system they may be encased in 150 mm concrete as a precautionary measure.

There is significant evidence of problems with old sewers; but these problems are confined largely to old systems, and modern systems tend to be root-tight. Furthermore, sewers are generally put in 2-3 m deep, which is below the main root zone of many trees.

On shrinkable soils, problems of swelling and shrinking due to tree roots may result in heave and fracture of gas pipes. There have also been cases where downward pressure from tree roots has caused pipes to fracture, but this is rare.

Damage by tree roots to electricity cables seems equally rare. Occasionally tree root expansion has been known to sever joints, but a more common problem is the restriction of access to cables because trees have been planted over them. If major roots are encountered in excavated trenches, it may be necessary to tunnel under and draw the cable through.

Telephone cables are now normally put underground, and there appears to be little evidence of loss of service due to tree roots.

Mains water pipes appear to suffer no real problems - these pipes are designed to be watertight!

Checklist

Proximity to buildings

Tree planting should take into account:

Foundation depths
Shrinkability of soil
Water demand of tree species
Mature height of trees
Climatic effect on moisture loss in soil

Building foundations

Construction of foundations should take into account:

Distance of trees from foundations
Shrinkability of soil
Water demand of tree species
Mature height of trees
Climatic effect on moisture loss in soil

Underground services and drainage

Location of tree planting with respect to service runs should take into account:

Potential root spread
Shrinkability of soil
Water demand of tree species
Mature height of trees
Climatic effect on moisture loss in soil

Bibliography

BRITISH STANDARDS INSTITUTION (1980) BS 5837: Trees in relation to construction

BUILDING RESEARCH ESTABLISHMENT (1985) The influence of trees on house foundations in clay soils, BRE Digest No. 298

DEEN, J. (1981) A hole lot of trouble, *GC and HTJ*, November 13

DEVOY, J. (1977) Tree roots in towns, *GC and HTJ*, April 8

FLORA, T. (1978) Treeless towns, *Landscape Design*, February

FLORA, T. (1978) What next, concrete trees?, *Housing review*, May/June

FLORA, T. (1978) Threat to our urban landscape, *Civic Trust News*, July/August

FLORA, T. (1979) Trees and building foundations, *Arboricultural Journal*, Vol. 3, No. 6

FLORA, T. (1980) Trees in relation to construction, *Housing Review*, July/August

NATIONAL HOUSE BUILDING COUNCIL (1985) Building near Tress, Practice Note 3

PYKE, J. F. S. (1978) Trees and buildings, *Arboricultural Journal*, No. 31

Detail sheets

9.1
Buildings - optimum distance
9.2
Buildings - optimum distance
9.3
Buildings - minimum distance
9.4
Buildings - minimum distance
9.5
Building - bridging foundation
9.6
Services - overhead clearance
9.7
Vehicle clearances
9.8
Vehicle clearances

Conversion Table			
mm	*ft. in*	*M*	*ft. in*
150	6"	0.8	2' 7"
		2.3	7' 6"
		4.3	14' 1"
		5.5	18' 0"
		9.3	30' 6"

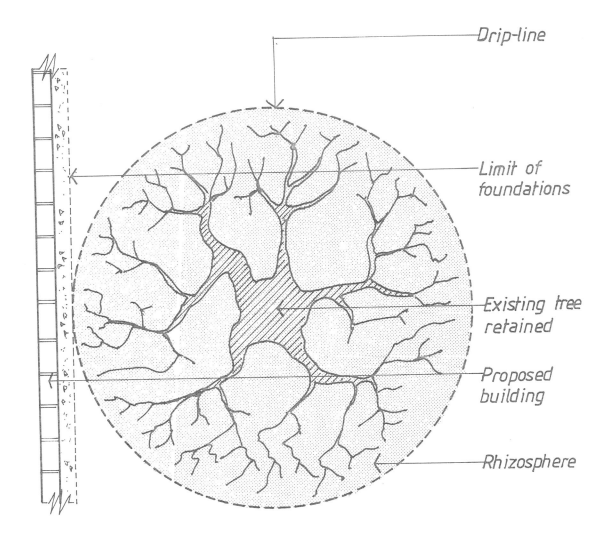

Drip-line

Limit of foundations

Existing tree retained

Proposed building

Rhizosphere

PLAN A

Scale 1:50

BUILDINGS
optimum distance

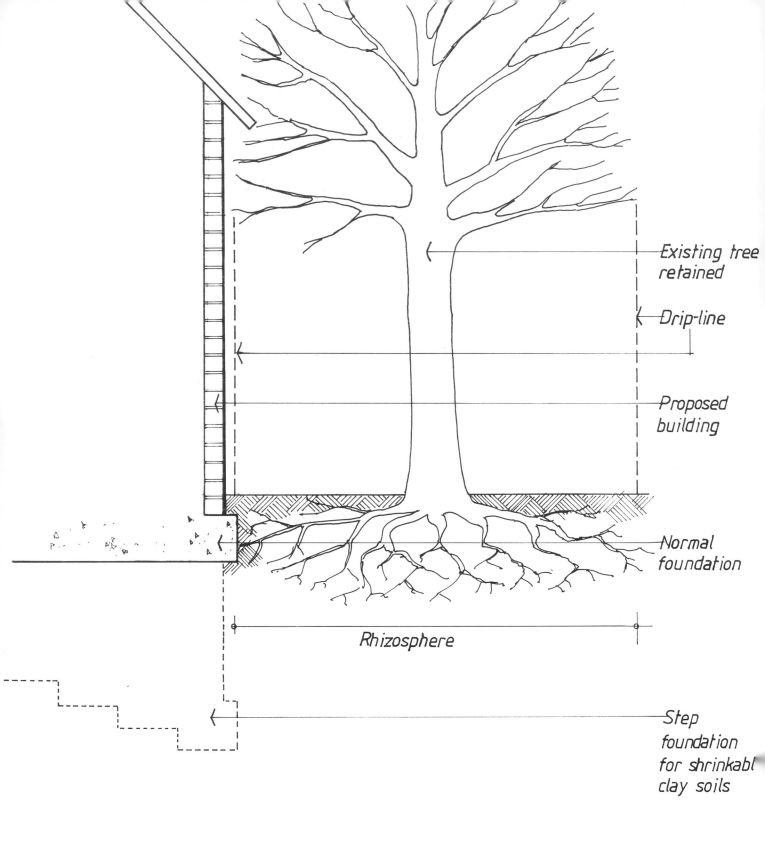

Existing tree retained

Drip-line

Proposed building

Normal foundation

Rhizosphere

Step foundation for shrinkabl clay soils

SECTION A

BUILDINGS
optimum distance

Scale 1:50

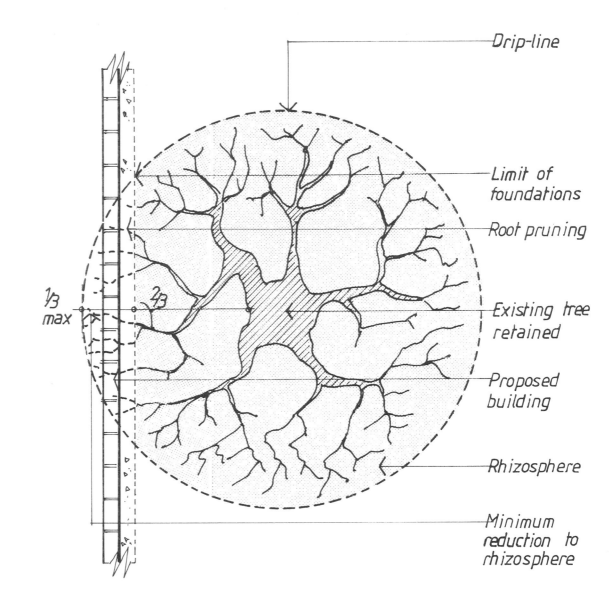

Drip-line

Limit of foundations

Root pruning

Existing tree retained

Proposed building

Rhizosphere

Minimum reduction to rhizosphere

⅓ max

⅔

PLAN B

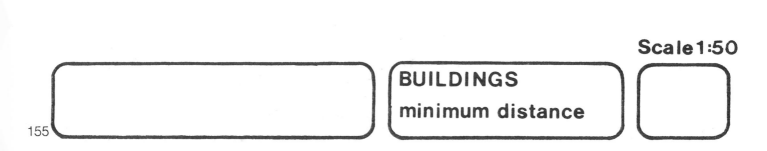

Scale 1:50

BUILDINGS
minimum distance

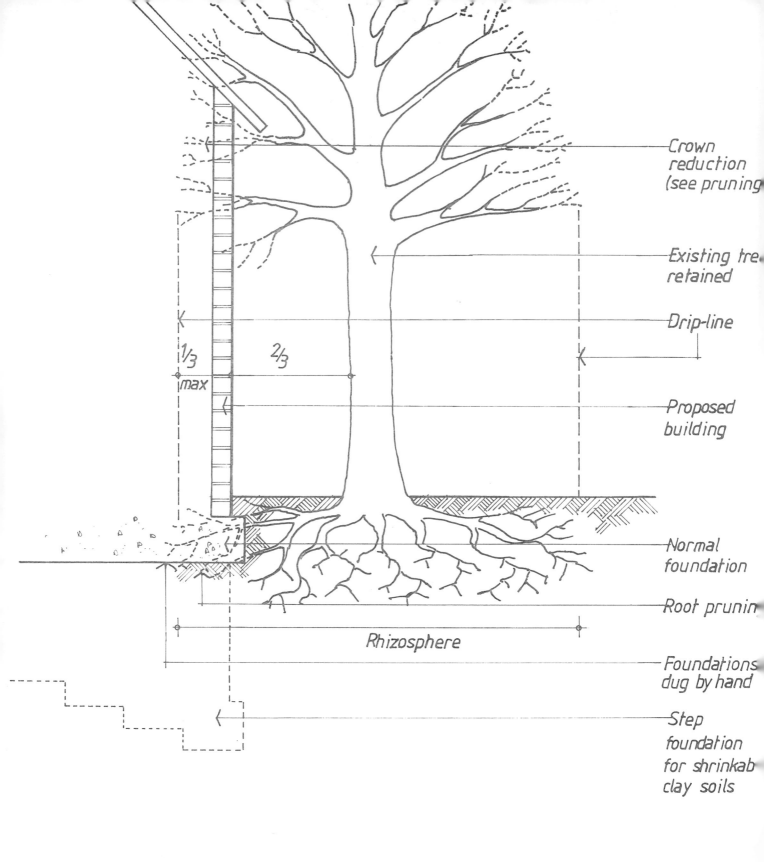

Crown reduction (see pruning

Existing tre retained

Drip-line

1/3 max

2/3

Proposed building

Normal foundation

Root prunin

Rhizosphere

Foundations dug by hand

Step foundation for shrinkab clay soils

SECTION B

Scale 1:50

BUILDINGS
minimum distance

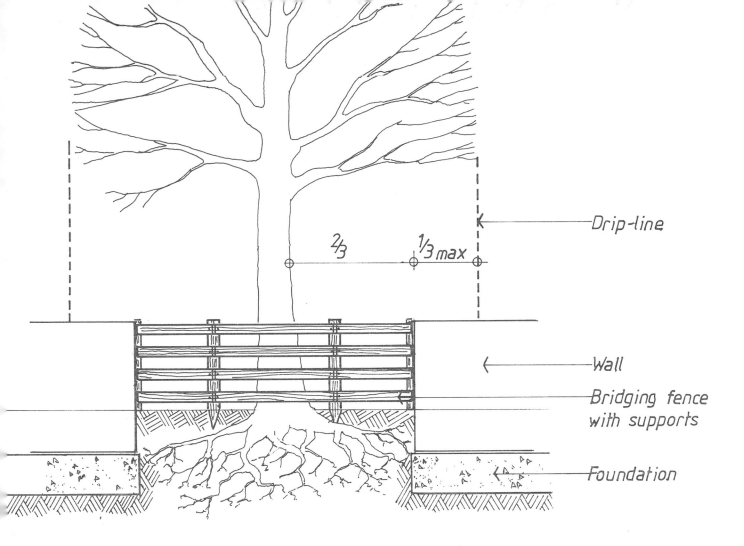

Drip-line

$\frac{2}{3}$ $\frac{1}{3}$ max

Wall

Bridging fence with supports

Foundation

SECTION

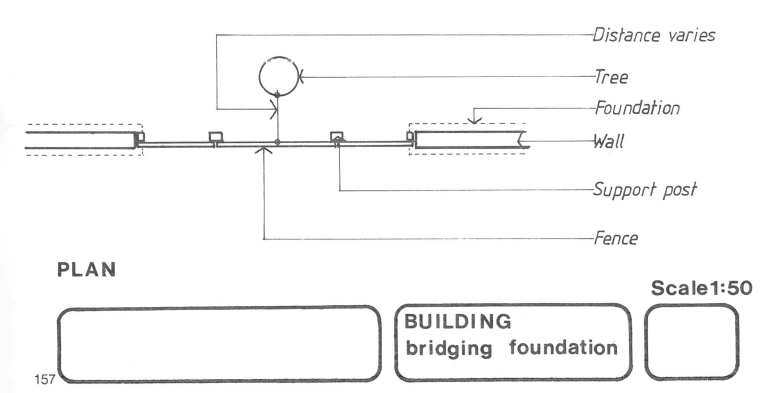

Distance varies

Tree

Foundation

Wall

Support post

Fence

PLAN

Scale 1:50

BUILDING bridging foundation

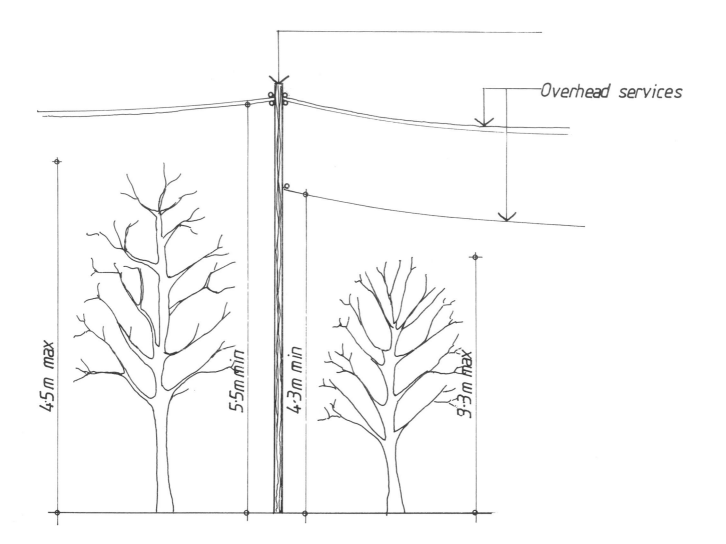

Overhead services

4·5m max

5·5m min

4·3m min

9·3m max

Note: Trees selected for use under overhead services must have an ultimate height no greater than 1·0m below the height of the services

NTS

SERVICES

overhead clearance

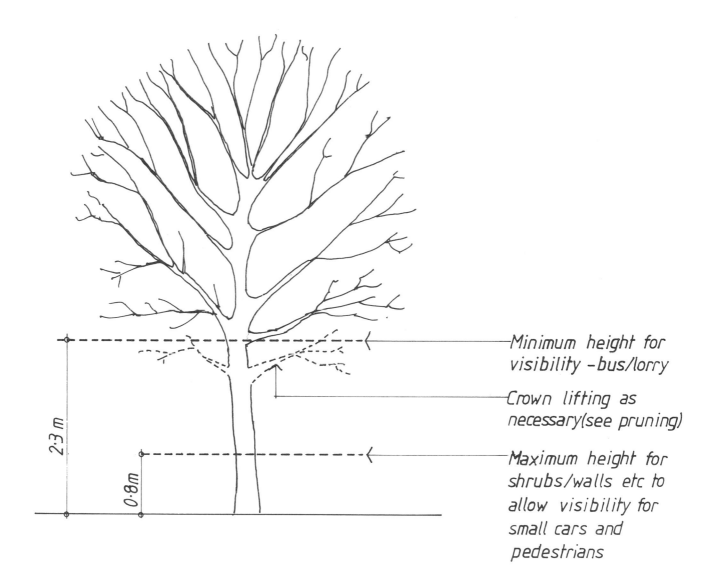

Minimum height for visibility –bus/lorry

Crown lifting as necessary (see pruning)

Maximum height for shrubs/walls etc to allow visibility for small cars and pedestrians

2·3 m

0·8m

VEHICLE
CLEARANCES

Scale 1:50

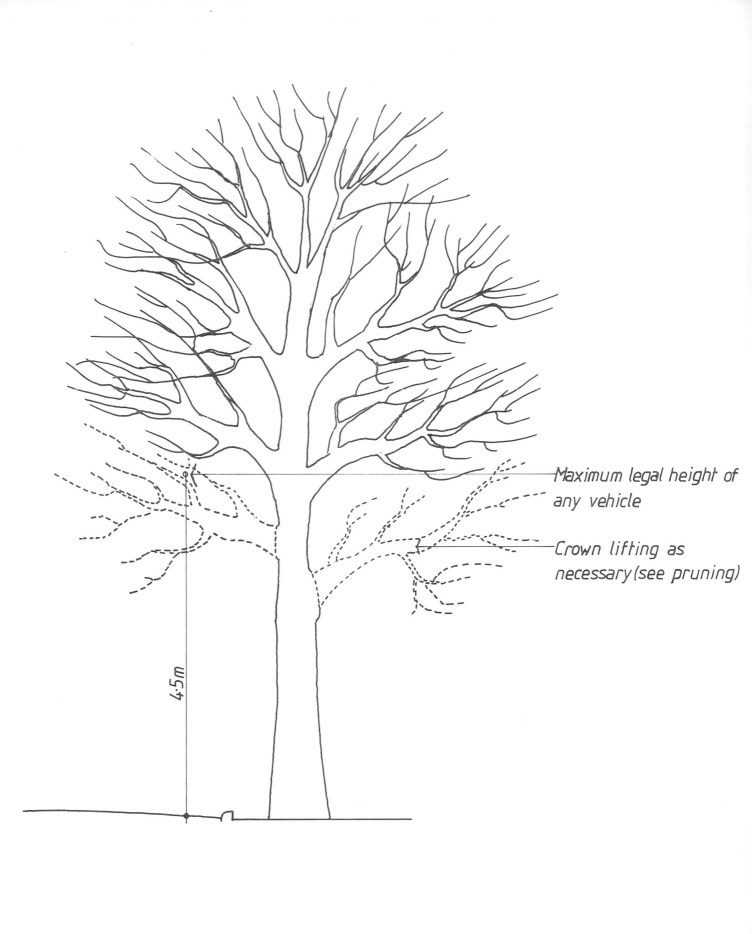

Maximum legal height of any vehicle

Crown lifting as necessary (see pruning)

4·5m

VEHICLE CLEARANCES

Scale 1:50

10 SURVEY AND EVALUATION

A landscape architect aims to make the best use of site assets; and in order to retain good trees and integrate them successfully into new developments, a good database is needed. Tree survey, evaluation and inspections provide the data for a full assessment. The level of research required will vary with the type of project.

Tree survey

Tree surveys collect a base of objective information. A typical survey records position, species, height, spread, girth and/or approximate age of a tree. The level at the base of the trunk is also useful, owing to its bearing on groundworks during development (cf. Chapter 5). It is usual to record information on forms and plans; examples of these are given below. Individual mapping of specimens is particularly important where more detailed design work is envisaged and where specimens are valuable for rarity or for historical or visual reasons.

A tree survey should be designed with a clear purpose in mind so as not to waste resources. For this reason computerised surveys are likely to be worthwhile only for large or long-term projects.

The Council for the Protection of Rural England (CPRE) suggests the following headings for classification of trees when making a survey:

Classification
Code

Single trees - T

Areas or linear belts of trees and hedges with significant trees.- A

Groups of trees (up to approx. 60) - G

Woods - W

Hedgerows - H

Single trees - T

These can be recorded on the map as a dot with the letter code T and its sequential number, e.g. * T1, * T2, * T3 etc. Record the number on the appropriate list and add the name and comments (if any), height, trunk diameter at breast height and amenity value.

Areas or linear belts of trees - A

These can be recorded on the map by outlining the area with a line and labelling with the letter A and its sequential number. They should include belts or linear groups where there are too many to label singly and only one or two trees in depth. They can also include overgrown hedges which have significant trees in them.

Groups - G

These can be recorded on the map by outlining the group with a line and labelling with the letter G and its sequential number. Groups may be considered as more than two trees in depth and up to about sixty trees in number. All tree types should be listed.

Woods - W

These can be recorded on the map by outlining the area and labelling with the letter W and its sequential number. They should include large areas of trees or woodlands, and they may be adjacent groups or areas. One should name as many species as can be seen, either directly or through binoculars; add a question mark if the identity is in doubt.

Hedgerows - H

These can be recorded on the map as vvvvv with the letter H and its sequential number. They should include hedges without significant trees; do not include scrub. One should note the main species present in any one hedge.

Mapping

Survey and mapping methods should take into account requirements and standards of local authorities. A common mapping technique is to colour code trees according to category, as follows:

Red block
Category 1 trees: to be retained

Red stripe
Category 1/2 and 2 trees: to be retained if possible

Yellow
Category 2/3 and 3 trees: not essential to retain

Green stripe
Category 3/4 trees: may need to be removed in the future

Green block
Category 4 trees: to be removed

Tree inspection

A closer inspection will usually be necessary in order to assess the safety, life-expectancy and condition of any particular tree; this must be carried out by an adequately trained person. It may involve climbing the tree, boring small-diameter holes in places where rot is suspected to be present, or digging holes to examine the extent and condition of the roots.

Tree evaluation (see also pp.164-6)

Tree evaluation involves more subjective interpretation, studying trees in relation to their setting and the proposed development rather than their individual qualities. The assessment made is basically in terms of amenity, and can be recorded on tree survey sheets as amenity value.

A system of evaluation for amenity has been developed by D. R. Helliwell (Tree Survey and Inspection). In this system, besides an assessment of the condition and life-expectancy of the tree, consideration is also given to its position in the landscape, shape, size and the presence of other trees.

Six factors are identified for each tree, plus any special factors such as historical associations or exceptional rarity. For each of these factors the tree is given a score of up to four points, and the scores for all the factors are then multiplied together to give an assessment of the amenity value of the tree.

162

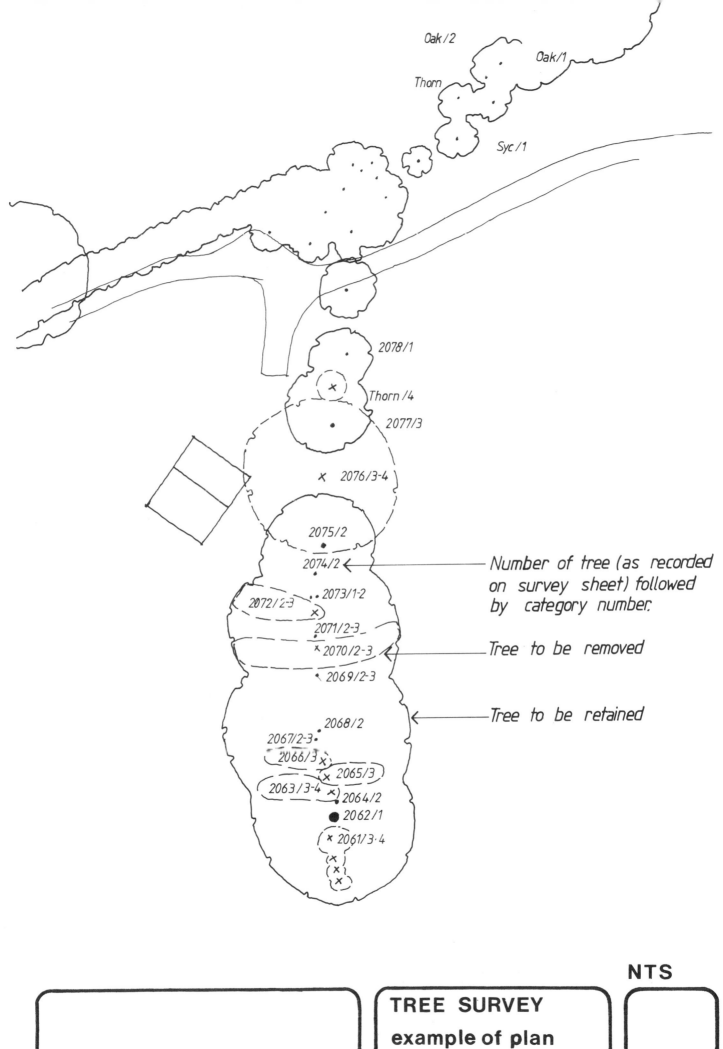

Oak/2

Oak/1

Thorn

Syc/1

2078/1

Thorn/4

2077/3

✗ 2076/3·4

2075/2

2074/2 ← Number of tree (as recorded on survey sheet) followed by category number.

2073/1-2

2072/2-3

2071/2-3

✗ 2070/2-3 ← Tree to be removed

2069/2-3

2068/2 ← Tree to be retained

2067/2-3

2066/3

2065/3

2063/3-4   2064/2

2062/1

✗ 2061/3·4

NTS

TREE SURVEY

example of plan

Tree Survey | **Date carried out:** | **Survey No**

Tree no.	Tree species	Height approx	Spread approx	Diam. of trunk	Ht. of clear trunk	Age New Yng.	Condition class 1234	Amenity value	Action recommended and notes

Legend and Definition of Terms

Condition

1 Sound and healthy

2 Defective, but defects can be rectified and tree should reach maturity

3 Defective, but defect cannot be rectified, although the tree still has a limited useful life

4 Defective to the point of being dangerous

Amenity value

A Tree of sufficient character and high quality that amenity loss will result if it is removed.

Its retention should therefore be of prime consideration in planning and development decisions.

B Good tree, good quality, every effort should be made to retain tree, but not of such value that its retention should necessarily override other vital factors.

C Tree of reasonable but not exceptional condition, worth retaining if it does not conflict with development proposals, but its removal would not necessarily reduce amenity.

D Tree of poor condition, appearance and value, which should be removed.

A B C D are value judgements which take into account condition. The fact that a tree needs tree surgery does not necessarily preclude it from being placed in A category.

Tree Surgery Recommendations — Abbreviations

O.K.	— No work required
Thin	— Lightly thin the crown
Dead wood	— Prune out dead wood
Snags	— Prune bad pruning snags
Sucker	— Prune out sucker growth
W/cup	— Drain water cup
Cav.	— Fill in cavity
Dis.	— Diseased

Tree Surveys

Guidance notes

Age

New — Newly planted

Yng — Young

Mat — Mature

Old — Old

General comments

Special comments should be added in the right-hand, i.e. Action column.

Transplanting — where trees which are suitable for transplanting cannot be retained in their present position TR should be inserted in the Action column.

Life expectancy — in certain cases, e.g. where the retention of certain trees is in doubt, the life expectancy should be noted in the Action column, e.g. "Life exptcy…yrs".

Retention for a limited period — in certain situations it may be worth retaining C or D trees for a period of years whilst young planting is establishing itself. In this case insert "Retain for…yrs".

Factor	Points			
	1	2	3	4
1 Size of tree	small	medium	large	very large
2 Useful life-expectancy	10-20 yrs.	20-40 yrs.	40-100 yrs.	100+ yrs.
3 Importance of position in landscape	little	some	considerable	great
4 Presence of other trees	many	some	few	none
5 Relation to the setting	moderately suitable	fairly suitable	very suitable	especially suitable
6 Form	poor	fair	good	esp. good
7 Special factors	none	one	two	three

Tree Inspection	Sheet No.	
Job No:		
Site:		
Project:		
Client:		
Inspected by:		
Plan code/No. from tree survey:	Date:	
Plan/drawing title:	National grid ref No:	
Tree name:	TPO:	
General surroundings:		
Site history:		
Buds/flowers/fruit:		
Leaves:		
Twigs and branch systems:		
Trunk:		
Base of tree and root system:		
General condition and health of tree:		
Climate:		
Conclusions:		
Leav samples taken:	Bark samples taken:	
Soil samples taken:	Insect samples taken:	
Photographs taken:	Root samples taken:	
Recommendations:		

If a tree fails to score on any of the first five factors it is given a nil rating for that factor and, therefore, a nil final score. Thus, if a tree is so small as to fail to reach the smallest size catagory, so rotten as to have less than ten years' useful life-expectancy, if it is completely hidden from view, or is totally unsuited to its setting, it is regarded as having no accountable amenity value. The only exception to this rule would be a tree with great rarity or historic value, whose size, visibility etc. would not affect the desirability of preserving it.

The assessment of some of the factors can be made with complete objectivity. For example, the size of the tree can be measured fairly simply, and the useful life-expectancy is a matter for expert opinion. With some of the factors, however, there must inevitably be a certain amount of subjectivity, and it may be that two people would assess the same tree differently, though in most cases the disagreement should not be very great

This method of assessment only takes account of the amenity value of a tree, and does not attempt to assess any costs which may be incurred in growing or maintaining the tree. Such costs are usually ascertainable, and if they exceed the calculated value a case could be made for removing the tree. On the other hand, it could be calculated that the planting of a tree in some other position would, in a few years' time, provide amenity in excess of the costs involved.

Explanatory notes

1.
The size of the trees taken as the height of the tree (in metres) multiplied by the mean crown diameter.
Small = 3 to 10 sq m (30-100 sq. ft)
Medium = 10 to 50 sq m (100-500 sq. ft)
Large = 50 to 200 sq m (500-2,000 sq. ft)

Very large = 200 sq. m or more.*

2.
The useful life-expectancy (in years) must take into account the position in which the tree is growing. For example a tree which overhangs a busy road must be absolutely sound in all respects, yet it may suffer from a variety of ill-effects from traffic fumes and roadworks. It would therefore have a lower useful life-expectancy than a similar tree in a large area of parkland, where the loss of a few twigs in a gale would do little harm and the tree is less likely to suffer damage from fumes, stray vehicles, or leaking gas mains. In most cases, the advice of an arboriculturist would be required if there is any doubt over this point.

3.
Importance of position in landscape/townscape. Many trees in well-wooded areas will have no individual importance, in that the loss of a single tree would not detract significantly from the amenities of the area.

"Little importance"
most trees in rural areas, back gardens, or in groups of trees etc.

"Some importance"
individual roadside trees in residential areas, trees close to busy roads, trees in public parks etc.

*Exceptional girth, where it adds to the visual value of the tree, could be taken to put the tree into a higher size category than its crown size alone would merit.

"Considerable importance"
prominent individual trees in well-frequented places such as town centres, shopping centres etc.

"Great importance"
trees which are of crucial importance to well-known places

4.
Presence of other trees:

Many
more than 30 per cent of the visual area (of which the tree is a part) covered by trees, and at least ten trees in total

Some
More than 10 per cent of the visual area covered by trees, and at least four trees in total

Few
less than 10 per cent of the visual area covered by trees, but at least one other tree present

None
no other trees present in the area under consideration

5.
Relation of species to the setting. This is probably the most difficult factor to define. As a very general rule, one should aim to have the largest and densest tree or group of trees that the available space will conveniently contain. Thus a small tree in a large space may appear insignificant; equally a large tree in a small space is not usually convenient, or is likely to appear overwhelming. Where trees are close to a building, light-foliaged trees, such as birch or false acacia, are likely to be more suitable than dense-foliaged species such as beech or sycamore, as

they will block out less light from the windows and will complement the appearance of the building rather than obscuring it. Where trees stand well clear of buildings, however, their visual impact will be greater if they are of the more dense-foliaged type. A single beech or sycamore standing on its own, for example, is likely to provide a greater visual impact than a single birch tree.

Sometimes a tree, or group of trees, is particularly suitable to a certain setting, in reflecting or emphasising the surrounding landform or architecture. Weeping willows hanging down into flowing water, cedars of Lebanon close to a mansion, or a row of elm trees in a country lane may be examples of successful juxtaposition. The question of the general desirability of a species should where necessary be allowed to affect the score under factor 5. Most would agree that for example a tulip-tree or a liquidambar, though not rare, should be preferred to, say, a sycamore.

6.
The form of a tree is, again, a matter which may be difficult to define precisely, although extreme examples of badly mutilated trees, or trees which have suffered damage from disease or storms, will be fairly obvious. Form need not necessarily be natural to be good: a good example of a pollarded tree may merit a high mark. Most trees will be rated "fair" or "good", with particularly beautiful specimens being rated "exceptionally good".

7.
Most trees will not have any "special factors". Some trees will have historical associations, and for a very few (say 10-20 in the whole of Britain) the historical

connections may be so strong as to place them outside the scope of this method of valuation. Some trees may also merit a higher valuation because of their great rarity, but this is likely to apply to very few trees outside arboreta and the grounds of stately homes. Generally speaking, if there are fewer than about three specimens of that type of tree in the county, it could be given a rating on this account. Other special cases may be where a tree obscures an unpleasant view, making it particularly important to keep it in that position, or where a tree forms part of a deliberate composition such as an avenue or group and its loss would detract from the value of the remaining trees, or within a conservation area whose listing is related to the trees in it.

Additional aspects which can usefully be researched include the relation of trees to views on site (e.g. whether they perform an essential function screening an unsightly view), how the tree may be affected physically by development and how the tree population in general will change with time.

In addition, cultural aspects should be considered: what is the historic significance of the tree? Is it part of a designed landscape such as an avenue? Is it subject to any restrictions such as Tree Preservation Orders?

Consideration of such questions will help decisions to be made about which trees should be retained and what restriction will influence development.

Helliwell does not make the attaching of a monetary value a main point of his recommendations, particularly because at the present time the rate of inflation cannot be ignored and any monetary unit decided on would have to be reviewed in the near future, possibly repeatedly.

The principal argument in favour of monetary evaluation must, however, be stated: only by being given a monetary value can trees take their rightful place in planning calculations, maintenance, budgeting etc. alongside other assets of known value. So long as amenity trees are excluded from balance sheets, they will be excluded from proper budgeting considerations.

Checklist

Tree survey

Record position, species, height, spread, girth and age of tree, as well as base level.

Design the survey with a clear purpose

Follow local authority standards.

Tree inspection

Must be carried out by an adequately trained person

Tree evaluation

Assess the amenity value of the tree, in relation to proposed development, in terms of:
position of the tree in the landscape;
relation to views;
cultural aspects;
and any restrictions such as TPOs on the tree.

Bibliography

HELLIWELL, D. R., et al. Tree Survey and Inspection, to be published by the Arboricultural Association

JACKSON, A. (1983) Can't see the wood, *GC and HTJ*, 29 July

LA DELL, W. T. (1986) Retaining Trees on Development Sites, A J Database C1/SFB, 19 February

TREE COUNCIL Trees in Towns and the Landscape, A method of evaluation (or later reference giving details of Helliwell method for valuation of Trees for Amenity)

APPENDICES

A GLOSSARY

Abiotic factors
Non-living components of the environment that directly affect plant life.

Abscission
The controlled shedding of a leaf or part of a plant.

Absorption
The active or passive uptake of water and solutes into the plant.

Acid rain
Rain with high levels of acidity caused by pollution with oxides of nitrogen and sulphur.

Adult leaves
The leaves on a stem which differ from the juvenile form.

Adventitious buds
Normally, growth buds develop between leaf and stem in a definite order. Adventitious buds are growth buds that arise without any relation to the leaves, usually in response to a wound. The shoots that arise from cut-back stems of a pollarded willow grow from adventitious buds.

Allergenic
A plant which produces rashes or irritation on contact.

Amphibious
A tree growing well on dry earth or in water-saturated earth.

Angiospermae
Flowering plants with enclosed seeds according to taxonomic classification (*see also* Gymnospermae).

Apex
The tip of a stem, hence *apical bud*, the uppermost bud on a stem, and *apical shoot*, the uppermost stem on a system of branches.

Apical dominance
The inhibition of development of lateral shoots/buds by the apical bud.

Arborescent
A plant with a perennial woody framework of branches (tree or shrub), as opposed to herbaceous.

Arboretum
A tree collection or tree garden.

Available moisture
The amount of moisture present in a soil between field capacity and the permanent wilting point (both gravitational and capillary water). This is the water which can be used by the plant.

Axil
The angle between a leaf and the stem on which it is growing. Hence *axillary bud*, the bud between leaf and stem, and *axillary shoot*, which arises between leaf and stem.

Backfil
See Fill.

Balled and burlapped (B & B)
Nursery stock in which the plant has been undercut to produce a fibrous rootball. Once dug up, the rootball is wrapped with burlap and tied with string. Plants (usually conifers and other evergreens) are available in this form for a very brief period during the winter.

Bare root
Another type of field-dug tree (usually deciduous); soil is absent from the roots, therefore root defects are easily

173

detected. Only available during winter (dormant) season.

Bark
All the tissues collectively lying outside of the vascular system.

Basal
The lowest part of the plant or of a stem, hence *basal growth*, *basal shoots* and *basal leaves*.

Beating up
A forestry term for the replacement of tree failures after planting.

Biome
A group of major regional terrestrial communities, each with its own type of climate, vegetation and animal life.

Binomial
The present system of classification of living organisms into a generic name and specific epithet, established by the Swedish biologist Carl von Linne (Linnaeus).

Bleeding
Loss of sap from a plant wound.

Blind shoot
A shoot which does not develop fully, in which the apical bud aborts and no further growth is made.

Bole
The unbranched section of a tree trunk.

Branch
A major limb or division from a tree's trunk.

Branched head
A branch system on a tree in which there is no central leader shoot.

Branchlet
Finer divisions of a branch.

Brashing
Removal of lower branches from forest trees.

Break
The development of lateral shoots as a result of pruning (stopping or pinching back) a shoot to an axillary bud.

Breaking bud
One that is in the process of opening.

Breastwood
Shoots which grow forward from trees or shrubs trained against walls, fences or other support structures.
Broadleaf evergreen
Evergreen tree having more or less

broad leaves (an angiosperm) similar to those of deciduous trees; leaves remain on branches for two or more years.

Bud
The embryonic shoot, flower or flower cluster, hence *growth bud*, *flower bud*.

Buffer
A chemical solution which counteracts changes in pH in the soil.

Calcicole
A plant which prefers soils with abundant free calcium.

Calcifuge
A plant which avoids soils with free calcium.

Callus
A mass of tissue formed over a wound.

Cambium
The lateral meristem in vascular plants.

Chimaera
A bigeneric graft hybrid.

Chlorosis
Intraveinal yellowing of leaves as a result of chlorophyll breakdown.

Climax vegetation
The final stable plant community within a region.

Clone
Genetically identical plants, maintained in cultivation by asexual propagation, all arising from the same individual parent plant.

Columnar
Very narrow 'pencil-like' tree form.

Competition
A situation where two or more organisms of the same or different species require and fight for the same limited resources.

Conical
A tree form where the shape of the tree forms a point.

Coniferales
A large order of gymnospermae (cone bearers).

Container-grown
Nursery stock grown in pots or containers throughout their nursery life.

Containerised
Nursery stock grown in open ground and potted or containerised just before sale/transportation.

Coppicing
The regular pruning of a tree or shrub close to ground level, resulting in the production of a quantity of vigorous basal shoots (*see also* Pollarding).

Coral spot
A common disease affecting trees, especially Acers, manifesting itself as orange spots on the bark.

Cordon
A normally branched tree or shrub restricted by spur pruning to a single stem.

Cosmetic pruning
Minor pruning of dead or spent flowers and thin weak or crossing shoots to keep a plant tidy and balanced in its overall shape.

Crown
(1)
The spreading mass of branches on a tree.

(2)
The base of a tree where the trunk meets the roots.

Cultivar
See Appendix B.

Current year's growth/wood
The shoots which have grown from buds during the present growing season.

Dead-heading
The removal of flowers to prevent seed formation or for aesthetic reasons.

Deadman
Underground support system for extra-large trees.

Deciduous
A tree that sheds all its leaves at one time.

Definite growth
A form of growth where a maximum size is reached beyond which no further increase occurs.

Delayed incompatibility
(Of grafting) the breaking down of the union long after the process was carried out.

Denitrification
The loss of nitrates from the soil to the atmosphere due to the action of denitrifying bacteria.

Dichotomous
Forking regularly and repeatedly on a branch.

Dominant species
The most abundant plant species in a community.

Dormant period
A period of plant rest triggered by low temperatures and short day-length.

Drawn shoots
Lanky weak growths caused by poor light conditions.

Drip-line
The ground below the outermost branches of a tree's crown, where most of the feeding roots are.

Ecology
Study of the inter-relationships between organisms and the environment.

Ecotype
A distinct population of plants within a species adapted genetically to its local habitat.

Edaphic factors
Soil factors (physical, chemical and biological).

Emergent tree
A tree whose crown emerges above other trees in a wood.

Endemic
(Of a plant species) growing only in a specific area.

Epicormic shoots
A cluster of shoots, derived from adventitious or dormant buds, on a main stem or branch after a wound or cut has been made (*see also* Watersprouts).

Espalier
Trees trained with a vertical main stem and horizontally trained branches in tiers usually about 15 inches apart. Four or five tiers are usual. In effect each branch is a horizontally trained cordon.

Evapo-transpiration
The loss of water to the atmosphere from both the plant by transpiration and the soil by evaporation.

Evergreen
A plant retaining its leaves throughout the seasons.

Exfoliate
Shedding of bark in layers.

Exotic
An alien (introduced) plant.

Extension growth
Shoots which develop as a result of the growth of the apical or terminal bud of a stem or branch. Used normally in reference to the current season's shoots.

Family
A taxonomic classification of related and similar genera.

Fan
A shrub or tree in which the main branches are trained like the ribs of a fan against a wall, fence or other support system.

Fastigiate
Branches erect and parallel.

Feathers
The lateral growths on a one-year old (maiden) tree.

Fibrous
A root system consisting of many thin roots rather than a taproot.

Field capacity
The maximum amount of water a soil can hold without draining away (i.e. against gravity).

Fill/backfill
A medium (e.g. gravel or soil) used to raise ground level.

Fissured
Deeply grooved bark.

Flaccid
Limp, dehydrated shoots.

Flocculation
The formation of a good crumb structure in clay by adding positively charged particles to the negatively charged clay colloidal solution.

Foliar feed
A fertiliser sprayed on to leaves which is then absorbed by the plant.

Form
Plant or tree shape or outline.

Framework
The "skeleton" of main branches of a tree or shrub.

Frost pocket
An area collecting cold air.

Genotype
The genetic constitution of the plant, as opposed to its physical appearance (*see* Phenotype).

Genus: see Appendix G

Globular
A round-headed tree form.

Grafting
A horticultural method of propagation to unite a shoot (or single bud) of one plant - the 'scion' - with the root system and stem of another - the 'stock'(rootstock).

Gravitational water
Excess water that drains away from the soil to the water table owing to gravity.

Growth bud
A bud that gives rise to a shoot.

Gymnospermae
Flowering plants with naked seeds, according to taxonomic classification (*see also* Angiospermae).

Habit
The general manner of plant growth.

Habitat
An area where organisms live.

Half-hardy
A tree not reliably hardy to cold in the environment where it is positioned; in Great Britain, such trees thrive only in the south and west.

Half-standard
A tree or shrub grown with 3-4 feet of clear stem.

Hardening
The gradual exposure of a plant to increasingly lower temperatures and harsher environmental conditions.

Hardiness
Refers to the cold-tolerance of a tree within its climatic environment, not its ability to withstand abuse or difficult growing conditions.

Head
The framework of branches on a tree.

Heading back
One of two types of pruning cuts in which a branch is cut back to a bud to increase bushiness, or limbs are cut back to reduce the size or height of a tree. (For the other type of cut, *see* Thinning).

Heartwood
The central part of the secondary xylem in arborescent plants, i.e. the wood.

Herbicide
Any chemical that will kill plants when applied to them.

Honeydew
Sticky, sugary solution deposited on leaves by aphids (*see* Sooty mould).

Humus
Complex organic matter (humic acids) resulting from the decomposition of plant and animal tissue and their wastes.

Hygroscopic water
Film of water only one molecule thick surrounding the soil particles; this moisture is held in the soil and is unavailable to plants because it is chemically attracted to the soil particles.

Indigenous
Native.

Internode
The section of stem between two nodes or joints.

Irregular
Of tree form.

Joint
See Node.

Juvenile leaves
The second leaves to appear from seedlings, in certain species varying greatly from adult leaves.

Lateral
A side growth which develops at an angle from the main axis. Lateral shoots are side shoots that grow from lateral buds on a main stem or leading stem.

Lateral branch
A branch arising from a bud on the side of the main trunk or leader; grows in a horizontal or upward-angled fashion.

Leaching
Loss of soil nutrients (salts) to the water table.

Leader
The shoot that terminates a branch and is actively growing and extending year by year (*see also* Apex *and* Terminal bud).

Leaf axil
See Axil.

Limb
A branch.

Lime requirement
The amount of lime required to raise the soil pH to 6.5 to a depth of 150 mm.

Liming
The addition of lime to the soil to raise soil pH.

Macro-nutrient
The main plant nutrients essential for good growth and required in large concentrations by most plants.

Maiden
A term used to describe a one-year-old tree or shrub, or occasionally, with fruit trees, one-year-old growth.

Matrix planting
A method of tree spacing based on a grid system.

Meristem
Live, actively dividing cells within plant tissue. There are two essential types: *apical* meristems, which occur in the root and shoot apexes, and are responsible for growth in the vertical plane; and *lateral* meristems, which occur in the trunks and branches and are responsible for growth in girth and wound healing.

Meristem culture
Micropropagation.

Microclimate
A significantly different climate within the regional climate; can be warmer or colder than the regional climate.

Micro-nutrient (trace element)
The essential plant nutrients needed in small concentrations by the plant.

Micropropagation
A system of plant production from a single or only a few cells from an apical meristem in a culture tube with a hormone-based culture solution.

Mildew
A fungus disease, usually made visible by a powdery or chalky substance on the leaves (the fruiting and growth structures of certain fungi).

Mineral matter
The sand, silt and clay portion of the soil.

Moribund
(Of a tree) past maturity and going into decline.

Mulch
A top dressing of organic material on the soil around a plant to reduce weed

growth and conserve moisture (may also be applied for aesthetic reasons).

Mycorrhiza
A symbiotic association between a fungus and plant roots (beneficial to both organisms).

New wood
Current season's growth.

Node
The point on a stem where a leaf or leaves arise.

Nodule
A small spherical swelling of plant tissue caused by infection of nitrogen fixing bacteria.

Notch planting
A forestry method of planting bare-root material. Its main value is speed. There are three types of notch planting: "L" notch, and two variations on it, "H" notch and "T" notch. (*See* the detail sheet in Chapter 2, *Planting*, 2.12.)

Old wood
Stem growth produced before the current season's growth.

Open centre
A tree or shrub in which the branch system is pruned and trained so that the centre of the framework is fairly open and free of main branches.

Organic matter
The part of the soil derived from once living organisms.

Ornamentals
Plants grown for their aesthetic value rather than their commercial usefulness or food value.

Ped
Soil particles aggregated into masses of various sizes and shapes.

Pendulous
"Weeping-like" tree form.

Permanent wilting point
When a plant wilts and will not recover on addition of water because the cells have collapsed.

pH
A measure of the hydrogen ion concentration in the soil.

Phenotype
The physical expression of the genotype as a result of the environmental influence.

Pinch back
To prune soft growth by cutting or nipping out with fingers the growing tip of a shoot (also known as stopping).

Pioneer species
A tree species selected because it is capable of re-vegetating a soil.

Pith
The central, cylindrical, often soft region of young stems.

Planting in arms
A forestry term where young trees are planted in the root arms of a felled tree stump.

Pollarding
The regular pruning of a tree or shrub back to the main stem or trunk (*see also* Coppicing).

Profile
A depth of soil showing the horizons.

Provenance
The geographical origin of tree seed.

Reaction wood
Structurally abnormal wood formed in response to stress (i.e. wind).

Recurrent flowering
The production of several crops of flowers during one season more or less in succession.

Renewal pruning
Pruning to obtain a constant supply of young shoots on a tree or shrub, so that vigour and freedom of flowering are maintained.

Resistance
The ability of a plant to tolerate the activities of pests, diseases and disorders.

Reversion
A shoot or growth from a cultivated or hybrid plant which genetically reverts to the natural form and is, consequently, different from the main plant.

Rhizosphere
The region of soil surrounding the root over which the roots exert some influence.

Rootstock
See Grafting.

Run-off
Water run-off from a surface.

Scaffold branches
The permanent branches of a tree that form its structure. Branches do not increase in height as a tree grows and always remain in the same position on the tree.

Scion
See Grafting.

Screefing
Scraping away of surface vegetation prior to notch planting of trees.

Secondary growth
Stem increment.

Second-year wood
Growth or shoots that are between one and two years old.

Seedling
A young plant. The progeny may differ significantly in characteristics from the parents (e.g. hardiness).

Semi-deciduous
A tree that retains some of its leaves during a mild winter (e.g. evergreen pear); it may lose all of its leaves during cold winters.

Semi-mature
Very large trees.

Shade plant
A plant tolerant to low light levels. Such plants are usually very dark green, with glossy leaves.

Snag
A short stump of a branch left after incorrect pruning.

Soil fertility
The ability of a soil to support plants.

Soil moisture deficit
The amount of water required to bring a soil to field capacity.

Soil structure
The arrangement of soil particles into peds.

Soil texture
The proportion of particles of different sizes.

Sooty mould
A black, fungal growth on honeydew.

Species
See Appendix B.

Spur
A slow-growing short branch system

that usually carries clusters of flower buds or fruit.

Stag heading
Die-back in the crown of old trees.

Standard
A tree grown with 5-6 feet of clear stem.

Stock
See Grafting.

Stopping
See Pinch back.

Stratification
Vegetation layers.

Sub-lateral
A side-shoot growing from a lateral shoot.

Sucker
A shoot arising from a root system (or occasionally another shoot) below or just at ground level. The term usually refers to unwanted growths from the rootstock of grafted or budded plants.

Sun plant
A plant thriving only in full light conditions (e.g. dominant trees).

Symbiosis
Two organisms living together for the benefit of one or both of the organisms.

Taproot
A persistent and robust primary root.

Temporary wilting point
When a plant wilts but will recover when water is applied.

Terminal bud,shoot
The uppermost, usually central, growth on a stem.

Thinning
(1)
Reducing the number of shoots in an overcrowded branch system so that the remaining shoots are evenly spaced to allow free air circulation and to let light reach the foliage in the centre of the plant.

(2)
Removing some trees to allow the remainder to mature.

Tilth
The size and stability of soil aggregates on the surface.

Tip bearers
Fruit trees which bear most of their fruits

179

at the tips of one-year-old shoots.

Topiary
Training and pruning of trees to create decorative shapes.

Topping
Applied occasionally to the stopping of shoots but more frequently to the removal of the top of a tree, leaving only a skeleton of the main branches (*see* Pollarding).

Top-worked
A standard or half-standard tree which has been grafted or budded at the top of the stem of the stock.

Trace element
See Micro-nutrient.

Transect
A line across an area, used for study of plant species distribution.

Transition region
The junction of stem and root at ground level.

Transpiration
The loss of water from the leaf surfaces.

Varietas
See Appendix B.

Variety
See Appendix B.

Vascular system
The transportation system within living plants, i.e. xylem and phloem.

Volunteer species
A tree that has grown from a self-sown seed.

Water holding capacity
The amount of water held in a soil at any given time.

Watersprouts (or watershoots)
Vigorous, often fairly soft, shoots that arise from adventitious buds on old wood when trees are growing very vigorously or have been damaged.

Water table
The natural level of water in a soil.

Weed
Any plant where it is not wanted.

Windbreak
Specialised shelter planting.

Wind-rock
The loosening of the root system of a shrub or tree by strong winds. Usually indicates a lack of balance between the root and shoot systems and can be avoided by firm staking and reduction of the branch system of top-heavy plants in autumn. May also be the result of root curl caused by container-growing systems, especially evident in certain plants, e.g. conifers and Eucalyptus spp.

Wolf
Mis-shapen trees in a woodland.

Wound wood
Callus.

B BOTANICAL NOMENCLATURE

Introduction

It is important to specify trees correctly, in order to avoid the confusion which can arise as a result of using common names.

Plant nomenclature is controlled by two standard internationally recognised codes:

1)
the International Code of Botanical Nomenclature, dealing with wild plants;

2)
the International Code of Nomenclature for Cultivated Plants, dealing with cultivars.

The taxonomy of plants is a complicated issue; it will be sufficient for the architect or landscape architect to understand the binomial system of classification.

Both codes use the binomial system of classification, as follows:

Genus
A group of homogeneous species. Always written in upper and lower case with a capital first letter, e.g. Betula. Usually a noun. A hyphenated word is acceptable but not two words.

Species
The basic unit of classification (specific epithet). Always written in lower case following the generic name. These are adjectives describing the genus. The ending of a specific name often agrees with the gender of the genus, e.g. Betula pendula.

Authorship
In some manuals and botanical works the species name is often followed by the name (or abbreviation for it) of the botanist who first named the wild plant; e.g. L. stands for Carl von Linne (Linnaeus). This need not be used when specifying trees.

varietas
One of the classifications below species level of naturally occurring types. Always written in lower case following the species name; often the prefix "var" is added.

e.g. Betula platyphylla japonica
or Betula platyphylla var japonica

Note
Do not confuse "varietas" with "variety", which is another term for cultivar.

Cultivar
An assemblage of cultivated plants distinguished by any characters, these characters being retained even through reproduction. Always written in upper and lower case, wih a capital first letter, following the species name. The cultivar name *must* either be in single inverted commas or prefixed with "c.v.".

e.g. Betula pendula "Tristis"
or Betula pendula c.v. Tristis

B i -generic hybrids There are two groups of these:

1)
Sexual crosses between species of two different genera. Always use the prefix "X" in upper case before the generic name.
e.g. X Cupressocyparis leylandii
2)
Graft hybrids, known as chimeras. Always use the prefix "+" in upper case before the generic name.

e.g. + Laburnocytisus adamii

Interspecific hybrids
Sexual crosses between two different
species of the same genus. Always use
the prefix "x" in lower case before the
specific name.

e.g. Betula x koehnei

Note
There is no standard code governing
the use of common names.

It is accepted practice when using
plant names in text either to underline
the name or to use italic type.

C BOTANICAL AND COMMON NAMES

Abies alba
European silver fir
Abies amabilis
Red silver fir
Abies balsamea
Balsam fir
Abies cephalonica
Grecian fir
Abies concolor
Colorado white fir
Abies grandis
Giant fir
Abies procera
Noble fir
Acacia dealbata
Silver wattle
Acer campestre
Field maple
Acer griseum
Paperbark maple
Acer macrophyllum
Oregon maple
Acer negundo
Box elder
Acer nikoense
Nikko maple
Acer platanoides
Norway maple
Acer pseudoplatanus
Sycamore
Acer rubrum
Canadian maple
Acer saccharinum
Silver maple
Acer saccharum
Sugar maple
Aesculus chinensis
Chinese horse chestnut
Aesculus flava
Sweet buckeye
Aesculus hippocastanum
Horse chestnut
Aesculus indica
Indian horse chestnut
Aesculus pavia
Red buckeye
Aesculus x carnea

Red horse chestnut
Ailanthus altissima
Tree of Heaven
Alnus cordata
Italian alder
Alnus glutinosa
Common alder
Alnus incana
Grey alder
Alnus rubra
Red alder
Alnus viridis
Green alder
Araucaria araucana
Monkey-puzzle tree
Arbutus andrachne
Grecian strawberry tree
Arbutus unedo
Killarney strawberry tree
Betula nigra
River birch
Betula papyrifera
Paper bark birch
Betula pendula
Silver birch
Betula pubescens
White birch
Betula utilis
Himalayan birch
Buxus sempervirens
Box
Calocedrus decurrens
Incense cedar
Carpinus betulus
Hornbeam
Carya ovata
Shagbark hickory
Castanea sativa
Sweet chestnut
Cedrus atlantica
Atlas cedar
Cedrus atlantica glauca
Blue cedar
Cedrus deodara
Deodar cedar
Cedrus libani
Cedar of Lebanon

Cercis siliquastrum
Judas tree
Chamaecyparis formosensis
Formosan cedar
Chamaecyparis lawsoniana
Lawson cypress
Chamaecyparis nootkatensis
Nootka cypress
Chamaecyparis obtusa
Hinoki cypress
Chamaecyparis pisifera
Sawara cypress
Chamaecypris thyoides
White cypress
Cordyline australis
Cabbage palm
Corylus avellana
Hazel
Corylus colurna
Turkish hazel
Crataegus laevigata
Midland thorn
Crataegus monogyna
Hawthorn
Cryptomeria japonica
Japanese cedar
Cupressus goveniana
Californian cypress
Cupressus macrocarpa
Monterey cypress
Cupressus sempervirens
Italian cypress
Diospyros kaki
Chinese persimmon
Elaeagnus angustifolia
Oleaster
Embothrium coccineum
Chilean fire tree
Eucalyptus dalrympleana
Broad-leaved kindling bark
Eucalyptus gunnii
Cider gum
Eucalyptus niphophila
Snow gum
Eucalyptus pauciflora
Cabbage gum
Fagus sylvatica
Beech
Fraxinus excelsior
Ash
Gingko biloba
Maidenhair tree
Gleditschia triacanthos
Honey locust
Ilex aquifolium
Holly
Juglans nigra
Black walnut
Juglans regia
Walnut
Juniperus communis
Common juniper
Laburnum alpinum
Scotch laburnum
Laburnum anagyroides
Common laburnum
Larix decidua
European larch

Larix kaempferi
Japanese larch
Larix occidentalis
Western larch
Larix x eurolipsis
Hybrid larch
Larix x pendula
Weeping larch
Laurus nobilis
Bay
Liquidambar styraciflua
Sweet gum
Liqustrum lucidum
Chinese privet/tree privet
Liriodendron tulipifera
Tulip tree
Magnolia campbellii
Pink tulip tree
Magnolia grandiflora
Bull bay
Malus sylvestris
Crab-apple
Mespilus germanica
Medlar
Morus alba
White mulberry
Morus nigra
Black mulberry
Morus rubra
Red mulberry
Nothofagus antarctica
Antarctic beech
Nothofagus obliqua
Roble beech
Nothofagus procera
Rauli
Nyssa sylvatica
Tupelo
Paulownia tomentosa
Foxglove tree
Phillyrea latifolia
Holm oak
Picea abies
Norway spruce
Picea brewerana
Brewer's weeping spruce
Picea glauca
White spruce
Picea mariana
Black spruce
Picea omorika
Serbian spruce
Picea orientalis
Oriental spruce
Picea pungens
Colorado spruce
Picea sitchensis
Sitka spruce
Pinus contorta
Beach pine
Pinus coulteri
Big cone pine
Pinus halepensis
Aleppo pine
Pinus nigra
Austrian pine
Pinus parviflora
Japanese white pine

Pinus pinaster
Maritime pine
Pinus pinea
Stone pine
Pinus radiata
Monterey pine
Pinus strobus
Weymouth pine
Pinus sylvestris
Scots pine
Pinus wallichiana
Bhutan pine
Platanus orientalis
Oriental plane
Platanus x acerifolia
London plane
Populus alba
White poplar
Populus balsamifera
Balsam poplar
Populus canescens
Grey poplar
Populus nigra
Black poplar
Populus nigra 'Italica'
Lombardy poplar
Populus nigra var betulifolia
Black poplar
Populus tremula
Aspen
Prunus avium
Gean or wild cherry
Prunus cerasifera
Myrobalan cherry plum
Prunus cerasus
Sour cherry
Prunus dulcis
Common almond
Prunus laurocerasus
Cherry laurel
Prunus padus
Bird cherry
Prunus persica
Peach
Prunus subhirtella
Spring cherry
Pseudotsuga menziesii
Oregon douglas fir
Pterocarya fraxinifolia
Caucasian wing nut
Pyrus communis
Wild pear
Pyrus salicifolia
Willow leaf pear
Quercus cerris
Turkey oak
Quercus coccinea
Scarlet oak
Quercus ilex
Holm oak
Quercus petraea
Sessile oak
Quercus robur
Common oak
Quercus rubra
Red oak
Quercus suber

Cork oak
Robinia pseudacacia
False acacia
Salix alba
White willow
Salix babylonica
Weeping willow
Salix caprea
Goat willow
Salix daphnoides
Violet willow
Salix fragilis
Crack willow
Salix matsudana
Peking willow
Salix pentandra
Bay willow
Sophora japonica
Pagoda tree
Sorbus aria
Whitebeam
Sorbus aucuparia
Rowan or mountain ash
Sorbus domestica
True service tree
Sorbus intermedia
Swedish whitebeam
Sorbus torminalis
Wild service tree
Taxodium distichum
Swamp cypress
Taxus baccata
Yew
Thuja occidentalis
American Arbor-vitae
Thuja orientalis
Chinese Arbor-vitae
Thuja plicata
Western red cedar
Tilia americana
American lime
Tilia cordata
Small-leaved lime
Tilia platyphyllos
Large-leaved lime
Tilia x europaea
Common lime
Trachycarpus fortunei
Chusan palm
Tsuga canadensis
Eastern hemlock
Tsuga heterophylla
Western hemlock
Ulmus carpinifolia
Smooth-leaved elm
Ulmus carpinifolia 'Cornubiensis'
Cornish elm
Ulmus carpinifolia 'Plotii'
Plot's elm
Ulmus glabra
Wych elm
Ulmus procera
English elm
Zelkova carpinifolia
Zelkova

D STANDARD GRAPHIC SYMBOLS

Symbols for proposed trees

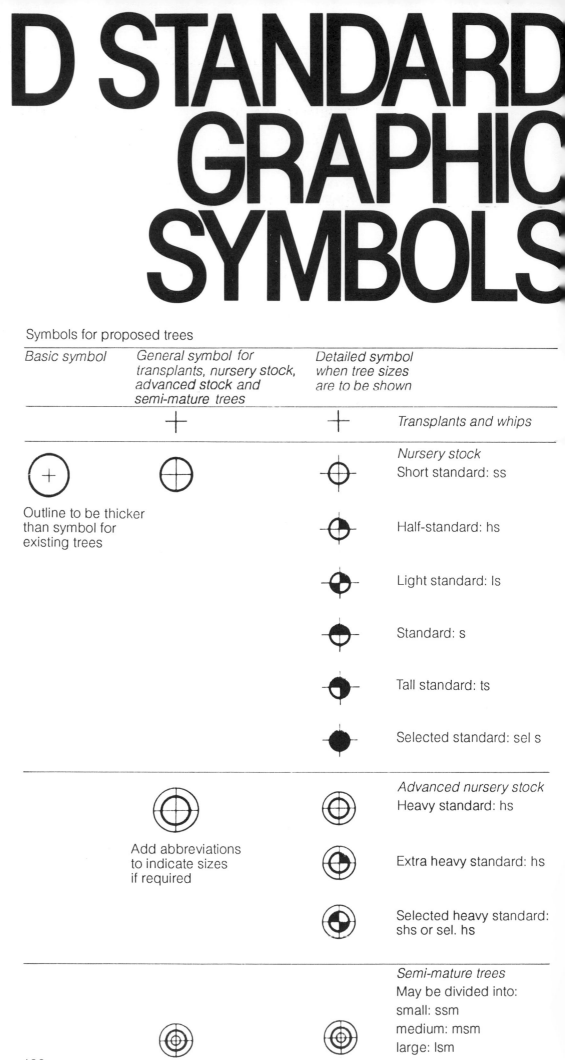

Basic symbol	General symbol for transplants, nursery stock, advanced stock and semi-mature trees	Detailed symbol when tree sizes are to be shown	
			Transplants and whips
Outline to be thicker than symbol for existing trees			*Nursery stock* Short standard: ss
			Half-standard: hs
			Light standard: ls
			Standard: s
			Tall standard: ts
			Selected standard: sel s
	Add abbreviations to indicate sizes if required		*Advanced nursery stock* Heavy standard: hs
			Extra heavy standard: hs
			Selected heavy standard: shs or sel. hs
			Semi-mature trees May be divided into: small: ssm medium: msm large: lsm

Item	Symbol	Comments
Trees of same species		Give number and species
Existing trees		Spread shown to scale
Proposed trees		Refer to symbols for proposed trees when size of tree is to be differentiated by symbol
Tree assessment: very good	A	Give details of species, size etc. on drawing or schedule
good	B	
fair	C	
dead/poor	D	
Existing trees to be protected temporarily during site works		Other planted areas requiring protection should be shown similarly
Existing or new trees to be protected permanently		Other planted areas requiring protection should be shown similarly
Tree pit		Drawn to scale, "hard" areas only
Trees to be removed		Show spread to scale. Give details of size and species on drawing or schedule
Woodland: existing		
proposed		Draw grid to scale when practical

Abbey Rose Gardens
Nashdom Lane, Burnham,
Buckinghamshire SL1 8NJ
Tel: 06286 3000

Aberdeen Tree Nurseries
Tillycorthie, Udny, Ellon,
Aberdeenshire AB4 0SD
Tel: 06513 2839

Aline Fairweather Ltd
The Garden Centre,
Beaulieu, Brockenhurst,
Hampshire SO4 7YB
Tel: 0590 612307

Allan, John, Ltd
Route de Plaisance,
St Pierre du Bois,
Guernsey,C.I.
Tel: 0481 64041

Allport, Roger, Nurseries
Parkstone, Newland,
Malvern, Worcestershire
Tel: 0886 32288 or 32000

Amenity Trees
16 Mill Lane, Arlesey,
Bedfordshire SG1 6RF
Tel: 0462 731340

Anderson, H.
87a The Lane, Awsworth,
Nottingham
Tel: 0602 301884

Angevin Nurseries
Caledonia Nursery, Fosse
Andre, St Peter Port,
Guernsey, Channel
Islands,
Tel: 0481 20141/24584
Telex: 419 602

**Anglia Group of
Nurseries Ltd**
46 Magdalen Street,
Thetford, Norfolk
IP24 2BN
Tel: 0842 4951
Telex: 817670

Arnot, C., & Sons (N) Ltd
Rosebank Nurseries,
Kingsmuir, Forfar
Tel: 0307 62139

Arundel Arboretum Ltd
Scotland Barn, Chichester
Road, Arundel,
West Sussex
Tel: 0903 883251

Aveland Trees
Dunsby, Bourne,
Lincolnshire PE10 0UB
Tel: 0778 35716

Badshot Farm Nurseries
Badshot Lea, Farnham,
Surrey GU9 9JX
Tel: 0252 313173

**Banff & Buchan
Nurseries Ltd**
Baley, Portsoy, Banff,
Scotland AB4 2YQ
Tel: 0261 8291
Telex: 73321

Bannatyne & Jackson
Smithycroft Nursery,
Carlisle Road, Hamilton,
Lanarkshire
Tel: 0698 286255

Barcham Farm Trees
Barcham, Soham, Ely,
Cambridgeshire CB7 5TN
Tel: 0353 720748

Barock F. G., & Co
Garden House Farm,
Drinkstone, Bury St
Edmunds, Suffolk
Tel: 0449 3249

Baronscourt Nurseries
Abercorn Estate,
Newtownstewart, Co
Tyrone, Northern Ireland
BT78 4EZ
Tel: 06626 61683
Telex: 748111

**Barters Farm Nurseries
Ltd**
Chapmanslade, Westbury,
Wiltshire
Tel: 037388 294

Barthelemy & Co
The Nurseries, Stapehill,
Wimborne, Dorset
Tel: 0202 874283

Bayley, E. J., & Sons Ltd
Bayston Hill Nurseries,
Bayston Hill, Shrewsbury,
Shropshire SY3 0DA
Tel: 0743 724261

Beauchamp Clark
The Nurseries, Mersham,
Ashford, Kent TN2 7HS
Tel: 023372 254

**Beckett, George,
Nurseries**
Compton Nursery, Main
Road, Compton,
Winchester, Hampshire
SO21 2DE
Tel: 0962 713732

Beechwood Nurseries
Crown Lane, Farnham
Royal, Slough,

Buckinghamshire
Tel: 02814 3108
Telex: 849325

**Belwood Landscape Co
Ltd**
Mauricewood Mains,
Penicuik, Midlothian
EH26 0NJ
Tel: 0968 736221
Telex: 728194

Benson, Clive
The Nurseries, Croston
Road, Farington, Preston,
Lancashire PR5 3PN
Tel: 0772 421543

**Bernhard's Rugby
Nurseries Ltd**
Bilton Road, Rugby,
Warwickshire CV22 7DT
Tel: 0788 811500
Telex: 312180 Bernex G

Berrydown Nursery
Berrydown Products
(Gidleigh) Ltd
Gidleigh, Chagford,
Devon TQ13 8HS
Tel: 06473 2373

Beverley Plant Center
Lond Lane, Beverley,
North Humberside
HU17 0RN
Tel: 0482 862513

Billen Ltd
Salisbury Road, Plaitford,
Romsey, Hampshire
SO51 6EE
Tel: 0794 22486

Blackmore & Langdon
Pensford, Bristol, Avon
BS18 4JL
Tel: 0272 332300

**Blakedown Nurseries
Ltd**
Belbroughton Road,
Blakedown,
Kidderminster, Worcs
DY10 3JD
Tel: 0562 700551
Telex: 334303

**Blooms of Bressingham
Ltd**
Bressingham, Diss,
Norfolk
Tel: 037988 464
Telex: 97335

Bluntington House Farm
Chaddesley Corbett,
Kidderminster,
Worcestershire DY10 4NP

Tel: 0562 730582

Boden Nurseries
Boden Hall, Scholar
Green, Cheshire
Tel: 09363 2032/6140

Boningale Nurseries Ltd
Holyhead Road,
Boningale, Albrighton,
Wolverhampton WV7 3AU
Tel: 090722 4276/7
Telex: 337818

Boosey, William & Son
Newton Bank, Middlewich,
Cheshire CW10 9EX
Tel: 060 684 2324

Border Woodlands Ltd
Rectory Nursery,
Richards Castle, Ludlow,
Shropshire SY8 4EE
Tel: 058474 338

**Border Tree & Shrub
Growers Ltd**
Monteviot Gardens,
Ancrum, Jedburgh,
Roxburghshire
Tel: 08353 239

Bottle Kiln Nursery
The Bottle Kiln,
West Hallam,
Derbyshire DE7 6HP
Tel: 0602 329442

**Boulton Bros
(Moddershall) Ltd**
The Nurseries,
Moddershall, Stone,
Staffordshire ST15 8TQ
Tel: 0785 813747

**Brackenwood Nurseries
Ltd**
Bradshaw Lane,
Greenhalgh, Kirkham,
Preston, Lancashire
PR4 3HQ
Tel: 0772 686232
Telex: 67242

**Bradford Estate Tree
Nursery**
Bradford Estate, Weston
under Lizard, Shifnal,
Shropshire TF11 8JU
Tel: 0952 76372

Bradshaw, J., & Son
Busheyfields Nursery,
Herne Bay, Kent
Tel: 0227 375415

**Brantling's Hay
Nurseries**
Sample Oak Lane,

Chilworth, Surrey
GU4 8RE
Tel: 0483 892582/893127

**Brechin Castle Gardens
& Nursery**
Dalhousie Estates,
Brechin, Angus, Scotland
DD9 6EL
Tel: 035 62 2689

**Breckland Garden
Centre**
Yaxham, Nr Dereham,
Norfolk
Tel: 0362 66 750

**Brentwood Moss
Nurseries**
New Moss Road,
Cadishead, Irlam,
Manchester M30 5TJ
Tel: 061 775 2257/7634
Telex: 665188

**Bridgemere Nurseries
Ltd**
Bridgemere, Nr Nantwich,
Cheshire CW5 7OB
Tel: 09365 264/375

Brinkley Nurseries Ltd
Fiskerton Road, Southwell,
Nottinghamshire
Tel: 0636 814501

Brinkman Bros Ltd
Walton Farm Nurseries,
Bosham, Chichester,
West Sussex
Tel: 0243 572221

Bristocks Ltd
School Road, West
Walton, Nr Wisbech,
Cambridgeshire
PE14 7DS
Tel: 0945 582633

**Broadhouse Farm
Nurseries**
Cutnall Green, Droitwich,
Worcestershire WR9 0LZ
Tel: 029923 338

Broadmead Trees
Silver Street, Sway,
Lymington, Hampshire
Tel: 0590 682409

Burrow Nursery
Herrings Lane, Cross-in-
Hand, Heathfields, Sussex
Tel: 04352 2992

Butcher, Thomas
60 Wickham Road,
Shirley, Croydon, Surrey
CR9 8AG

Tel: 01 654 3720

Caldwell & Sons Ltd
The Nurseries and Garden
Centre, Knutsford,
Cheshire WA16 8LX
Tel: 0565 4281/2

Cants of Colchester Ltd
Agriculture House,
305 Mile End Road,
Colchester, Essex
CO4 5EB
Tel: 0206 844008

Caradoc Acre Nurseries
The Levons, Hazler Road,
Church Stretton,
Shropshire SY6 7AQ
Tel: 0694 722475

Cardwell Nursery
Lunderston Bay,
by Gourock, Ayrshire,
Scotland PA19 1BB
Tel: 0475 521536 Ext. 28

Central Alpines
17 Ball Street, Aston,
Oxford, OX8 2DN
Tel: 0993 850979

Challis of York Ltd
Northfield Nurseries,
Poppleton, York
Tel: 0904 796161
Telex: 57621

Chantry Nursery
Combe Raleigh, Honiton,
Devon EX14 0TQ
Tel: 0404 2981

Cheshire Nurseries
Siddington, Macclesfield,
Cheshire SK11 9LH
Tel: 026 04 428

Chessum, Paul
21 High Street, Great
Barford, Bedfordshire
MK44 3JH
Tel: 0234 870182

Chichester Trees
The Mill Yard, Beaulieu,
Hampshire, SO4 7ZN
Tel: 0590 612198

**Christies (Fochabers)
Ltd**
The Nurseries, Fochabers,
Moray, Scotland
Tel: 0343 820362

Civic Tree Care Ltd
PO Box 23, Tring,
Hertfordshire HP23 4AF

Tel: Head office—
044282 5401,
Sales office—01 950 4491
Telex: 826715

**Clarke, Peter,
Cultivation Ltd**
Boundary Farm,
Perton Road, Compton,
Wolverhampton WV6 8DJ
Tel: 0902 761237

Clayton, J. & M.
Ewbank Field Nurseries,
Farnham Lane, Farnham,
Knaresborough,
North Yorkshire
Tel: 09014 484

Coblands Nurseries Ltd
Trench Road, Tonbridge,
Kent TN10 3HQ
Tel: 0732 359666

**Cocker, James, & Sons
(Rose Specialist)**
Whitemyres, Lang Stracht,
Aberdeen AB9 2XH
Tel: 0224 313261

**Commercial Landscapes
Ltd**
The Nursery, Paices Hill,
Aldermaston, Berkshire
Tel: 073 56 6111/6161

Conifox Nurseries
Foxhall, Kirkliston,
West Lothian,
Scotland EH29 9ER
Tel: 031 333 3334
Telex: 727905

**Conway Valley
Nurseries**
Tyn-y-Groes, Nr Conwy,
Gwynedd LL32 8SS
Tel: 049267 228

**Copenhagen Nurseries
Ltd**
Bradford Road,
Sandbeds, Keighley,
Yorkshire BD20 5NP
Tel: 0274 564557

Cranage Nursery
Northwich Road, Cranage,
Nr Knutsford, Cheshire
CW4 8HL
Tel: 0477 32431

Crowder, W., & Sons Ltd
Thimbleby Nurseries,
Horncastle, Lincolnshire
LN9 5LZ
Tel: 06582 6363
Telex: 946240

**Crown Estate
Commissioners**
Crown Estate Office, The
Great Park, Windsor,
Berkshire
Tel: 0753 860222

Darby Nursery Stock Ltd
Old Feltwell Road,
Methwood, Thetford,
Norfolk IP26 4PW
Tel: 0366 728380

Deacons Nursery
Moor View, Godshill, Isle
of Wight PO38 3HW
Tel: 0983 840750

Daydawn Nurseries
Station Road, Chobham,
Woking, Surrey GU24 8AS
Tel: 09905 7448

Dingle Nurseries
Welshpool, Powys, Wales
SY21 9JD
Tel: 0938 2587

Double, Paul
Nursery Gardens,
Woolverstone, Ipswich,
Suffolk
Tel: 047 384 322

**Double Yew Nurseries
Ltd**
Northorpe, Bourne,
Lincolnshire
Tel: 0778 424181

Dovecote Nurseries
Church Road, Emneth,
Wisbech, Cambridgeshire
PE14 8AA
Tel: 0945 583925

**Duff, Wm., & Son
(Forfar) Ltd**
West Craig Nurseries,
Forfar, Scotland DD8 1XE
Tel: 0307 63621

**Duncan & Davies (UK)
Ltd**
Highleigh Nurseries,
Highleigh Road,
Sidlesham, Nr Chichester,
West Sussex PO20 7NR
Tel: 0243 56711
Telex: 86345

**Eames & Son
(Nurserymen) Ltd**
Newark Nurseries
84 Eye Road
Peterboro PE1 4SQ
Tel: 0733 62739

Eastcote Nurseries (Solihull) Ltd
Wood Lane, Barston, Solihull, West Midlands B92 0JL
Tel: 067 55 2033

Economic Forestry Group plc
Market Street, Fordham, Cambridgeshire
Tel: 0638 720455
Telex: 817165 and
Maelor Nursery, Conery Lane, Bronington, Whitchurch, Shropshire
Tel: 094873 555
Telex: 35534 and:
Aberdeen Tree Nurseries, Tillycorthie, Udney, Aberdeen AB4 0SD
Tel: 065 132 839

Elliott, J. W., & Sons (West End) Ltd
Fenns Lane Nurseries, West End, Woking, Surrey GU24 9QE
Tel: 04867 2210

Ellis Brothers
Dumbleton Nurseries, Dumbleton, Nr Evesham, Worcestershire WR11 6QW
Tel: 0386 881897

Emerald Vale Nursery
Arcadia, Rackenford, Tiverton, Devon EX16 8ER
Tel: 088488 231

Emwood Nurseries Ltd
Ash Lane, Martin Hussingtree, Nr Worcester WA3 8TB
Tel: 0905 58558

English Woodlands Ltd Oare Nursery
Bradley Court Road, Chieveley, Berkshire
Tel: 0635 248589 and:
Burrow Nursery, Herrings Lane, Cross-in-Hand, Heathfield, Sussex
Tel: 04352 2992

Everton Nurseries Ltd
Lymington, Hampshire SO4 0JZ
Tel: 0590 42155

Exbury Trees
Otterwood, Exbury Road, Beaulieu, Brockenhurst, Hampshire SO4 7YS
Tel: 0590 612278

F & R Nurseries (Woking) Ltd
Warbury Lane, Knaphill, Woking, Surrey GU24 4XS
Tel: 09905 7969

Fairley, James, & Co
Main Street, Cairney Hill, Fife, Scotland KY12 8QT
Tel: 0383 880223

Fargro Plants
Toddington Lane, Littlehampton, West Sussex BN17 7PP
Tel: 0903 722737
Telex: 877575

Finalystone Estate Gardens
Finlaystone, Langbank, Renfrewshire, Scotland PA14 6TJ
Tel: 047 554 235

Forde Abbey Forest Nursery
Chard, Somerset TA20 4LU
Tel: 0460 20231

Fords Nursery Stock Ltd
Carthouse Lane Nurseries, Carthouse Lane, Horsell, Woking, Surrey GU21 4XS
Tel: 09905 7969

Foxhall & Gyle Nurseries Ltd
Brigton of Ruthven, Meigle, Perthshire, Scotland PH12 8RQ
Tel: 082 84 219
Telex: 76192

Fresh Acres Nurseries Ltd
Roundstone Lane, Angmering, West Sussex DN10 4AU
Tel: 0903 785123/771659

Frost, D. W., (Wholesale Nurseries)
Fosseway Nurseries, Car Colston, Bingham, Nottinghamshire NG13 8JA
Tel: 0949 20445

Gandy's Roses Ltd
North Kilworth, Lutterworth, Leiciestershire LE17 6HZ
Tel: 0858 880398

Gemmell, H. K.
Blairside Nursery, Kilwinning, Ayrshire,

KA13 6PD
Tel: 0294 52589

Goldsmith, Douglas Ltd
Crown Nursery, School Lane, Ufford, Woodbridge, Suffolk IP13 6DY
Tel: 0394 460755

Green, S. W., & Sons
Ringbeck, Ellerker, Brough, North Humberside
Tel: 04302 2256

Greenfield Horticulture Ltd
Plumbs Farm, Sutton Road, Terrington-St-Clement, Norfolk
Tel: 0553 828699

Greenfingers (Kenilworth) Ltd
Wholesale Nursery, Kington Lane, Claverdon, Warwickshire CV35 8PP
Tel: 092684 2797

Green Leaf Nurseries (NI) Ltd
Milecross Road, Newtownards, Co Down, Northern Ireland
Tel: 0247 810077

Grove Farm Nurseries
Pirbright, Woking, Surrey GU24 0JY
Tel: 04867 2039

Hewton Trees & Shrubs
Bere Alston, Yelverton, Devon PL20 7BW
Tel: 0822 840460

Higher Heath Forest Nurseries
The Meadows, Higher Heath, Whitchurch, Shropshire SY13 2JA
Tel: 0948 840120

Hill, John, & Sons
Spot Acre Nurseries, Stone, Staffordshire
Tel: 088 924 388

Hill, R., & Son
The Nurseries, Appleton, Abingdon, Oxfordshire OX13 5QN
Tel: 0865 862081

Hillier Nurseries (Winchester) Ltd
Ampfield House,

Ampfield, Romsey,
Hampshire SO51 9PA
Tel: 0794 68733

Hilling, T., & Co Ltd
The Nurseries, Bagshot
Road, Chobham, Woking,
Surrey
Tel: 09905 7101

Holmes Nurseries
South Drive, Littleton,
Winchester, Hampshire
SO 22 6PY
Tel: 0962 882020

Huverba (UK) Ltd
Fairview Nurseries,
Church Road, Emneth,
Wisbech, Cambridgeshire
PE14 8AP
Tel: 0945 64383/583591

Hydon Nurseries Ltd
Clock Barn Lane,
Hydon Heath, Godalming,
Surrey GU8 4AZ
Tel: 048 632 252

J & J Nurseries Ltd
Showborough Lodge,
Twyning, Tewkesbury,
Gloucestershire GL20
6DN
Tel: 0684 293583

**Johnson, E. R.,
(Nurseries) Ltd**
The Nurseries, Whixley,
York YO5 8AQ
Tel: 0901 30234

**Jones, C & K,
International Rose
Specialists**
Golden Fields Nursery,
Barrow Lane, Tarvin,
Chester CH3 8JF
Tel: 0829 40663

**Jones, J. A., & Sons
(Churchtown)**
Bankfield Nurseries,
99 Bankfield Road,
Southport, Lancashire
PR9 7NT
Tel: 0704 28235

Jungman, P.
Hacks Drove, Baston-Fen,
Peterborough,
Cambridgeshire
Tel: 07786 392

**Juniper Hill Nurseries
Ltd**
Mickleham, Surrey
RH5 6DB
Tel: 0372 375004

Juniper Nurseries
Foxhole Farm, Little
Horwood Road, Winslow,
Buckinghamshire
MK18 3JW
Tel: 029671 3820

Kennedy's Nurseries
Green Lane, Shamley
Green, Guildford, Surrey
GU5 0RD
Tel: 0483 893337

Keydell Nurseries
Keydell Avenue,
Horndean, Hampshire
PO8 9TE
Tel: 0705 59839

Kingsfield Tree Nursery
Winsham, Chard,
Somerset TA20 4JF
Tel: 046 030 697

Knight's Nurseries Ltd
Park Road, Hellingly, East
Sussex BN27 1PB
Tel: 0323 842454

Knowl Park Nurseries
Knowl Road, Mirfield,
West Yorkshire WF14 9UU
Tel: 0924 492645

**Koolbergen & Ramsay
Ltd**
Bell Lane, Birdham,
Chichester, West Sussex
PO22 7HY

Ladybrook Nursery
37 Ravenoak Park Road,
Cheadle Hulme, Cheshire
SK8 7EH
Tel: 061 440 8060

Layham Nurseries
Summerfield, Staple,
Canterbury, Kent CT3 1LD
Tel: 0304 611380

Ledaig Nursery
Ledaig, Oban, Argyll,
Scotland PA37 1SA
Tel: 063 172401

Lees & Co
Portmore, Lymington,
Hampshire SO4 8RA
Tel: 0590 75446
Telex: 47674

Lowlands Nursery
Waterbeach Fen,
Waterbeach, Cambridge
CB5 9LR
Tel: 0223 861424

M&S Young Plants

Wilmoor Lane, Sherfield-
on-Loddon, Basingstoke,
Hampshire RG27 0JD
Tel: 0256 882239

Mahood Bros Ltd
Burscough Nurseries,
Ring O'Bells Lane,
Lathom, Ormskirk,
Lanchire L40 5US
Tel: 0704 892150
Telex 677406

Mallet Court Nursery
Mallet Court, Curry Mallet,
Taunton, Somerset
TA3 6SY
Tel: 0823 480 748

Mandry, Maurice, Ltd
Durnford Nurseries,
Ottershaw, Surrey
KT16 0QT
TEL: 719 3218

**Manor Farmhouse
Nursery**
37 East Lane, West
Horsley, Leatherhead,
Surrey KT24 6HQ
Tel: 048 65 3482

Manor Nursery
Kilham Lane, Winchester,
Hampshire SO22 5QD
Tel: 0962 52844

Marleybrooks Nurseries
Preston, Canterbury, Kent
CT3 1ED
Tel: 0227 722385

Mathews Fruit Trees Ltd
Thurston,
Bury St Edmunds, Suffolk
IP31 3RN
Tel: 035 70263

**Matthews, A.P.,
Nurseries Ltd**
Thurlwood Farm, Rode
Heath, Stoke-on-Trent,
Staffordshire ST7 3RN
Tel: 09363 2371

Matthews, Frank P., Ltd
Berington Court, Tenbury
Wells, Worcestershire
WR15 8TH
Tel: 0584 810214
Telex: 312242

Matthews, S. E.
Alderley Park Nurseries &
Garden Centre, Nether
Alderley, Macclesfield,
Cheshire
Tel: 0625 582087

Mattock, John, Ltd
Nuneham Courtney,
Oxford, OX9 9PY
Tel: 086 738 265/454

May, Robert M.
Box Cottage Nursery,
Inkpen, Newbury,
Berkshire
Tel: 04884 427

Mears Ashby Nurseries Ltd
Glebe House, Glebe
Road, Mears Ashby,
Northampton NN6 0DL
Tel: 0604 811811

Medrum, D., & Sons
Prior Road, Forfar, Angus,
Scotland DD8 3EJ
Tel: 0307 62565

Meldrum Nurseries
Silverwells, Montrose
Road, Arbroath, Tayside
DD11 5RA
Tel: 0241 72286

Microplants Ltd
Longnor, Buxton,
Derbyshire SK17 0NZ
Tel: 029883 585
Telex: 668135

Middleton, J.D., Shelley Common Nursery
Shelley Lane, Ower,
Nr Romsey, Hampshire
Tel: 0794 23323

Midland Nurseries Ltd
Kenilworth Road,
Hampton in Arden,
Solihull, West Midlands
Tel: 06755 2132
Telex: 337624

Mile Tree Nurseries
Mile Tree Lane, Wisbech,
Cambridgeshire PE13 4TR
Tel: 0945 87557

Mill House Nursery
Gressenhall, Dereham,
Norfolk NR20 4EB
Tel: 0362 860612

Mill Race Nursery
New Road, Aldham,
Colchester, Essex
CO6 3QT
Tel: 0206 24324

Minier Nurseries
Ilmer Nurseries, Ilmer,
Aylesbury,
Buckinghamshire
Tel: 08444 453

193

Monarch Horticulture
Deer Park Nurseries,
Northampton Road, Crick,
Northampton NN6 7SQ
Tel: 0788 823888

Morrey, F., & Son
Forest Nursery Kelsall,
Tarporley, Cheshire
CW6 0SW
Tel: 0829 51342

Mount Pleasant Trees
Rockhampton, Berkeley,
Gloucestershire GL1 9DU
Tel: 0454 260348

Nettletons Nursery
Ivy Mill Lane, Godstone,
Surrey
Tel: 0883 842426

Newland Nursery
Coppice Lane, Middleton,
Nr Tamworth,
Staffordshire
Tel: 021 308 7197

Northern Garden Supplies
Garden Centre &
Nurseries, Blyth Road,
Oldcotes, Worksop, Notts
S8A 8JE
Tel: 0909 731024

Northgate Horticultural Services
698 Harrogate Road
Greengates, Bradford,
West Yorkshire BD10 0QE
Tel: 0274 611608

North Hill Nurseries
Scotts Grove Road,
Chobham, Woking, Surrey
GU24 8DW
Tel: 099505 8800

North Surrey Nursery Group Navara Nurseries
Lightwater, Surrey
GU18 5SN
Tel: 0276 72186 also
Martin Robert
Stafford Lake Nursery,
Knaphill, Surrey
Tel: 04867 6367
Woodcote Park Nurseries
Ripley Road, Send, Nr
Woking, Surrey

Norton Ash Nursery
Norton Crossroads,
Norton, Sittingbourne,
Kent
Tel: 0795 521549

Nostell Priory Rose Gardens
Nostell, Wakefield, West
Yorkshire WF4 1QE
Tel: 0924 862248

Notcutts Nurseries Ltd
Woodbridge, Suffolk
IP12 4AF
Tel: 03943 3344

Notcutts, Waterers Nurseries
Jenkins Hill, Bagshot,
Surrey GU19 5DG
Tel: 0276 72109

Nuthatch Nurseries
Schoolhouse Cottage,
Stockley Hill, Peterchurch,
Herefordshire HR2 0ST
Tel: 09816 601

Oakover Nurseries Ltd
Calehill Stables,
The Leacon, Charing,
Ashford, Kent
Tel: 023371 3016

Old England Nurseries
Sutton-on-Trent, Newark,
Notts NG23 6QA
Tel: 0636 821436

Oldfield Nurseries
Trowbridge Road, Norton
St Phillip, Bath, Somerset
BA3 6NG
Tel: 022 122 2104

Otter Nurseries Ltd
Gosford Road, Ottery St
Mary, Devon EX11 11LZ
Tel: 040481 3341

Oxford Botanic Nursery
Noke, Oxford OX3 9TU
Tel: 086 75 3068

Oxford Ground Cover
Northmoor,
Oxon OX8 1AX
Tel: 086 731 737

Pacific Nurseries
Chester Road, Aldridge,
Walsall, West Midlands
WS9 0PH
Tel: 021 353 4017

Palmers Nurseries Ltd
Worcester Garden Centre,
Droitwich Road,
Worcester WR3 7SW
Tel: 0905 51231

Palmstead Nurseries
Upper Hardres,
Canterbury, Kent CT4 6EF

Tel: 022 787 414

Parks Farm Nurseries
Newent, Gloucestershire
GL18 1DL
Tel: 0531 820620

Pengethy Nurseries
Peterstow, Ross-on-Wye,
Herefordshire HB9 6LL
Tel: 098 987 284

Pennell's Nurseries
Brant Road, Lincoln
LN5 9AF
Tel: 0522 721684

Pennine Nurseries
Shelley, Huddersfield
HD8 8LG
Tel: 0484 605511

Pine Tree Nursery
Conscience Lane,
Rowdenfield, Devizes,
Wiltshire SN10 2LY
Tel: 0380 2899

Prefix Ltd
Hirstwood Nurseries,
Hirstwood Lock, Hirst
Lane, Saltaire Shipley,
West Yorkshire BD10 0QE
Tel: 0274 591251

Plandorex (France)
UK Agent Mrs J. Morris,
Long Acre, Micklepage,
Nuthurst, Horsham,
Sussex RH13 6RG
Tel: 0403 76577
Telex: 877427

**Plantscape Nursery
Stock**
Station Road,
Groombridge, Tonbridge
Wells, Kent TN3 9NJ
Tel: 0892 76852

Plumridge, A.
The Nurseries, Mill Road,
Walpole Highway,
Wisbech, Cambridgeshire
PE14 7QP
Tel: 0945 780203

Pople Landscape Ltd
Elmstree Farm, Heath
Chesterfield, Derbyshire
S44 5SA
Tel: 0246 850059 also at
Dunston Road Nursery,
Newbold, Chesterfield,
Derbyshire S41 9RL
Tel: 0246 452328 and
Cromford Nursery, Derby
Road, Matlock Bath,
Derbyshire
Tel: 062 982 4990

**Pye, W. E., (Forestry)
Ltd**
Lee Nursery, Staunton-on-
Arrow, Pembridge,
Leominster, Herefordshire
HR6 9LF
Tel: 05447 397

Quatford Nurseries
Quatford, Bridgnorth,
Shropshire WV15 6QB
Tel: 07462 4491

Quaymont Ltd
The Nurseries, Wereham,
King's Lynn, Norfolk
PE33 9AY
Tel: 0366 500240

Radclive Nurseries Ltd
Folly Farm, Stanford Road,
Faringdon, Oxfordshire
SN7 8ER
Tel: 0367 20053
Telex: 449359

Read's Nursery
Hales Hall, London,
Norfolk NR14 6QW
Tel: 050846 395

Rearsby Roses Ltd
Melton Road, Rearsby,
Leicester LE7 8YP
Tel: 0533 601211

Reddish Wood Nurseries
124 Woodsmore Lane,
Stockport, Cheshire
SK3 8TJ
Tel: 061 456 3326 or
061 439 8088

Redman, T. A. Ltd
Elms Farm, Ancton Lane,
Middleton-on-Sea, Bognor
Regis, Sussex PO22 6NJ
Tel: 0243 694447

Reed, A. N., & Son
Shipton Nurseries,
Shipton-by-
Benningbrough,
York YO6 1BW
Tel: 0904 470232

Reid, Ben, & Co Ltd
Pinewood Park Nurseries,
Countesswells Road,
Aberdeen AB9 2QL
Tel: 0224 318744

Reuthe, G., Ltd
Foxhill Nurseries, Jackass
Lane, Keston, Bromley,
Kent BR2 6AW
Tel: 0689 52249

Richalps
Alpine Lodge, Land of
Nod, Grayshott Road,
Headley Down, Hants
GU35 8SH
Tel: 0428 712968

**Richards, John,
(Wholesale Nurseryman)**
No 1 Camp Hill, West
Malvern, Worcestershire
WR14 4BZ
Tel: 06845 5382/
0684 40790

Rivendell Nurseries Ltd
Mill Lane, Widnes,
Cheshire WA8 0UL
Tel: 051 423 2638

**Roberts, A. E., (Fruit
Grower & Nurseryman)
Ltd**
Frith Farm, Wickham,
Fareham, Hampshire
PO17 5AW
Tel: 0329 833730

**Robertson, D., of
Broomhouse**
5 Church Street,
Uddingston, Glasgow
G71 7PT
Tel: 0698 814972

**Rochford, Joseph,
Gardens Ltd**
Pipers End, Letty Green,
Hertfordshire SG14 2PB
Tel: 07072 61370

Roda Nurseries
Green Lane, Winster,
Windermere, Cumbria
LA23 3NL
Tel: 09662 4653

Roger, R. V., Ltd
The Nurseries, Whitby
Road, Pickering, North
Yorkshire YO18 7HG
Tel: 0751 72226

Rosehaven Nurseries
Borras, Wrexham, Clwyd
LL13 9TL
Tel: 097 883 2367

Roseland Nurseries
Clappers Farm, Pennypot
Lane, Chobham, Woking,
Surrey GU24 8DG
Tel: 09905 8989/8980

Ross, David G.
Kettleshulme, Whaley
Bridge, Nr Stockport,
Cheshire SK12 7RD
Tel: 06633 2555

Row Farm Nursery Ltd
Chapmanslade, Westbury,
Wiltshire BA13 4AB
Tel: 037388 260

Rowhook Nursery
Rowhook Hill, Horsham,
West Sussex RH12 3PU
Tel: 0403 790472

Rumwood Nurseries
Langley, Maidstone, Kent
ME17 3ND
Tel: 0622 861477

St Bridget Nurseries Ltd
Old Roydon Lane, Exeter,
Devon EX2 7JY
Tel: 039 287 3672

Salisbury Nurseries
Moulton, Northampton
Tel: 0604 47849

Scandaplants
Bankfield Nurseries, Black
Moss Lane, Scarisbrick,
Nr Ormskirk, Lancashire
Tel: 0704 880186

Scotsdale Nursery Ltd
120 Cambridge Road,
Great Shelford,
Cambridge CB2 5JT
Tel: 0223 842777

Scotstock Nurseries Ltd
Melville Nurseries,
Lasswade, Midlothian,
Scotland EH18 1AZ
Tel: 031 663 1944

**Scottish Landscaping
Ltd**
Broompark Farm,
Mid Calder, Livingstone,
West Lothian EH53 0EB
Tel: 0506 881513

**Scotts Nurseries
(Merriot) Ltd**
Merriott, Taunton,
Somerset, TA16 5PL
Tel: 0460 72306

Sealand Nurseries Ltd
(Bees of Chester),
Sealand, Chester
CH1 6BA
Tel: 0244 880501
Telex: 61457

Shrublands Nurseries
Motcombe, Shaftesbury,
Dorset SP7 9PT
Tel: 074 76 2591

Simmons, D. & R., Ltd
45 Market Way, Spalding,

Lincolnshire PE11 3PE
Tel: 0775 3320

**Simpsons of Lower
Peover**
Tree Tops, Crown Lane,
Lower Peover, Knutsford,
Cheshire WA16 9QA
Tel: 056 581 2306

Slocock Nurseries
Barrs Lane, Knaphill,
Woking, Surrey GU21 2JW
Tel: 04867 81212

Smeaton Nursery
East Linton, East Lothian
Scotland
Tel: 0620 860501

Smith, Chas, & Son
Caledonian Nursery,
PO Box 19, St Peter Port,
Guernsey
Tel: 0481 20141

**Smith, James, (Scotland
Nurseries) Ltd**
Tansley, Matlock,
Derbyshire DE4 5GF
Tel: 0629 3036

Soames Plants
Soames Lane, Ropley,
Hampshire SO24 0ER
Tel: 096277 3350

**Spains Hall Forest
Nursery**
Spains Hall Farm House
Finchingfield, Essex
CM17 4NJ
Tel: 0371 81056/
079986 506

Specimen Trees
High Legh Estate Office,
High Legh, Knutsford,
Cheshire WA16 0QW
Tel: 092 575 5204/0599

Springhill Nurseries Ltd
Lang Stracht, Aberdeen
AB2 6HY
Tel: 0224 693788 or 0330
6246

Starborough Nursery
Starborough Road, Marsh
Green, Edenbridge, Kent
Tel: 0732 865614

Stewarts Nurseries
God's Blessing Lane,
Broomhill, Wimborne,
Dorset
Tel: 0202 882462

Stichill Forest Nursery
Stichill, Kelso,
Roxburghshire TD5 7TD
Tel: 05737 261

**Stone Cottage Gardens,
The**
95 The Highway,
Hawarden, Clwyd
Tel: 0244532 678

Street, Henry
Surrey Rose Nurseries,
Guildford Road, West
End, Woking, Surrey
GU24 9HP
Tel: 04867 3253

Sutton, G. T., Ltd
School Road, West
Walton, Wisbech,
Cambridgeshire
PE14 7DS
Tel: 0945 582683

Swallownest Nurseries
Swallownest, Sheffield
S31 0TT
Tel: 0742 872240

Tacchi's Nurseries Ltd
Banks End, Wyton,
Huntingdon,
Cambridgeshire
Tel: 0480 53338

**Tandee Nursery
Suppliers**
Barnwell Depot, Thrapston
Road, Barnwell, Oundle,
Peterborough
Tel: 0832 73478

Tean Nurseries
Tean, Staffordshire
ST10 4JW
Tel: 0538 722599

**Thames Valley Rose
Growers**
Staines Road, Laleham,
Nr Staines, Middlesex
TW18 2SF
Tel: 0784 55209

Theed Amenity Trees
Monksilver, Taunton,
Somerset TA4 4JG
Tel: 09846 56284

Thistle Hill Nurseries
Thistle Hill,
Knaresborough, North
Yorkshire HG3 8LS
Tel: 0423 868452

Thorp Perrow Nurseries
Bedale, North Yorkshire
Tel: 0677 22974

Tilhill Forestry Ltd
(Nurseries Division),
Greenhills, Tilford,
Farnham, Surrey
GU10 2DY
Tel: 025 3265 Ext 33

Timsbury Nursery
Jermyns Lane, Romsey,
Hampshire
Tel: 033528 68236

Tittenhurst Nurseries
London Road, Sunninghill,
Berkshire SL5 0PN
Tel: 0990 25828/23576

Tooby, John & Co Ltd
Bransford Nurseries,
Bransford, Worcester
WR6 5JB
Tel: 0886 32369

Topline (New Zealand)
UK Agent Mrs J. Morris,
Long Acre, Micklepage,
Nuthurst, Horsham,
Sussex RH13 6RG
Tel: 040376 577
Telex: 877427

Totties Nurseries
Greenhill Bank Road, New
Mill, Holmfirth,
Huddersfield, West
Yorkshire DH7 1UN
Tel: 0484 683363

Toxward Nursery
Sedgwick Lane, Horsham,
West Sussex RH13 6QE
Tel: 0403 53608

Trehane Camellias
Camellia Nursery,
Stapehill Road,
Hampreston, Wimborne,
Dorset BH21 7LE
Tel: 0202 873 490

Trenear, Peter
Chantryland, Chequers
Lane, Eversley Cross,
Hampshire RG27 0NX
Tel: 0734 732300

**Treswithian Down
Nurseries**
Camborne, Cornwall
TR14 0BT
Tel: 0209 713333

Trewince Nurseries
St Issey, Wadebridge,
Cornwall
Tel: 020881 2006

Trinkle, G., & J.
8 Tail Mill, Merriott,

Somerset TA16 5PF
Tel: 0460 74394

Twin Acre Nurseries
Hulme Hall Lane,
Allostock, Nr Knutsford,
Cheshire WA16 9JN
Tel: 056 581 2013

**Twyford Plant
Laboratories Ltd**
Baltonsborough,
Glastonbury, Somerset
Tel: 0458 50576
Telex: 449325

Walker, J., Henry
Ankerdine, Knightwick,
Worcestershire WR6 5PH
Tel: 0886 21288

**Warley Rose Gardens
Ltd**
Warley Street, Great
Warley, Brentwood, Essex
CM13 3JH
Tel: 0277 221966

Warwick Farm Nursery
Cley Lane, Saham Toney,
Thetford, Norfolk IP25 7HE
Tel: 0945 884109

Watts, Edgar, Ltd
Willow Works, Bungay,
Suffolk NR35 1BW
Tel: 0986 2751

Wellington Nurseries
Brandon Crescent,
Shadwell, Leeds
LS17 9JH
Tel: 0532 892601

Wells, Tim, Nurseries
Hoe Lane, Ware, Herts
SG122 9NY
Tel: 0920 69441

Welsh Tree Services Ltd
Abergavenny Road,
Raglan, Gwent NP5 2BH
Tel: 0291 690 751

**West Lancashire
Nurseries Ltd**
Wigan Road, Leyland,
Lancashire PR5 2UD
Tel: 0772 432611
Telex: 67109

Wheal Vor Nurseries
Carlean Breage, Helston,
Cornwall
Tel: 073 676 2365

Wheatcroft Roses Ltd
Edwalton,
Nottinghamshire

NG12 4DE
Tel: 0602 216061
Telex: 377560

Willows Nurseries
Sherwood Lodge, Grove
Coach Road, Retford,
Nottinghamshire
DN22 0PW
Tel: 0777 02638

**Windlesham Court
Nursery Ltd**
London Road,
Windlesham, Surrey
GU20 6LJ
Tel: 0990 21456

Winrow Nursery
Lewis Drove, Godney,
Wells, Somerset
Tel: 0934 712571

Wisbech Plant Co Ltd
Walton Road, Wisbech,
Cambridgeshire PE13 3EF
Tel: 0945 582588

**Woodbridge Nurseries
Ltd**
Rectory lane, Longworth,
Abingdon, Oxfordshire
OX13 5DZ
Tel: 0865 820300

Woodcote Park Nursery
Ripley road, Send,
Woking, Surrey GU23 7LT
Tel: 0483 223504

**Woodham Mortimer
Nurseries Ltd**
Walhampton, Lymington,
Hampshire SO4 8AS
Tel: 0590 72534

**Woodland Improvement
(Nurseries) Ltd**
Newent Lane, Huntley,
Gloucestershire GL19 3EY
Tel: 0452 830344

**Woodlands Services
Supplies Ltd**
Brooklands, Mardy,
Abergavenny, Gwent
NP7 6NU
Tel: 0873 5431

**Woodshoot Nurseries
Ltd**
King's Bromley, Burton-
on-Trent, Staffordshire
DE13 7HY
Tel: 0543 472233

Woodside Nurseries
84 Old Belfast Road,
Sainfield, Co Down

Tel: 0238 510591

Worcester Nurseries Ltd
Pear Tree Farm,
Broomhall, Norton,
Worcester WR5 2NY
Tel: 0905 357570

Worley, J. A., Ltd
Bockingfold, Ladham
Road, Goudhurst,
Kent TN17 1LY
Tel: 0580 211647

Wyevale Nurseries Ltd
Kings Acre, Hereford
HR4 0SE
Tel: 0432 265474
Telex: 35519

**Wyevale-Hawkins
Specimen Trees**
Thinghill Court,
Withington, Herefordshire
HR4 0SE
Tel: 0432 265474

Wykeham Trees Ltd
Wykeham Estate,
Wykeham, Scarborough,
North Yorkshire
YO13 9QD
Tel: 0723 862406
Telex: 527192

Yeoman Gardeners
Newcourt Road,
Topsham, Exeter EX3 0BU
Tel: 039 287 3339

**Chapter 1: European
suppliers**

Faassen Tegelen bv
PO Box 3088, 5930 AB
Tegelen, Holland
Tel: 010 31 77 737000

Felix & Dykhuis bv
PO Box 16, 2770 AA
Boskoop, Holland
Tel: 010 311 727009

**Frederiksens, Poul
Planteskole**
PO Box 104, Lojtoftevej
205, 4900 Nakskov,
Denmark
Tel: 010 453923366
Telex: 47554

Gan Adam Nurseries
Moshav Beit Halevy, D.N.
Lev Hasharon, Israel,
42870
Tel: 010 9729 8522

Gaultier, F., Pepinières
13670 St Andiol, France
Tel: 010 3390950255
Telex: 431231

**Gebr Mohr
Pflanzenhandels-
gesellschaft mbH**
D-2200 Elmshorn-
Langelohe, Postfach 805,
West Germany
Tel: 010 49412171041
Telex: 218454

**Georges, Richard,
Pepinières**
Rue Mont-Coris II, 6698
Grand-Halleux, France
Tel: 010 3280 215720

Green Inter Trade
Hoolstraat 36, 4847AC
Teteringen, Holland
Tel: 010 3176710878
Telex: 54373

**Grootendorst, F. J., &
Sons bv**
Laag-Boskoop 16, PO Box
130, 2770 AC Boskoop,
Holland
Tel: 010 3117273344

**Grootendorst, Peter, en
Zn**
PO Box 38, Boskoop,
Holland
Tel: 010 3117272148
Telex: 39863

**Growers Association de
Boskoopse Veiling ba**
PO Box 93, Boskoop,
Holland
Tel: 010 3117272960
Telex: 39966

**Guldemond Bros
Boskoop Ltd**
Reyerskoop 150a
Boskoop, Holland
Tel: 010 311727 6261
Telex: 39811

Hardijzer, Hanno, bv
Rietkraág 10, 2771 KX
Boskoop, Holland
Tel: 010 311 7274226

Hooftman, Wm. J.
Biezen 122, PO Box 76,
Boskoop, Holland
Tel: 010 3117272369

**Horticulture A., van
Heck**
Zeveneken Dorp 132,
9130 Lochristi, Belgium
Tel: 010 32 91 555235

Huibers, G., & Zonen bv
Hamsestraat 70, 4043 ZG,
Opheusden, Holland
Tel: 010 31 8887 1911
Telex: 48463

**Innocenti & Mangoni
Piante**
51030-Chiazzano, Pistoia,
Italy
Tel: 010 39539259
Telex: 572058

**Jardinart-Van Mulders
pvba**
Meerstraat 11, B3018-
Wijgmaal-Leuven,
Belgium
Tel: 010 3216445071

**Kloosterhuis, Jan H., &
Son bv**
Zuiderveen 46, PO Box
127, 9670AC Winschoten,
Holland
Tel: 010 31597015050
Telex: 77156

Kromhout & Co
PO Box 98, 2770 AB
Boskoop, Holland
Tel: 01031 1727 3434

Kruijer, J., & Sons bv
PO Box 6, 9610 AA
Sappemeer, Holland
Tel: 010 31598092504
Telex: 53377

Kuiper, F., bv
PO Box 57, Veendam,
Holland
Tel: 010 31598719410
Telex: 77203

Lapair W. G.
Boskoopseweg 4b, PO
Box 89, 2770 AB,
Boskoop, Holland
Tel: 010 3117275005
Telex: 39810

**Mesman, William, &
Sons bv**
PO Box 105, 2770 AC
Boskoop, Holland
Tel: 010 3117274348

Model Nursery
Horseleap, Moate, Co
Westmeath, Eire
Tel: 010 3535 0635 116

Moerheim Nurseries Ltd
Moerheim St 78, 7701GC
Dedemsvaart, Holland
Tel: 010 31 5230 12345
Telex: 11987

Nieuwesteeg, Jan
Lansing 14, PO Box 180,
2770 AD Boskoop,
Holland
Tel: 010 31 1727 5466
Telex: 39 789

Nieuwesteeg, W., & Zn
Lansing 7, PO Box 113,
2770 AC Boskoop,
Holland
Tel: 010 31 1727 6600
Telex: 39701

The Old Farm Nurseries
H. den Ouden & Son bv,
PO Box 1,2770 AA,
Boskoop, Holland
Tel: 010 3117274442
Telex: 39810

Otto & Sons bv
PO Box 44, 2770 AA
Boskoop, Holland
Tel: 010 3117273186

**Pepalbrac Export
Nurseries**
Massemenstwg 61, B9200
Wetteren, Belgium
Tel: 010
3291691801/691458

Plandorex (France)
Long Acre, Micklepage,
Nuthurst, Horsham,
Sussex
Tel: 0403 76577

Proost pvba
Antwerpse Weg 54,
2340 Beerse, Belgium
Tel: 010 320 14612321

Ravenhorst Bros
Zijde 123, Boskoop,
Holland
Tel: 010 311727100
Telex: 39915

Rentes Nurseries
Moyvalley, Co Kildare,
Ireland
Tel: 040551237

**Renz, Martin, Nachf
GmbH & Co KG,
Forstbaumschulen**
D-7272 Nagold-
Emmingen, West
Germany
Tel: 010 497 4524073

Rey, Jean, Pepinières
Route de Carpentras,
84150 Jonquieres, France
Tel: 010 3390706113

Rosarbo Nursery
Nieuwstraat 65, 9209 B
Serskamp, Belgium
Tel: 010 3291 690177

Rosen-Union
D-6350 Bad Nauhaim-
Steinfurth, Steinfurther
Hauptstrasse 25, West
Germany
Tel: 010 49603282068

Salling Planteskole A/S
Jebjerg, DK-7870 Roslev,
Denmark
Tel: 010 457574333
Telex: 66715

SAP Nurseries Ltd
Carbury, Co Kildare,
Ireland
Tel: 0405 51166

Schepers, Norbert
Planterystraat A1, B9880
Aalter, Belgium
Tel: 010 32 9174 1451

Sonneville Luc
Artwerpse, Sleenweg 98,
B9130 Lochristi, Belgium
Tel: 010 32 9155 6319
Telex: 12439

**Spaargaren, W. J.,
Export Nurseries**
Laag-Boskoop 11, PO Box
18, Boskoop, Holland
Tel: 010 3117277071
Telex: 39847

Stolker, F., & Zn bv
Goudse Ryweg 130, 2771
AT Boskoop, Holland
Tel: 01031 1727 3468

Stolwyk, G. C., & Co bv
Postbox 15-2770 AA
Boskoop, Holland
Tel: 010 3117276040

Sylvia Nurseries
't Hand 10, 9950
Waarschoot, Belgium
Tel: 010 3291772217
Telex: 11904

To, Nicola, & Co NV
Gorsemdorp 51, 3803
Sint-Truiden, Belgium
Tel: 010 32 11 68 3774

Topline (New Zealand)
Long Acre, Micklepage,
Nuthurst, Horsham,
Sussex
Tel: 0403 76577

Topplant, N. V.
Haagstraat 9, 8588-
Spiere-Helkijin, Belgium
Tel: 010 32 56455681

Van den Berk Bros Ltd
PO Box 130, 5490 AC Sint
Oedenrode, Holland
Tel: 010 31 41387233

Van Eck Boskoop Ltd
Biezen 86, 2771 CN
Boskoop, Holland
Tel: 010 31 172 74848
Telex: 39737

Van Eygen, A., Nursery
Keerken 4, B9 258,
Oosterzele, Belgium
Tel: 091 625568

**Van Ginneken, Charles,
& Son**
Royal Wilhelmina
Nurseries
Meirseweg 26a, 4881 DJ
Zundert, Holland
Tel: 010 311 6962210

**Van Hauwaert, Martin,
pvba**
Gistelsteenweg 462, 8200
Sint-Andries-Brugge,
Belgium
Tel: 010 3250387737

**Van Herreweghe,
Charles, pvba**
52 Nieuwstraat B-9209,
Serskamp, Belgium
Tel: 010 3291690424

**Van Herreweghe, Johan,
Nurseries**
Dendermondse Steenweg
120, B-9208, Schellebelle-
Wichelen, Belgium
Tel: 010 3291693170
Telex: 12664

Van Herreweghe, Willem
Nieuwstraat 50, B-9209,
Serskamp-Wichelen,
Belgium
Tel: 010 3291690176

**Van Hevele-Van Hulle,
Ghislain**
Saint-Laureiosesteenweg
12, B9900 Eeklo, Belgium
Tel: 010 32 91774141

**Van Hulle-De
Baerdemaecker**
Koning Albertlaan, 26b-
9990 Maldegem, Belgium
Tel: 010 3250712570
Telex: 82011

Van Hulle Hubbert Export Nurseries
Aalterbaan 234-9990
Maldegem, Belgium
Tel: 010 3250715961

Van Hulle, Lois
Leopoldlaan 70, B9900
Eeklo, Belgium
Tel: 010 32 91771774
Telex: 11336

Van Hulle-Wallyn & Zn
Aardappelstraat 9, 8030
Beernem, Belgium
Tel: 010 3250788617
Telex: 81875

Van Kerckhove, Alfons Ltd
Oordegemse Steenweg
179, B9200, Wetteren,
Belgium
Tel: 010 3291691691
Telex: 12621

Van der Poel, Wim, & Alphons
Burg Smitweg 64, 2391
NG Hazerswoude,
Holland
Tel: 010 3117289905

Van Wengerden, JAC
Valkenburgerlaan 105,
2771 CZ Boskoop,
Holland
Tel: 010 3117277406

Vanucci Piante
Via Pratese 238, 51110
Pistoia, Italy
Tel: 010 39573735483

Verwey, J., bv
Export Nurseries,
Voorweg 153, 2391 AJ
Hazerwsoude-dorp,
Holland
Tel: 010 3117273213

Von Hellms, H., Export Nurseries
Box 1507, D-2080
Pinneberg, Holstein, West
Germany
Tel: 010 4941017766

Wezelenburg, K., & Son
Royal Nurseries, PO Box
7, 2390 AA-Hazerswoude,
Holland
Tel: 010 3117272575
Telex: 39781

Wezelenburgh, T., Nurserymen bv
Long Boskoop 41, 2771
GW Boskoop, Holland
Tel: 010 3117272051

Telex: 39612

Windhorst, Messrs. L..
Biezen 138, 2771 CP
Boskoop, Holland
Tel: 010 3117277421

Chapter 2: Soil and ameliorants

Agricultural Polymers Ltd
Pillar and Lucy House,
Merchants Road,
Gloucester GL1 5RG
Tel: 0452 21733

Avena Research Ltd
Warwick House, Forge
Lane, Minworth, Sutton
Coldfield, West Midlands
B76 8AH
Tel: 021 351 5806

Banks Horticultural Products Ltd
3 Angel Court, off High
Street, Market
Harborough,
Leicestershire LE16 7NL
Tel: 0856 64346

Bord na Mona
36 King Street, Bristol
BS1 4DP
Tel: 0272 211666
Telex: 44709

Bradco Ltd
Linces Farm, Kimpton
Road, Welwyn AL6 9NL
Tel: 043871 6874

Bulrush Peat Co Ltd
Newferry Road, Bellaghy,
Magherafelt, Co
Londonderry, Northern
Ireland BT45 8ND
Tel: 064886 555
Telex: 74435

Camelot Peat
Puriton, Bridgwater,
Somerset TA7 8BQ
Tel: 0278 683383

Camland Products Ltd
Fordham House,
Fordham, Cambridgeshire
Tel: 0638 721100
Telex: 81254

D L Coutts (Horticulture) Ltd
Roundstone Lane,
Angmering, Littlehampton,
Sussex
Tel: 0903 771861
Telex: 877435

Cowpact Products
PO Box 595, Adstock,
Buckinghamshire
MK18 2RE
Tel: 029671 3838

Croxden Horticultural Products Ltd
Cheadle, Stoke-on-Trent,
Staffordshire ST10 1RH
Tel: 0538 723641
Telex: 367429

Duckbill Earth Anchors Ltd
Unit 5E, Vallance by
Ways, Lowfield Heath
Road, Charlwood, Horley,
Surrey
Tel: 0293 862989

Eden Park Ltd
Tunstall, Sittingbourne,
Kent ME9 8DY
Tel: 0795 71583/78108

Fargro Ltd
Toddington Lane,
Littlehampton, Sussex
BN17 7PP
Tel: 0903 721591
Telex: 877575

Farmura Ltd
Stone Hill, Egerton, near
Ashford, Kent
Tel: 023376 241
Telex: 966125

Fisons plc (Horticulture Division)
Paper Mill Lane,
Bramford, Ipswich, Suffolk
IP8 4BZ
Tel: 0473 830492
Telex: 98168

E J Godwin (Peat Industries) Ltd
Meare, Glastonbury,
Somerset
Tel: 04586 644/5

Harrison Clark (Manchester) Ltd
29 Rainforth Street,
Longsight, Manchester
Tel: 061 224 2955

ICI Plant Protection Division
Woolmead House East,
Woolmead Walk,
Farnham, Surrey
GU9 7UB
Tel: 0252 724525
Telex: 858347

A W Maskell and Sons Ltd
Maskell Estate,
Stephenson Street,
London E16 4SA
Tel: 01 476 6321

Melcourt Industries Ltd
Three Cups House,
Tetbury, Gloucestershire
GL8 8JG
Tel: 0666 52711/53919
Telex: 43144

Monro Horticulture Ltd
Morwick Hall, York Road,
Leeds LS15 4NB
Tel: 0532 738282

Northern Bark Ltd
6 Northern Road,
Belfast,Northern Ireland,
BT3 9AL
Tel: 0232 754936

George A Palmer Ltd
Oxney Road,
Peterborough PE1 5YZ
Tel: 0733 61222
Telex: 32465

Penicuik Peat Co Ltd
Springfield Road,
Penicuik, Midlothian
EH26 8PR
Tel: 0968 78082

Rathmoor Peat Co
Preston Brockhurst,
Shrewsbury SY4 5QA
Tel: 0939 28253

Regional Peat Supplies Ltd
23 Rectory Road,
Burnham-on-Sea,
Somerset TA8 2BZ
Tel: 0278 782116

Rigby Taylor Ltd
Rigby Taylor House,
Garside Street, Bolton,
BL1 4AE
Tel: 0204 394888

Scottish Agricultural Industries plc
Firth Road, Houston
Industrial Estate,
Livingston, West Lothian,
Scotland
Tel: 0506 39281
Telex: 727145

Seery's Peat Products
Lewis Drove, Godney,
Near Wells, Somerset
Tel: 0934 712128/713229

Silvaperl Products Ltd
PO Box 8, Department
16S, Harrogate, North
Yorkshire
Tel: 0423 870370
Telex: 57406 SILVAP

Sinclair Horticulture and Leisure plc
Firth Road, Lincoln
LN6 7AH
Tel: 0522 37561
Telex: 56367

Sportsmark Group Ltd
Sportsmark House, Ealing
Road, Brentford, London
TW8 0LH
Tel: 01-560 2010

Wessex Peat Co Ltd
South Newton, Salisbury,
Wiltshire SP2 0QW
Tel: 0722 742500

White Moss Peat Co Ltd
Simonswood Moss Works,
North Perimeter Road,
Simonswood, Kirby,
Liverpool L33 3AN
Tel: 051-547 2979

Chapter 2 Planting: Fertilisers

Alginure Products Ltd
Bells Yew Green,
Tunbridge Wells, Kent
Tel: 089275 664
Telex: 95303 (COMALG)

BASF United Kingdom Ltd
Lady Lane, Hadleigh,
Ipswich IP7 6BQ
Tel: 0473 822531
Telex: 987752

Brinkman Horticultural Services Ltd
Dunswell Lane, Dunswell,
Hull, North Humberside
Tel: 0482 842123/4/5
Also: Unit 8, Thorgate
Road, Lineside Industrial
Estate, Littlehampton,
West Sussex
Tel: 0903 723826

British Seed Houses Ltd
Bewsey Industrial Estate,
Pitt Street, Warrington,
Cheshire
Tel: 0925 54411
Telex: 627353

Chase Organics (Great Britain) Ltd

Coombelands House,
Addlestone, Weybridge,
Surrey KT15 1HY
Tel: 0932 858511

Chempak Products
Geddings Road,
Hoddesdon, Herts
EN11 0LR
Tel: 0992 441888

Chipman Ltd
The Goods Yard,
Horsham, West Sussex
RH12 2NR
Tel: 0403 60341
Telex: 8772233

Cowpact Ltd
PO Box 595, Adstock,
Buckingham MK18 2RE
Tel: 029 671 3838

Envhy Ltd
Padholme Road,
Peterborough
Tel: 0733 47881

Fargro Ltd
Toddington Lane,
Littlehampton, West
Sussex BN17 7PP
Tel: 0903 64411

Farmura Ltd
Stone Hill, Egerton, Near
Ashford, Kent
Tel: 023 376 241
Telex: 966125

Farrant Chemicals Ltd
37/39 Southgate Street,
Winchester SO23 9EH
Tel: 0962 51226
Telex: 477104

Fisons plc - Horticulture Division
Paper Mill Lane,
Bramford, Ipswich, Suffolk
IP8 4BZ
Tel: 0473 830492

ICI Professional Products
Woolmead House East,
Woolmead Walk,
Farnham, Surrey
GU9 7UB
Tel: 0252 724 525
Telex: 858347 ICI FAR G

Inter Seeds Ltd
Southern Avenue
Industrial Estate,
Leominster, Herefordshire
HR6 0QF
Tel: 0568 6363
Telex: 35307 INTERS G

A W Maskell and Sons Ltd
Stephenson Street,
London E16 4SA
Tel: 01-476 6321

Maxicrop International Ltd
21 London Road, Great
Shelford, Cambridge
CB2 5DF
Tel: 0223 844024
Telex: 81277

Maxwell Hart Ltd
612 Reading Road,
Winnersh, Wokingham,
Berkshire RG11 5HF
Tel: 0734 785655
Telex: 848669
(Northern sales and
distribution: 17 Adlington
Court, Birchwood,
Warrington WA3 6PL
Tel: 0925 825501

Palmers Horticulture and Amenity
Oxney Road,
Peterborough PE1 5YZ
Tel: 0733 61222
Telex: 32465

Pan Britannica Industries Ltd
Britannica House,
Waltham Cross,
Hertfordshire
Tel: 0992 23691
Telex: 23957

Phosyn Chemicals Ltd
Manor Place, The Airfield,
Pocklington, York YO4 2NR
Tel: 0759 302545
Telex: 57679

Rigby Taylor Ltd
Rigby Taylor House,
Garside Street, Bolton,
Lancashire BL1 4AE
Tel: 0204 394888

Scottish Agricultural Industries plc
Firth Road, Houston
Industrial Estate,
Livingston, West Lothian
Tel: 0506 39281
Telex: 727145

Sierra United Kingdom Ltd
116a Melton Road, West
Bridgford, Nottingham
NG2 6EP
Tel: 0602 45510
Telex: 377557

Silvaperl Products Ltd
PO Box 8, Department
16S, Harrogate, North
Yorkshire
Tel: 0423 870370
Telex: 57406 SILVAP

Sinclair Horticulture and Leisure Ltd
Firth Road, Lincoln
Tel: 0522 37561
Telex: 56367

Sportsmark Group Ltd
Sportsmark House, Ealing
Road, Brentford,
Middlesex TW8 0LH
Tel: 01-560 2010/2

Supaturf Products Ltd
Oxney Road,
Peterborough,
Cambridgeshire
Tel: 0773 68384
Telex: 32465; also at
Hartlebury Trading Estate,
Kidderminster
Tel: 0299 250087;
Normanon, Wakefield,
West Yorkshire
Tel: 0924 891000 and Iver
Heath, Buckinghamshire
Tel: 0895 832626

Vitax Ltd
Palais Buildings, Liverpool
Road North, Burscough,
Ormskirk, Lancashire
L40 0SB
Tel: 0704 893311
Telex: 628781

Chapter 2: Suppliers

Acorn Planting Products
Mornington, Walnut Hill,
Surlingham, Norwich
Tel: 05088 279

A'Dare Products
PO Box 1, Knighton,
Powys
Tel: 0547 528908

Durston (Somerset) Woodlands
Elmfield, Higher Durston,
Taunton, Somerset
Tel: 0823 412387

EFG Nurseries
Conery Lane, Bronington,
Whitchurch, Shropshire
Tel: 0948 73 555

Euro-Trac Ltd
Flockton House, Audby
Lane, Wetherby, West

Yorkshire
Tel: 0937 64548

Exenco Ltd
PO Box 81, Tadley,
Hampshire
Tel: 07356 6588

C Wm Jorgensen
Morton, Keighly, Yorkshire
Tel: 027 4564557

Michael Richmond
5-15 Weyhill, Haslemere,
Surrey
Tel: 0428 4394

W E Pye (Forestry) Ltd
Lee Nursery, Staunton-on-
Arrow, Leominster,
Herefordshire
Tel: 05447 397

Reekie Plant Ltd
South Road, Cupar, Fife
Tel: 0334 52481

Reynolds Boughton Ltd
Bell Lane, Amersham
Common,
Buckinghamshire
Tel: 02404 4411

Sachs Dolmar (UK) Ltd
Offterton Industrial Estate,
Hempshaw Lane,
Stockport, Cheshire
Tel: 061 477 2790

Stanton Hope Ltd
422 Westborough Road,
Westcliff-on-Sea, Essex
Tel: 0702 351281

J Toms Ltd
Wheeler Street, Headcorn,
Ashford, Kent
Tel: 0622 891111

Chapter 3: Pruning and surgery

May and Baker (Seal and Heal wound paint)
Agrochemicals Division,
Regent House, Hubert
Road, Brentwood, Essex
CM14 4TZ
Tel: 0277 261414

Chapter 4 and 5: Protection of new trees; Protection of existing trees

British Gates and Timber Ltd

Biddenden, Near Ashford,
Kent
Tel: 0580 291555

Crendon Timber Fencing
Thame Road, Long
Crendon, Aylesbury,
Buckinghamshire
HP18 9BB
Tel: 0844 201020

English Woodlands Ltd
125 High Street, Uckfield,
East Sussex TN22 1EG
Tel: 0825 4235

Ferrous Gate Company
Green-Street-Green Road,
Dartford, Kent DA1 1QQ
Tel: 0322 72119

Forest Fencing Ltd
Stanford Court, Stanford
Bridge, Near Worcester,
Worcestershire WR6 6SR
Tel: 08865 451

Larch-Lap Ltd
PO Box 17, Lichfield
Street, Stourport-on-
Severn, Worcestershire
DY13 9ES
Tel: 02993 3232

**Longlyf Treated Timber
Products**
Tilhill Forestry Ltd,
Greenhills, Tilford,
Farnham, Surrey
GU10 2DY
Tel: 025 125 3265

M and M Timber Co Ltd
Hunt House Sawmills,
Clows Top, Near
Kidderminster,
Worcestershire DY14 9HY
Tel: 029922 611

**D G Masters and Co
(Oakhill Forge) Ltd**
The Old Railway Station,
Haybridge, Near Wells,
Somerset BA5 2AW
Tel: 0749 72984

Sika Ltd
Watchmead, Welwyn
Garden City, Hertfordshire
AL7 1BQ
Tel: 07073 29241

Rusticraft
The Forge, 17A Burton
Street, Melton Mowbray,
Leicestershire LE13 1AE
Tel: 0664 69965

**Tinsley Wire (Sheffield)
Ltd**
PO Box 119, Shepcote
Lane, Sheffield, South
Yorkshire S9 1TY
Tel: 0742 443388

**Trentwood Timber
Supplies Ltd**
Victoria Street Sawmills,
Hartshill, Stoke-on-Trent,
Staffordshrie ST4 6HD
Tel: 0782 632113

Chapter 6: Tree surrounds

Monomet Ltd
3 Church Road, Croydon,
Surrey CR0 1SG
Tel: 01-689 8990

Broxap and Corby Ltd
Walker Street, Radcliffe,
Manchester M26 9JH
Tel: 061 773 7831

Townscape Products Ltd
Fulwood Road South,
Sutton in Ashfield,
Nottinghamshire
NG17 2JZ
Tel: 0623 513355

**Furnitubes International
Ltd**
29 Leegate, London
SE12 8SS
Tel: 01-463 0507

Chapter 7: Trees in containers and roof gardens

ARC Leca Aggregate
Mill Lane, Ongar, Essex
Tel: 0277 363388

Chapter 8: Maintenance and management

Agrichem Ltd
Padholme Road,
Peterborough,
Cambridgeshire PE1 5XL
Tel: 0733 47881

BASF UK Ltd
Agrochemical Division,
Lady Lane, Hadleigh,
Ipswich IP7 6BQ
Tel: 0473 822531

Bayer UK Ltd
Agrochem Division,
Eastern Way, Bury St
Edmunds, Suffolk
IP32 7AH

Tel: 0284 63200

Bos Chemicals Ltd
Paget Hall, Tydd St Giles,
Wisbech, Cambridgeshire
PE13 5FL
Tel: 0945 870014

Burts & Harvey
Crabtree Manorway North,
Belvedere, Kent
DA17 6BQ
Tel: 01-311 7100

**J. D. Campbell & Sons
Ltd**
and **J. D. Campbell
(Sales) Ltd**
18 Liverpool Road, Great
Sankey, Warrington,
Cheshire WA5 1QR
Tel: 0925 33232/3

J. W. Chafer Ltd
Chafer House, 19 Thorne
Road, Doncaster, South
Yorkshire DN1 2HQ
Tel: 0302 67371

Chipman Ltd
The Goods Yard,
Horsham, Sussex
RH12 2NR
Tel: 0403 60341/5

**Ciba-Geigy
Agrochemicals**
Whittlesford, Cambridge
Tel: 0223 833621

Dow Agriculture
Latchmore Court, Brand
Street, Hitchin,
Hertfordshire SG5 1HZ
Tel: 0462 57272

DuPont (UK) Ltd
Agricultural Products
Department, Wedgwood
Way, Stevenage,
Hertfordshire SG1 4QN
Tel: 0438 734457

Elanco Products Ltd
Kingsclere Road,
Basingstoke, Hampshire
Tel: 0256 53131

Fisons plc
Horticulture Division,
Paper Mill Lane,
Bramford, Ipswich,
Suffolk,
Tel: 0473 830492

Hoechst UK Ltd
Agricultural Division, East
Winch, King's Lynn,
Norfolk PE32 1HN
Tel: 0553 841581

Hortichem Ltd
2 Edison Road,
Churchfields Industrial
Estate, Salisbury, Wiltshire
Tel: 0722 20133

ICI Midox
Woolmead House West,
Bear Lane, Farnham,
Surrey GU9 7UB
Tel: 0252 724525

**ICI Professional
Products**
Woolmead House East,
Woolmead Walk Farnham,
Surrey GU9 7UB
Tel: 0252 724525

May & Baker Ltd
Agrochemicals Division,
Regent House, Hubert
Road, Brentwood, Essex
CM14 4TZ
Tel: 0277 230522

Monsanto plc
Agricultural Division,
Thames Tower, Burleys
Way, Leicester LE1 3TP
Tel: 0533 20864

Octavius Hunt Ltd
5 Dove Lane, Redfield,
Bristol B25 9NQ
Tel: 0272 556107

**Pan Britannica
Industries Ltd**
Britannica House,
Waltham Cross,
Hertfordshire
Tel: 0992 23691

Rigby Taylor Ltd
Rigby Taylor House,
Garside Street, Bolton
BL1 4AE
Tel: 0204 394888/389888

Rohm & Haas (UK) Ltd
Lenning House, 2 Mason's
Avenue, Croydon, Surrey
Tel: 01-686 8844

SDS Biotech UK Ltd
Bayhead House,
4 Fairway, Petts Wood,
Orpington, Kent BR5 1EG
Tel: 0689 74011

Schering Agriculture
Nottingham Road,
Stapleford, Nottingham
NG9 8AJ
Tel: 0602 390202

Shell Chemicals UK Ltd
Agricultural Division, 39-

41 St Mary's Street, Ely,
Cambridgeshire CB7 4HG
Tel: 0353 3671

Synchemicals Ltd
44 Grange Walk, London
SE1 3EN
Tel: 01-232 1225

Union Carbide UK Ltd
Agricultural Chemicals
Division, Springfield
House, King's Road,
Harrogate, North
Yorkshire HG1 5JJ
Tel: 0423 509731/3

**Universal Crop
Protection Ltd (Unicrop)**
Park House, Maidenhead
Road, Cookham,
Maidenhead, Berkshire
Tel: 06285 26083

**Chapter 9: Building,
engineering and trees**

**Malcolm Ogilvie and Co
Ltd (Wyretex)**
31 Constitution Street,
Dundee DD3 6NL
Tel: 0382 22794

F ASSOCIATIONS AND INSTITUTES

Arboricultural Association
Ampfield House
Ampfield
nr Romsey
Hants SO5 9PA
0794 68717

British Association of Landscape
Industries (BALI)
Landscape House
Henry Street
Keighley
W. Yorkshire BD2 3DR
0535 606139

Cement and Concrete Association
Wexham Springs
Frounwood Road
nr Slough
Bucks SL3 6PL
0281 62727

Civic Trust
17 Carlton House Terrace
London SW1Y 5AW
01 930 1914

Forestry Commission Research Station
Alice Holt Lodge
Wrecclesham
Farnham
Surrey GU10 4LH
0420 22255

Garden History Society
12 Charlbury Road
Oxford OX2 6UT

Horticultural Trades Association
18 Westcote Road
Reading
Berks RG7 5AH
0734 303132

Institute of Horticulture
PO Box 313
80 Vincent Square
London SW1P 2PE
01 834 4333

Institute of Leisure and Amenity
Management
Lower Basildon Road
Reading
Berks RG8 9NE

Institute of Terrestrial Ecology
Monks Wood Experimental Station
Abbot Ripton
Huntingdon
Cambs PE17 2LS

International Geotextile Society
c/o EDANA
51 Avenue des Cerisiers
B-1040 Brussels
Belgium
(02) 7349310

Ministry of Agriculture,
Fisheries and Food,
Agricultural Development Advisory
Service
Check the telephone directory for your
local office

Landscape Institute
Nash House
12 Carlton House Terrace
London SW1Y 5AH
01 839 3855

Meteorological Office
London Road
Bracknell
Berks RG12 2SZ
0344 420242

Royal Forestry Society
102 High Street
Tring
Herts HP23 4AH
044 282 2028

Royal Horticultural Society
80 Vincent Square
London SW1P 2PE
01 834 4333

Society of Landscape and Garden
Designers
23 Reigate Road
Ewell
Surrey DT17 1PS
01 840 1188

Tree Council
Room C10/13
2 Marsham Street
London SW1P 3EB
01 235 8854

G FURTHER READING

Appendix G

Arnold, H. F.: Trees in Urban Design (Van Nostrand Reinhold, New York)

Badmin, S. R. and Colvin, B.: Trees for Town and Country (Lund Humpries)

Bean, W. J.: Trees and Shrubs Hardy in the British Isles, Vols. 1-4 (John Murray)

Beckett, K. and G.: Planting Native Trees and Shrubs (Jarrold)

Brennan, G., Patch, D., and Stevens, F. R. W.: Tree Roots and Underground Pipes (Arboricultural Research Notes 36/85/TRL)

Bridgeman, P. H.: Tree Surgery (David and Charles)

Brown, G.: The Pruning of Trees, Shrubs and Conifers (Faber and Faber)

British Standards Institution: Progress v Preservation: Trees in Relation to Construction (Seminar Papers)

Civic Trust: Moving Big Trees

Civic Trust: The Civic Trust Trees Campaign

Civic Trust Trees Campaign: Practice Notes on the Transplanting of Semi-mature Tress

Clouston, B. (ed.): *see* Landscape Institute

Clouston, B. and Stansfield, K.: Trees in Towns: Maintenance and Management (Architectural Press)

Cutler, D. F. and Richards, I. B. K.: Tree Roots and Buildings (Construction Press)

Davies, R. J.: Do Soil Ameliorants Help Tree Establishment (Arboricultural Research Notes, 69/87/SILS)

Davies, R. J.: A Comparison of the Survival and Growth of Transplants, Whips and Standards, With and Without Chemical Weed Control (Arboricultural Research Notes 67/87/ARB)

Davies, R. J. and Gardiner, J. B. H.: The Effect of Weed Competition on Tree Establishment (Arboricultural Research Notes 59/85/ARB)

Downing, H. F.: Landscape Construction (E. and F. N. Spon)

Gilchrist, T. D.: Trees on Golf Courses (Arboricultural Association)

Greater London Council, Department of Architecture and Civic Design: The Design of Urban Space (Architectural Press)

Gruffydd, B.: Tree Form, Size and Colour - A Guide to Selection, Planting and Design (E. and F. N. Spon)

Haller, J.: Tree Care

Handisyde, C.: Hard Landscape in Brick (Architectural Press)

Harris, R. W.: Arboriculture: Care of Trees, Shrubs and Vines in the Landscape (Prentice-Hall)

Hicks, P.: The Care of Trees on Development Sites (Arboricultural Booklet Number 69, HMSO Publications)

Hillier, H. G.: Hillier's Manual of Trees and Shrubs (David and Charles)

HMSO Publications: Individual Tree Protection (Arboricultural Research Notes No. 10)

HMSO Publications: Removal of Tree Stumps (Arboricultural Booklet No. 7)

HMSO Publications: Trees and Water (Arboricultural Booklet No. 6)

Innes, J. L.: Acid Rain, Air Pollution and Trees (Arboricultural Research Notes, 111/87/SSS)

Innes, J. L.: Surveys of Tree Health 1987 (Arboricultural Research Notes, 70/87/SSS)

Insley, H., and Patch, D.: Root Deformation by Biodegradable Containers (Arboricultural Research Notes 22/80/ARB)

Landscape Institute: Landscape Design with Plants, ed. Brian Clouston (Heinemann)

Langer, R. H. S.: How Trees Grow (Edward Arnold Studies in Biology No. 39)

Littlewood, Michael: Landscape Detailing (Architectural Press)

Lonsdale, D.: A Definition of the Best Pruning Position (Arboricultural Research Notes 48/83/PATH)

McCavish, W. J. and Insley, H.: Herbicides for Use with Broadleaved Amenity Trees (Arboricultural Research Notes 27/83/SILS)

Mercer, P. C.: Treatment of Tree Wounds (Arboricultural Research Notes 28/81/PATH)

Mitchell, A.: A Field Guide to Trees of Britain and Northern Europe (Collins)

Mitchell, A.: The Native and Exotic Trees in Britain (Arboricultural Research Notes 29/81/SILS)

Mitchell, A., and Jobling, J.: Decorative Trees for Country, Town and Garden (HMSO Publications)

Morling, R. J.: Trees including Preservation, Planting Law and Highways (The Estates Gazette Ltd)

Nadel, I. B. and Oberlander, C. H.: Trees in the City (Pergamon, New York)

National House Building Council: Building near Trees (Practice Notes 3)

National House Building Council: A quick way to find the right depth of foundations on clay soils (Supplement to Practice Notes 3)

Patch, D.: Tree Staking (Arboricultural Research Notes 40/84/ARB)

Patch, D., Coutts, M. P., and Evans, J.: Control of Epicormic Shoots on Amenity Trees (Arboricultural Research Notes 54/84/SILS)

Pepper, H. W.: Plastic Net Tree Guards (Arboricultural Research Notes, 5/83/WILD)

Pirone, P. P.: Tree Maintenance (Oxford University Press, New York)

Reynolds, E. R. C.: Tree Roots and Foundations (Arboricultural Research Notes 24/80/SILS)

RIBA Publications Ltd: Frost Damage to Trees and Shrubs

Rose, D. R.: Lightning Damage to Trees in Britain (Arboricultural Research Notes, 68/87/PAT)

Skinner, D. N.: Planting Success Rates - Standard Trees (Arboricultural Research Notes, 66/86/EXT)

Sole, J. S. P., and Mason, W. L.: Alternatives to Simazine for Weed Control in Transport Lines and Shrubberies at Time of Planting (Arboricultural Research Notes, 65/86/SILS)

South Hams District Council: The Management and Treatment of Trees in Designated Conservation Areas (Recommended Code of Practice)

South Hams District Council: The Management and Treatment of Trees Which Are the Subject of Tree Preservation Orders (Recommended Code of Practice)

South Hams District: Trees on Building Sites (Recommended Code of Practice)

Southern Tree Surgeons: The Care of Trees (Richmond Press Ltd)

Tabbush, P. M.: Rough Handling Reduces the Viability of Planting Stock (Arboricultural Research Notes, 64/86/SILN)

Tabbush, P. M.: The Use of Co-Extruded Polythene Bags for Handling Bare Rooted Planting Stock

(Arboricultural Research Notes,
110/87/SILN)

Tandy, C. (ed.): Handbook of Urban
Landscape (Architectural Press)

Tuley, G.: Shelters Improve the Growth
of Young Trees (Arboricultural
Research Notes 49/84/SILS)

University of Bath: Tree Establishment
(University of Bath Symposium
Proceedings)

Weddle, A. E.: Landscape Techniques
(Heinemann)

Zion, R. L.: Trees for Architecture and
the Landscape (Van Nostrand
Reinhold)

H BOOK SUPPLIERS AND PUBLISHERS

Academic Press
Harcourt Brace Jovanovich
24/28 Oval Road
London NW1 7DX
01 267 4466

(Scientific titles)

Butterworth Architecture
Borough Green
Sevenoaks
Kent TN15 8PH

(Many related titles)

British Standards Institution
Linford Wood
Milton Keynes MK14 6LE
0908 320033

Daniel Lloyd (D. & E. Lloyd)
Heather Lea
4 Hillcrest Avenue
Chertsey
Surrey KT16 9RD
01 940 2512

(Superb stock of rare and out of print
botanical, horticultural and related
titles)

Forestry Commission Research Station
Alice Holt Lodge
Wrecclesham
Farnham
Surrey GU1D 4LH
0420 22255

(Excellent research notes and booklets)
Georges Bookshops
Park Street

Bristol BS1 5PW
0272 276602

(Excellent stock of books; will also do a
search for rare or out-of-print
publications)

Grower Books (Publications) Ltd
50 Doughty Street
London WC1N 2LP
01 405 7135

(Several useful titles)

HMSO Bookshops
49 High Holborn
London WC1V 6HB
01 211 5656

Also at:
PO Box 276
London SW8 5DT
01 622 3316

13a Castle Street
Edinburgh EH2 3AR
031 453 5610

80 Chichester Street
Belfast BR1 4JY
0232 234488

Brazenose Street
Manchester M60 8AS
061 834 7201

258 Broad Street
Birmingham B1 2HE
021 643 3740

Southey House
Wine Street
Bristol BS1 2BQ
0272 264306

(Many useful titles related to trees)

Landsmans Postal Bookshop
Buckenhill
Bromyard
Herefordshire HR7 4PH
0885 83420

(Comprehensive stock of agricultural,
horticultural and related titles)

National House Building Council
Chiltern Avenue
Amersham
Bucks HP6 5AR
0240 034477

(Some good research notes)

N. J. Ogilvie
Airile House
Ansford
Castle Cary BA7 7AJ
0963 50512

(Good for rare and out-of-print books)

RIBA Publications Ltd
Finsbury Mission
Moreland Street
London EC1V 8VB
01 251 0791

Royal Horticultural Society Enterprises
Ltd
RHS Garden
Wisley
Woking
Surrey GU23 6QB
0483 224163

University of Bath Publications
A Wilson, Horticulture Group
School of Biological Sciences
University of Bath
Claverton Down
Bath BA2 7AY
0225 826826

(Three useful titles)

I UNIVERSITIES COLLEGES

Degree courses in forestry and land management

University of Bath
School of Biological Sciences, Claverton Down, Bath BA2 7AY

Wye College
Ashford, Kent TN25 5AH

Department of Agricultural and Forest Sciences
South Parks Road, Oxford OX1 3RB

University of Reading
Faculty of Agriculture and Food, Whiteknights, Reading RG6 2BU

University College of North Wales
School of Agriculture, Memorial Buildings, Bangor, Gwynedd LL57 2DG

BTech and Diploma Courses in Arboriculture

Royal Botanic Gardens
Edinburgh EH3 5LR

Royal Botanic Gardens
Kew, Richmond, Surrey TW9 3AB
Royal Horticultural Society
Wisley Gardens, Woking, Surrey GU23 6QB

Local arboricultural courses

England

Bedfordshire
Bedford College Farm, Silsoe, MK45 4OU

Berkshire
Berkshire College of Agriculture, Hall Place, Burchetts Green, Maidenhead, Berks

Buckinghamshire
Education Office, County Offices, Walton Street, Aylesbury HP20 1UZ

Cambridgeshire
Isle of Ely College of Further Education and Horticulture, Ramnoth Road, Wisbech PE13 2JE

Cheshire
Cheshire College of Agriculture, Reaseheath, Nantwich, CW5 6DF

Cleveland
The Education Office, Woodlands Road, Miiddlesbrough TS1 3BW

Cornwall
Agricultural Education Section, Room 26, Old County Hall, Truro TR1 3BA
Cumbria
Cumbria College of Agriculture and Forestry, Newton Rigg, Penrith

Derbyshire
The Derbyshire College of Agriculture, Broomfield, Morley, Derby DE7 6DN

Devon
Bicton College of Agriculture, East Budleigh, Budleigh, Salterton EX9 7BY

Dorset
Dorset College of Agriculture, Kingston Maurward, Dorchester, Dorset

Durham
Durham Agricultural College, Houghall, Durham HD1 3SG

Essex
Writtle Agricultural College, Writtle, Chelmsford CM1 3RR

Gloucestershire
Gloucestershire College of Agriculture, Hartpury House, Nr Gloucester

Hampshire
Hampshire College of Agriculture, Sparsholt, Winchester

Hereford and Worcester
Pershore College of Horticulture, Avonbank, Pershore WR10 3JP
Hertfordshire
College of Agriculture and Horticulture, Oaklands, St Albans, Herts

211

Humberside
Bishop Burton College of
Agriculture, Beverley
HU17 8AG

Isle of Wight
Isle of Wight College of
Arts and Technology,
Newport, Isle of Wight

Kent
Hadlow College of
Agriculture and
Horticulture, Hadlow,
Tonbridge, Kent
TN11 0AL

Lancashire
College of Agriculture,
Myerscough Hall,
Bilsborrow, Preston PR3
0RY

Leicestershire
Brooksby Agricultural
College, Brooksby, Nr
Melton Mowbray,
Leicestershire LE14 2LJ

Lincolnshire
Kesteven Agricultural
College, Caythorpe Court,
Grantham, NG32 3EP

Lindsey College of
Agriculture, Riseholme,
Lincoln LN2 2LG

**London Borough of
Ealing**
Norwood Hall Institute of
Agricultural and
Horticultural Education,
Norwood Green, Southall,
Middlesex UB2 4LA

**London Borough of
Enfield**
Capel Manor Institute of
Horticulture, Bullsmoor
Lane, Waltham Cross
EN1 4RW

Norfolk
Norfolk College of
Agriculture and
Horticulture, Easton,
Norwich NR9 5DX

Northamptonshire
Northamptonshire College
of Agriculture, Moulton,
Northampton NN3 1RR

Northumberland
Northumberland College
of Agriculture, Ponteland,
Newcastle-upon-Tyne,
NE20 0AQ

Nottinghamshire
Nottinghamshire College
of Agriculture,
Brackenhurst, Southwell,
Notts

Oxfordshire
Rycotewood College,
Priest End, Thame
OX9 2BR

Salop
Shropshire Farm Institute,
Walford, Baschurch,
Shrewsbury

Somerset
Somerset College of
Agriculture and
Horticulture, Cannington,
Bridgwater TA5 2LS

Staffordshire
Staffordshire College of
Agriculture, Rodbaston,
Penkridge, Stafford

Suffolk
East Suffolk College of
Agriculture and
Horticulture, Otley,
Ipswich IP6 9EY

Surrey
Merrist Wood Agricultural
College, Worplesdon, Nr
Guildford GU2 3PE

Sussex: East Sussex
Plumpton Agricultural
College, Plumpton, Nr
Lewes

Sussex: West Sussex
West Sussex College of
Agriculture, Brinsbury
Estate, North Heath,
Pulborough RH20 1DL

Warwickshire
Warwickshire College of
Agriculture, Moreton Hall,
Moreton Morrell, Warwick
CV35 9BL

Wiltshire
Lackham College of
Agriculture, Lacock,
Chippenham SN15 2NY

**Yorkshire: North
Yorkshire**
Askham Bryan College of
Agriculture and
Horticulture, Askham
Bryan, York YO2 3PR

Wales

Clwyd
The Welsh College of
Horticulture, Northop, Nr
Mold CH7 6AA

Dyfed
Carmarthen Technical and
Agricultural College,
Pibwrlwyd, Carmarthen

Gwent
The Usk College of
Agriculture, Usk NP5 1XJ

Gwynedd
Glynllifon College of
Further Education,
Clynnog Road,
Caernarvon LL54 5DU

Mid Glamorgan
Mid Glamorgan College of
Agriculture and
Horticulture, Pencoed,
Bridgend

Powys
Montgomery College of
Further Education,
Newtown, Powys

Scotland

Borders, Central

Lothian
The East of Scotland
College of Agriculture,
West Mains Road,
Edinburgh

Oatridge Agricultural
College, Ecclesmachan,
Broxburn, W Lothian

Dumfries and Galloway
The National Trust for
Scotland, Threave School
of Practical Gardening,
Castle Douglas,
Kirkcudbrightshire,
DG7 1RX

Fife
Elmwood Agricultural and
Technical College,
Canslogie Road, Cupar,
Fife

Highlands and Islands

Grampian
The North of Scotland
College of Agriculture,
581 King Street, Aberdeen
AB9 1UD

Strathclyde
The West of Scotland
Agricultural College,
Auchincruive, Ayr
KA6 5HW

Woodburn House Further
Education of Horticulture,
Buchanan Drive,
Rutherglen, Glasgow
GT3 PF

Tayside
Kingsway Technical
College, Old Glamis
Road, Dundee

Northern Ireland

Antrim
Greenmount Agricultural
and Horticultural College,
22 Greenmount Road,
Antrim

Republic of Ireland

Dublin
Faculty of Agriculture,
University College,
Belfied, Dublin 4

Kilkenny
College of Agriculture and
Horticulture, Kildalton,
Piltown, Co Kilkenny

Louth
I C A College of
Horticulture,
Termonfeckin, Co Louth

Meath
Salesian College of
Agriculture, Warrenstown,
Drumree, Co Meath